*Progress and Pragmatism*

# CONTRIBUTIONS IN AMERICAN STUDIES

Series Editor: *Robert H. Walker*

# Progress and Pragmatism

## James, Dewey, Beard,
## and the American Idea of Progress

David W. Marcell

*Ͷ*

Contributions in American Studies, Number 9

Greenwood Press
Westport, Connecticut    ●    London, England

*B832*
*M18*

**Library of Congress Cataloging in Publication Data**

Marcell, David W
   Progress and pragmatism.

   (Contributions in American studies, no. 9)
   Bibliography: p.
   1. Pragmatism. 2. Progress. 3. James, William,
1842-1910. 4. Dewey, John, 1859-1952. 5. Beard,
B832.M18         191         72-818
ISBN 0-8371-6387-0

Library of Congress Catalog Card Number: 72-818
ISBN: 0-8371-6387-0

First published in 1974
Greenwood Press, a division of Williamhouse-Regency Inc.
51 Riverside Avenue, Westport, Connecticut 06880


Manufactured in the United States of America

To my mother and father
—and to Mary and Gretchen—
I dedicate this book with love
and gratitude

# Contents

# Preface

It seems clear that the world view that blended pragmatism and the idea of progress into the theoretical foundation of twentieth-century liberalism has now gone into something of an eclipse. Pragmatism today is generally regarded as philosophically passé and psychologically naive; liberalism seems to have vastly misconstrued both the nature of postindustrial power and the real possibilities of human rationality; and progress—or what has usually been regarded as such—apparently exacts its own grim compensation for every facet of social and technological advance. That liberal optimism proclaiming its faith in progress through a humanistic, experimental science has been greatly eroded in the past decade. The dominant mood in America today swings from a shallow nostalgia through existential resignation to what Theodore Roszak has called "that dispiriting conviction of cosmic absurdity" haunting contemporary culture.

One reason for this general lapse from optimism and confidence may lie, ironically, largely within the compass of pragmatic liberalism itself, for to score its own telling blows against the regnant orthodoxy of late nineteenth-century rationalism and conservatism, pragmatic liberalism may have both overdramatized the accomplishments it portended and underestimated the ease and the speed with which they were to be accomplished. The requirements of the pragmatic faith may have caused liberals to envision more progress than American culture could realistically deliver, and its failures have thus become a reproach to the cluster of ideas and assumptions that raised such optimistic possibilities in the first place. But whatever the reasons for the lapse, the time is ripe for a close, careful scrutiny of the mode of pragmatism on which so many liberals grounded their conceptions of social change, intelligence, morality, and history during the first decades of this century.

It has become almost ritual for students of American thought to treat pragmatism as part of a unique intellectual tradition stretching back to the practical theology of Massachusetts Bay, the empirical Calvinism of Jonathan Edwards, and the democratic common sense of Benjamin Franklin. Developing in time, this heritage comes to nurture such luminaries as Thomas Jefferson, Ralph Waldo Emerson, Henry Thoreau, and Walt Whitman, branches out to include Josiah Royce and Chauncey Wright, and finally flowers in the blooming, native American school of pragmatism: Charles S. Peirce, William James, John Dewey, George Herbert Mead, and perhaps a few others.

While there are compelling historical reasons for locating pragmatism in the context of the "great American thinkers," in the pages that follow I have chosen a somewhat different course. My reasons are several. In the first place, pragmatism is so varied and protean a mode of philosophy that lumping Peirce, James, Dewey, and Mead into a "school" may justifiably raise eyebrows. Early in this century A. O. Lovejoy identified thirteen pragmatisms, and one can argue that each has since proliferated. In the second place, there is considerable question as to the real influence early American thinkers had on late nineteenth- and early twentieth-century thought; such implied continuity seems to meet the organizational requirements of historians of thought more than it does to explain the development of philosophy. Finally, it seems to me that there is another tradition in which pragmatism should be placed in an effort to explain its particularly American features, its popular attractiveness, and its unquestionable diversity and vitality: the tradition of the idea of progress in America.

This context has led me to focus on three of America's most influential pragmatists: William James, John Dewey, and Charles Beard. The three are linked not so much by agreement on the technicalities of pragmatism (Beard, indeed, scarcely mastered them) as by their common perception of the intellectual crisis of their times and by the kinds of responses they made to that crisis. My contention is that pragmatism in their hands became explicitly a philosophy of progress and that, in turn, their recasting of the idea of progress helps to locate and identify pragmatic liberalism in the broad reach of American intellectual history. Specifically, I hope to show how their thought bridged the gap between the traditional national faith in progress and the more scientific, critical approach to history, morality, and experience characterizing the twentieth century.

This concern explains both the structure of the book and my selection of James, Dewey, and Beard as its main subjects. Other pragmatists who were important thinkers in their own right failed to achieve as wide an influence on the public mind, and I therefore elected not to treat them. Their neglect is merely a function of my own purposes and not a judgment, covert or otherwise, on the value or importance of their thought.

James, Dewey, and Beard each attained unrivaled influence in his own intellectual sphere, and each produced a distinctive, significantly different version of the idea of progress. Nevertheless, they shared a common skepticism of absolutes, wholes, certainties, and finalities and a common faith in the efficacy of the will, in the compatibility of science and democracy, and in the sufficiency of experience as the source of knowledge of the good and the true. The balance between their faith and their skepticism differed in certain particulars, but the three maintained a similar kind of activist, progressive equilibrium. The extent to which they did so went a long way toward defining the intellectual world they so clearly dominated, and their successes and failures provide a convenient yardstick by which to measure that world.

# Acknowledgments

No book is the product of any one person, yet I blush to think how many of my friends and acquaintances have, sometimes advertently, shared in the construction of this one. To my students and colleagues at Skidmore College who have listened long and tolerantly and, most importantly, critically, I owe the largest obligation. Robert Orrill and Erwin Levine have been sharp-eyed and helpful, and their comments have been especially valued. Edwin Moseley, Skidmore's provost and dean of faculty, provided encouragement and support for which I am deeply grateful. While a graduate student at Yale, I had the good counsel of John Morton Blum, R. W. B. Lewis, John E. Smith, and the late David Potter, all of whom generously helped bring order—and progress—out of my investigation of pragmatism. Then, and more recently when I had the opportunity to return to New Haven for a year of study, I found Norman Holmes Pearson an unfailing source of wisdom and shrewd advice. William Goetzmann of the University of Texas provided a welcome critique of my estimate of Beard. During my undergraduate days, I was fortunate enough to find a mentor in John A. Hague, whose intellectual integrity and boundless enthusiasm for studying the American heritage is a continuing inspiration. To all of these friends

and contributors—and to the others I must omit—my
heartfelt thanks.

A research grant from the American Philosophical
Society in 1967 enabled me to begin the revisions of
the present manuscript, and several grants from the
Skidmore Faculty Research Fund provided additional
support. A sabbatical leave from Skidmore in 1970-
1971, during which I held a Post-doctoral Research
Fellowship in American Studies at Yale, afforded a crucial, uninterrupted block of time for study and writing.
The staffs at Yale's Sterling Library and at Harvard's
Houghton Library were most cooperative. Special
thanks go to Selma Harwood for her cheerful and
accurate typing of an often illegible manuscript.

Parts of this book have appeared previously in print
in different form. Portions of chapters three and four
appeared in *The Journal of American History* in 1970; sections of chapter six appeared in *American Quarterly* in
1969; a fragment of chapter three appeared in an essay
in *Challenges in American Culture*, Ray Browne, editor,
in 1971; all have been reprinted with permission.

I would like especially to express gratitude to my
wife Gretchen, whose comradeship and affection have
contributed more than she will ever know to the completion of my book.

Saratoga Springs, New York
January 1, 1973

# Progress and Pragmatism

# 1

# *Formalism, Degradation, and Pragmatism*

In February 1910, Henry Adams sent a copy of his recently published *Letter to American Teachers of History* to his old friend and former colleague at Harvard, William James. The essay, a deliberately provocative meditation on the law of cosmic degradation, had been submitted to the *American Historical Review* some months earlier, but the editor had not found it suitable for inclusion in the self-consciously professional journal. So Adams, as he had done with both *Mont-Saint-Michel and Chartres* (1904) and its sequel, *The Education of Henry Adams* (1907), had the essay printed privately for his friends. Several hundred copies were sent out; Adams expected perhaps three or four disputing acknowledgments. For once he was too hopeful; by June, only William James, then weeks away from death, had dissented.[1]

Adams's *Letter* and James's reply were the two friends' last excursion into history, into what Adams called "this old thicket of ignorance." They emerged, as they had entered, on diverging philosophical paths leading in different metaphysical directions. Adams's path led back toward the past, toward the nineteenth

3

century's hope of blending empirical science and cosmic philosophy in a vast and comprehensive system that afforded scientific certainty of the curve of history. James's path led toward the future, toward the twentieth century's more limited, pragmatic interpretation of progress and historical experience. In 1910, as Adams and James both knew, and as their exchange revealed, historical understanding stood at the crossroads.

Henry Adams and William James had known each other for more than forty years, and, as befit their long acquaintance, they chided each other candidly for what each regarded as the other's temperamental excesses and philosophical wrongheadedness. Their letters over the years expressed continuing affection and a growing, mutual exasperation. Adams once referred peevishly to the "contempt" he imagined James felt for him after reading the *Education*, and James in turn bluntly told Adams that the *Letter* "doesn't impress me at all, save by its wit and erudition."[2] Yet James took time to write a lengthy, thoughtful reply to the *Letter* at a time when any exertion at all had become excruciating, and Adams, who had carefully read and commented upon James's *Principles of Psychology* in 1902,[3] was deeply grieved by the news of his death in August. The following winter he wrote to William's brother Henry and apologized for not having written sooner, explaining that "I felt the loss myself rather too much to talk about it."[4] But friendship notwithstanding, Adams's and James's disagreements were real and basic; on the profound questions of historical determinism and free will, the two had long since parted ways. Their correspondence over Adams's *Letter* was a fitting end to their protracted, fundamental differences of opinion, differences that harked back to their early days together as young professors at Harvard.

Four years older than James, Adams had already graduated from Harvard and embarked for London to become private secretary to his father, then American minister to England, when James matriculated at Harvard's Lawrence Scientific School in the fall of 1861. The war years and their travels during the aftermath prevented the two from meeting until 1870 when Adams returned to Cambridge to commence a seven-year professorship in history. In the fall of that year, the two were dining together regularly at the monthly meetings of "the Club," an informal gathering of friends whose intellectual interests, and, in some cases, bachelor estates, drew them together. The club included, among others, such notables as William's brother Henry (with whom Adams was more intimate than he was with William), Oliver Wendell Holmes, Jr., William Dean Howells, John Fiske, John C. Gray, Francis Parkman, and James Ford Rhodes.[5] In 1872, President Charles Eliot invited James to teach physiology and hygiene to Harvard undergraduates, and for the next five years, until Adams resigned to return to Washington, D.C., and his researches in American history, their careers overlapped and their paths crossed frequently. After Adams's departure, the two met only occasionally, although they did take pains to seek each other out whenever their travels brought them within hailing distance.

Separation did not, however, prevent the two from keeping up with each other's works and whereabouts and from exchanging what were sometimes pungent letters of criticism. One such exchange took place five years after Adams left Harvard. In the summer of 1882, during those wonderfully happy years before his

wife's tragic suicide, Adams wrote to James in response
—one is tempted to say reaction—to two of James's
recent essays which had attracted much attention: "The
Sentiment of Rationality," which appeared in *Mind* in
1879, and "Rationality, Activity and Faith," published
in the *Princeton Review* in 1882.[6] The essays contained
in rudimentary form much of what James was later to
expand into the philosophy of pragmatism, and
Adams's rejoinder revealed his discomfort with James's
tough-minded relativism, a discomfort that was to grow
as the years passed.

Arguing in these essays that rationality was at bottom
merely "unimpeded mental function," the feeling of
well-being and ease the mind knows when it has
reached a sensible solution to some problem, James
went on to sketch the kind of universe such a notion
of rationality implied.[7] If rationality was indeed a feeling of completeness, then it somehow had to give
assurance that the future was not entirely uncertain.
Yet forever and forever such assurance seemed to
recede before the advance of the synthesizing, simplifying process of rationality; just when men think they
have reduced experienced complexities to the final
resolution, "the craving for further explanation, the
ontological wonder-sickness," would inevitably strike
again.[8] In such circumstances, the mind did not recoil
from functioning; rather, it continued to act upon the
faith that the experiences it recorded and abstracted
from were somehow congruous with the future.
Sometimes this meant choosing to believe in a future
that would not have come about without that act of
choice. *"There are then,"* James insisted, *"cases where faith
creates its own verification."*[9] Only in a universe open and
yielding to the conceptualizing individual mind could
there be morality and ethics, and with this kind of universe James cast his lot. In the ultimate philosophy, he

concluded, there must be always "another realm into which the stifled soul may escape from pedantic scruples and indulge its own faith at its own risks; and all that can here be done will be to mark out distinctly the questions which fall within faith's sphere."[10]

Henry Adams was not impressed. The "ultimate philosophy" for him had a great deal more to do than simply raise questions about what an individual's mind and faith could or could not do in time. Having recently completed a four-volume life and edited writings of Albert Gallatin in 1879, his anonymous novel, *Democracy*, in 1880, a life of John Randolph in 1882, and the draft of the first two volumes of what would become his definitive *History of the United States during the Administrations of Jefferson and Madison*, in addition to numerous essays and reviews on historical subjects, Adams had convictions about history and the role of the individual that took a vastly different tack from James's estimate. As a scientific historian, Adams was increasingly committed to the belief that history had an overriding framework, that it functioned, like physics, according to fixed laws and discernible forces of measurable intensity. The philosophy needed by the historian had to contain a firm sense of the mechanics of time, an explanation of the laws that governed the past and would determine the future. As he had written to his former student and protégé Henry Cabot Lodge in 1878, "Unless you can find some basis of faith in general principles, some theory of the progress of civilization which is outside and above all temporary questions of policy, you must infallibly think and act under the control of the man or men whose thought, in the times you deal with, coincides most nearly with your own prejudices."[11]

Yielding to another's intellectual posture was never one of Adams's weaknesses. While James was implicitly

branding "faith in general principles . . . outside and
above all temporary questions of policy" an intellectual
chimera, Adams was decrying the loss of disinterested-
ness and moral standards those general principles
required. Accordingly, in his reply to James's essays,
he conveyed his dissatisfaction with James's too exuber-
ant dismissal of historical determinism in favor of some
arbitrary allegiance to free will. While James could live
comfortably in a pluralistic world that was somehow
both lawful and plastic, in which there was both continuity and inception, Adams could not. Indeed, the
two extremes were for him mutually exclusive, and a
universe made up of both was an absurdity. "As I
understand your Faith," he wrote to James,

> . . . it is the old question of Free Will over again.
> You choose to assume that the will is free. Good!
> Reason proves that the will cannot be free. Equally
> good! . . . If the orthodox are grateful to you for
> such gifts, the world has indeed changed, and we
> have much to thank God for, if there is a God,
> that he should have left us unable to decide
> whether our thoughts, if we have thoughts, are
> our own or his'n. . . . With hero-worship like Car-
> lyle's I have little patience. In history heroes have
> neutralysed each other, and the result is no more
> than would have been reached without
> them. . . .[12]

James's essays had adumbrated what he was later to
call "the will to believe," a pragmatic philosophical perspective that accepted a loose, sometimes incongruous
universe held together as much by human experience
and purpose as by any external adhesive. Offered the
choice between a monistic, deterministic view of reality
and a pluralistic indeterminacy, James unhesitatingly

opted for the latter. Indeterminacy meant freedom for the mind to choose, to create, to add onto the sum of things in existence; in this creative possibility was the very substance of intelligent, meaningful life. Fundamental to James's pragmatism was the notion that the individual's mind could, within limits, create history out of its own acts of choice. The reputation he was to gain as a philosopher around the turn of the century derived from his elaboration and defense of this position.

For Adams, the alternatives had different connotations. The choice was not whether there was freedom to alter the flow of time by electing this or that option, but whether amid or beyond the chaos of history there was some knowable regularity, some law or laws the human mind could discover and abide by. Such laws would, of course, encompass the thought processes and choices of the human mind and thus provide a unified framework for interpreting the past, comprehending the present, and predicting the future. It was for this reason that Adams reacted so strongly against James's voluntarism. Adams always sought unity behind the multiplicity of life; he always sought synthesis and order within the flow of the past and present. Just as James's reputation was staked on indeterminacy and pluralism, so Adams came to be noted for his dogged quest for unity, for the monolithic, rational resolution of the vexing, often incomprehensible puzzle of historical change.

For nearly three decades after Adams's letter to James in 1882, the two struggled in their own ways with the problems of order and chaos, unity and multiplicity, determinism and free will. If they could not agree on solutions to these questions, however tentatively expressed, at least they agreed on what were the central intellectual issues of the day. By spring 1910,

they had reached their separate conclusions; they could
but agree to disagree. Each had written volumes about
these problems and made a name for himself by his
distinctive, highly idiosyncratic answers. The two could
have hardly been further apart. Adams's *Letter* and
James's reply to it were their last words together on
all that had preoccupied them for so many years.
There was, as Adams liked to put it, nothing more to
say; silence was best.

James had again embarked for Europe in April on
another of his vain searches for relief from depression
and angina, the latter having of late become increasingly painful and constant. Characteristically, his
antidote for fatigue and heart strain was renewed exertion. Since the fateful day in July 1898 when he had
exhausted himself mountain climbing in the Adiron-
dacks, his heart condition had progressively worsened.
James refused, as he put it, to "give up to it," and by
1907 he had to retire from Harvard. Retirement, however, did not mean idleness; in 1908, he delivered the
prestigious (but taxing) Hibbert Lectures at Oxford,
and the following year he published *A Pluralistic
Universe* and *The Meaning of Truth*. By the spring of
1910, he was—as he well knew—mortally ill. Still
undaunted, he resolved to have another round in the
enervating baths at Nauheim, Germany, and to visit his
brother Henry, who was also ailing, near London on
the way.[13]

At Lamb House, while waiting for Henry to improve,
James discovered a copy of *Mont-Saint-Michel and
Chartres*, which Adams had sent to his brother but
had neglected to send to him.[14] James had read the
*Education* with pleasure and had remembered to
bring his copy of *Letter to American Teachers of History*
with him to Europe, but he was saving it to read at
Nauheim. *Mont-Saint-Michel and Chartres* impressed him

immensely, and he wrote at once to Adams, then in Paris: "[I] can't help sending you a paean of praise. From beginning to end it reads as from a man in the fresh morning of life, with a frolic quality of power unusual in historical literature so far as yet revealed to me, and I have found it powerful instructive. Where you stole all that St. Thomas, I shd. like to know! Of course I skipt much of the architectural detail, and found myself wishing that you would reprint the whole thing with innumerable fotografs or other designs —I'm sure it will last in literature—and in that case one will not feel inclined to skip."[15]

In May, James traveled to Paris to consult a heart specialist, and during his stay he visited with Adams. He had not yet read the *Letter*, though, and did not do so until some weeks later in Nauheim. It was from the German spa that he penned his reactions to his friend's final speculation about history.

The *Letter to American Teachers of History* was Adams's last attempt to suggest a comprehensive, scientific synthesis of historical movement. It represented the culmination of a series of inquiries he had begun in the early 1890s that led first to his presidential message to the American Historical Association in 1894, "The Tendency of History," and later to *Mont-Saint-Michel and Chartres*, the *Education*, and "The Rule of Phase Applied to History" (1909). In "Tendency," Adams had written that "any science assumes a necessary sequence of cause and effect, a force resulting in motion which cannot be other than what it is. Any science of history must be absolute, like other sciences, and must fix with mathematical certainty the path which human society has got to follow."[16] He had then, with that characteristic perversity which was almost playful, gone on to demonstrate all the reasons why such a science of history could never be achieved. In the *Letter*, however, again in that spirit of play which was so desperately serious, he attempted what he had earlier proclaimed to be impossible.

Henry Adams had long been piqued by the failure of historians to make use of the data and methods of modern science to renovate their discipline. History, he had written in the *Education*, was still "a hundred years behind the experimental sciences."[17] In centuries gone by, the problem had not become crucial because the forces of social change had not reached the critical levels of intensity that the late nineteenth century witnessed. Now, in the twentieth century, with the secrets of nuclear energy promising to deliver a new and awesome source of power into the hands of men, the need for a unifying, scientific explanation of historical force was imperative. None of the nineteenth-century historical syntheses were any longer viable: Auguste Comte, Charles Darwin, Charles Lyell, Henry Buckle, Herbert Spencer—all had given interpretations that antedated or failed to consider the implications of modern physics for history.[18] The great syntheses of the nineteenth century had been based on biological or mechanical analogies that were now outmoded. A modern historical synthesis had to derive from physics and mathematics, since these were the sciences producing the incredible new history-making energies.

Two nineteenth-century hypotheses—Lord Kelvin's (William Thompson) second law of thermodynamics, or entropy, and Josiah Willard Gibbs' rule of phase—provided Adams with the principles for his theorizing.[19] In "The Rule of Phase Applied to History," Adams had drawn an analogy between Gibbs' idea of the stages of equilibrium through which chemical compounds pass—solid, fluid, vapor, electricity, ether—when subjected to variations in pressure, temperature, and volume, and the stages of the concentration and expenditure of energies in history. Just as changes in the temperature of and pressure on water transform it from a fluid to a gaseous state, so changes in human thought and social institutions transform history in a measurable, deterministic fashion: "Under the Rule of Phase . . . man's Thought, considered as a single substance passing through a series of historical phases, is assumed to follow the analogy of water, and to pass from one phase to another through a series of critical points which are determined by the three factors of Attraction, Acceleration, and Volume, for each change of equilibrium."[20] Adams had even gone so far as to plot the trajectory of how the accelerating phase-changes of history threatened to bring thought itself to the "limit of its possibilities in the year 1921."[21] Geometric increases in the volume of thought operating under the law of inverse squares were propelling man to a point beyond which equilibrium would soon no longer be physically possible, and, presumably, cosmic chaos would then reign.

A basic assumption of "The Rule of Phase" was that thought, like electricity or gravity, was a form of energy. As such, it functioned according to invariable physical laws. This being true, the historian's task was greatly simplified: all he needed now was to master certain physical principles and axioms and apply them to history. In one sense, the historian's job was finished. In place of him stood the physicist; art was to yield to science. "Sooner or later, every apparent exception, whether man or radium, tends to fall within the domain of physics."[22] In the *Letter*, Adams exchanged his artist's palette for the physicist's slide rule.

The physical principle Adams rested his case on in the *Letter* was Lord Kelvin's second law of thermodynamics, or entropy, which had been set forth in 1852 and which Adams seems to have discovered

shortly after the turn of the century.[23] As Adams
understood it, the law posited that the fixed amount
of energy the universe began with was being dissipated
with every expenditure of physical or mental effort in
the cosmos: "granting that the universe was a closed
box from which nothing could escape,—the higher
powers of energy tended always to fall lower, and . . .
this process has no known limit."[24] As degeneration,
or degradation, as Adams called it, inexorably proceeded, the universe moved from primal heat and
motion toward coldness, stillness, and a final resting
place somewhere near minus 273 degrees centigrade.
All of life, society, and history had to yield before this
total, constant, accelerating dissipation of heat and
energy. The sun would condense and wither, the stars
would grow cold, eternal night would descend; given
the law of entropy, the end of the universe was
assured.

To support his point, Adams cited a variety of current authorities in physics, mathematics, natural
philosophy, geology, and anthropology, all of whom
concurred that the cosmic energies were irrecoverably
dissipating themselves at what Adams suggested was at
an accelerating rate. Generally, however, this scientific
consensus was being ignored by students of society,
particularly in the United States.[25] This, to Adams, was
an intolerable oversight. "If the entire universe, in
every variety of active energy, organic and inorganic,
human and divine, is to be treated as a clockwork that
is running down, society can hardly go on ignoring the
fact forever. . . . The universe has been terribly nar-
rowed by thermodynamics."[26] Historians especially
seemed to resist entropy and its implications. Committed to an archaic progressivism based on an uncritical acceptance of Darwin, Comte, Spencer or some vag-
rant Germanic idealism, professors of history shunned

entropy in favor of sentiment. Adams's goal was to shake his fellow historians out of their vast complacency by forcing them to take entropy into account in their systems and theories.[27]

The vision of history contained in the *Letter* systematically took the dominant assumptions of American historians in 1910 and stood them on their collective heads. Under the law of degradation, the most recent and advanced developments in thought and society became, by inversion, the latest and most powerful contributions to that ultimate extinction toward which all tended. Civilization itself, far from representing the culmination of upward-moving historical tendencies, was but the most recent, and most pervasive, form taken by energy as it dissipated. So too with man and his works, his will, and his intellect. Appearing late in the sequence of creation did not mean that man was the ultimate, the highest product of cosmic teleology, but simply that he was the most recent (and hence lowest) form of universal degradation. The more refined and powerful his achievements, the more degrading were their implications. All that current opinion pointed to with pride—industrialization, technology, science, art—became evidence of the charging, impending doom toward which all human energies were directed. Adams's theory of degradation inverted the mainstream of contemporary historical opinion and turned progress against itself: silence and death were to be the ultimate rewards of human effort. The *Letter* was Adams's impious rebuttal to the cheerful orthodoxy of evolutionary progressivism.

Adams's tirade was directed particularly against Darwinian evolutionism and the progressive interpretations of natural selection. Darwin and his interpreters had assumed that cosmic energies were constant and that energy conserved itself; they assumed the validity of the ancient first law of thermodynamics. The newer law of entropy, however, extended equally to organic and inorganic nature, both of which showed "a universal tendency toward the dissipation of energy." The evolutionist, though possibly correct in certain short-run instances, had to admit many exceptions to his generalization; moreover, he had to admit (and this was crucial) that "nature shows no known machinery for restoring the energy that she dissipates." If evolution were true on the cosmic scale, the evolutionist would have proof "that man alone enjoys the supernatural power of consciously reversing nature's process, by raising her dissipated energies, including his own, to higher intensities. That is to say, man must possess the exclusive power of reversing the process of extinction inherent in other activities of nature." Rather than this, man showed himself to be anything but a conserver of nature's energies; every exercise of his will and genius produced newer and more virulent dissipations. His use of natural resources, his conversion of the environment to a vast habiliment, his labor-saving (but energy-expending) inventions and machinery—all demonstrated that "from the physicist's point of view, Man, as a conscious and constant, single, natural force, seems to have no function except that of dissipating or degrading energy."[28] The logic of degradation inverted evolutionism's assumptions about directionality and value in history.

This inversion was especially evident when it came to the function and consequences of human thought. Most evolutionists regarded man's cerebral capacities as the most advanced—the highest—response that organic creation had made to the natural environment. But if thought was, as the evolutionists insisted, a natural product not independent of the laws governing the development of matter and motion, it too was subject to the same degenerative imperatives, to the "steady and fated enfeeblement and extinction of all nature's energies."[29] If thought was energy, it also represented a debased, latter-day advance over some more primitive but originally potent instinct or capacity for action. Thus, Adams carried his assault even to the level of reason and intelligence, to the holy of holies of the Progressive era. The result was a resplendent irony, the kind of suspension Adams delighted in: "From the beginnings of philosophy and religion, the thinker was taught by the mere act of thinking, to take for granted that his mind was the highest energy of nature. . . . As a force [reason] must obey the laws of force; as an energy it must content itself with such freedom as the laws of energy allow; and in any case it must submit to the final and fundamental necessity of Degradation. The same law, by still stronger reasoning, applies to the Will itself."[30] Even the discovery of the second law of thermodynamics and its application to history represented but the most recent and hence degraded of acts. Adams's own intellectual endeavors, as he best knew and appreciated, were nothing more than further dissipations of an already enfeebled energy!

There was in all of this so strong an element of Adams's dyspeptic personality and declining circumstances in life that at least one critic has dismissed the *Letter* as "irony and tomfoolery," as Adams's last wry, mocking joke on those who took science and scientism as the alpha and omega of modern knowledge.[31] And there was, to be sure, a puckish, gleeful aspect to Adams's demolition of the prevailing historical refraction of his day. Adams had taken a familiar, apocalyptic vision, once couched in terms of Christian eschatology, and translated it into the formalistic parlance of modern science. Traditional absolutism and modern empiricism were thus smitten in one outrageous stroke.

Yet Adams's taste for irony and his penchant for shocking the bourgeois have, in the last analysis, little bearing on whether the *Letter* was meant as a joke. The point, on the contrary, is that when Adams turned to science and history for a unifying principle with which to broach and comprehend the cosmos, the substance of the *Letter* was the result. Joke or not, Adams certainly expected to be taken seriously, for he could weave no wider net for snaring the vicissitudes of time. If the net was spun in the pattern of his own eccentric biases, it was still his instrument, his entrapment for meaning, and it had, at least in his mind, to be reckoned with.

Adams could not, in truth, resist putting human history in some cosmic frame of reference, for only in such a context could he perceive it as having meaning. But that history turned out to be regressive was not, as Adams tried to make it appear, incidental to the framework; Adams's affinity for the degradationist viewpoint had long been evident in his work, and, as William Jordy has shown, in the *Letter* Adams tailored a variety of current theories to fit his leanings.[32] Adams was careful, however, to give the impression of a relentless, even reluctant, presentation of the hard facts of life. If man and his illusions about progress crumbled in the process, there was apparently little Henry Adams could do about it. That was damage for others to repair—if they could. The *Letter* dared them to try.

It was appropriate, then, that only William James took time to dissent, for James had a well-deserved reputation for intellectual dauntlessness. As might be expected, his reaction was highly critical. Adams had postulated so much in the *Letter* that was anathema to

James that he must scarcely have known where to begin his attack. The formalistic conception of the universe as a box with fixed contours and preestablished boundaries, the debauched inversion of man's will and intellect into some diabolical machinery for ultimate self-destruction, the assumption that the historian (or anyone else) could infer the beginning and end of the cosmos from a fragment of experience and then plot an absolute, deterministic curve between the two—all were points against which James had written numerous pragmatic disquisitions. Adams's *Letter* cut diametrically across the grain of James's faith in human thought and will and their role in history. James's pragmatism had projected a universe as experienced by individuals that was open, vital, and amenable to human effort and energy, neither of which seemed noticeably on the decline. But if time and energy were not necessarily running out for mankind, they were for James, and he had to satisfy himself with a trenchant rebuttal that went to the heart of the *Letter*'s thesis: he attacked Adams's conception of history itself.

Conceding that the conventional wisdom of modern science did, for the moment, lean toward a theory of universal degradation, James confined his remarks to "some of the specifications of the great statistical drift downwards of the original high-level energy." Theories of beginnings and ends of time, however scientific and current, were essentially in the nature of "conventions and fashions," and James generously did not question that Adams had represented the physicists accurately. What he did question was what all this meant for man as he lived out his allotted three-score years and ten, what history as degradation meant in terms of human experience. James speaks best for himself:

To begin with, the *amount* of cosmic energy it costs

to buy a certain distribution of fact which humanely we regard as precious, seems to me to be an altogether secondary matter as regards the question of history and progress. Certain arrangements of matter *on the same energy-level* are, from the point of view of man's appreciation, superior, while others are inferior. Physically a dinosaur's brain may show as much intensity of energy-exchange as a man's but it can do infinitely fewer things, because as a force of detent it can only unlock the dinosaur's muscles, while the man's brain, by unlocking far feebler muscles, indirectly can by their means issue proclamations, write books, describe Chartres Cathedral, etc., and guide the energies of the shrinking sun into channels which never would have been entered otherwise—in short, *make* history. Therefore the man's brain and muscles are, from the point of view of the historian, the more important place of energy-exchange, small as this may be when measured in absolute physical units.

The "second law" is wholly irrelevant to "history"—save that it sets a terminus—for history is the course of things before that terminus, and all that the second law says is that, whatever the history, it must invest itself between that initial maximum and that terminal minimum of difference in energy-level. As the great irrigation-reservoir empties itself, the whole question for us is that of the distribution of its effects, of *which* rills to guide it into; and the size of the rills has nothing to do with their significance. Human cerebration is the most important rill we know of, and both the "capacity" and the "intensity" factor thereof may be treated as infinitesimal. Yet the filling of such rills would be cheaply bought by the waste of whole sums spent in getting a little of the down-flowing torrent to enter them. Just so of human institutions—their value has in strict theory nothing whatever to do with their energy-budget—being wholly a question of the form the energy flows through. Though the *ultimate* state of the universe may be its vital and psychical extinction, there is nothing in physics to interfere with the hypothesis that the penultimate state might be the millennium—in other words a state in which a minimum of difference of energy-level might have its exchanges so skillfully *canalisés* that a maximum of happy and virtuous consciousness would be the only result. In short, the last expiring pulsation of the universe's life might be, I am so happy and perfect that I can stand it no longer. You don't believe this and I don't say I do. But I can find nothing in "Energetik" to conflict with its possibility. You seem to me not to discriminate, but to treat quantity and distribution of energy as if they formed one question.

There! that's pretty good for a brain after 18 Nauheim baths—so I won't write another line, nor ask you to reply to me. In case you can't help doing so, however, I will gratify you now by saying that I probably won't jaw back.—It was pleasant at Paris to hear your identically unchanged and undegraded voice after so many years of loss of solar energy.[33]

Not jawing back was too much to expect from James, however, and two days later he was again writing to Adams:

P.S. Another illustration of my meaning: The clock of the universe is running down, and by so

doing makes the hands move. The energy
absorbed by the hands and the *mechanical* work
they do is the same day after day, no matter how
far the weights would have descended from the
position they were originally wound up to. The
*history* which the hands perpetrate has nothing to
do with the *quantity* of this work, but follows the
*significance* of the figures which they cover on the
dial. If they move from 0 to XII, there is
"progress," if from XII to 0, there is "decay," etc.
etc.

W.J.[34]

Adams discreetly avoided James's challenge. In a letter from Paris dated June 20, he replied that it was
not he who was "making trouble," but rather the thinkers and scientists he cited in the *Letter*, none of whom
would rise in response to the long-term implications
which Adams saw in their views for history. He himself
was "not asserting or rejecting anything." Indeed, he
never had:

Never have I held an opinion of my own, or ven-
tured to trust a judgment. With humble heart I
have chased the flying philosopher, trying to find
out *his* opinion that I might guide my own steps;
and a wearier task I know not. My philosopher
runs like a rabbit when I seek his burrow. He
denies frenziedly that he has ever expressed an
opinion at all. He hides his tail. . . . I come as
a student in a spirit of love and moral chastity,
but I see them already running away till they
darken the field, and leave me alone, scattering
carrots and turnips—or whatever it is to scat-
ter,—to entice them back.[35]

This elicited from James one last comment, again an illustration of the point he had been trying to make in his letter of June 17:

> Yours of the 20th, just arriving, pleases me by its docility of spirit and passive subjection to philosophic opinion. Never, never pretend to an opinion of your own! that way lies every annoyance and madness! You tempt me to offer you another illustration—that of the *hydraulic ram* (thrown back to me in an exam. as a "hydraulic goat" by an insufficiently intelligent student). Let this arrangement of metal, placed in the course of a brook, symbolize the machine of human life. It works, clap, clap, clap, day and night, so long as the brook runs *at all*, and no matter how full the brook (which symbolizes the descending cosmic energy) may be, it works always to the same effect, of raising so many kilogrammeters of water. What the *value* of this work as history may be, depends on the uses to which the water is put in the house which the ram serves.[36]

In effect, James was saying that the *Letter* and its elaborate web of scientific evidence still allowed history to escape. For all his efforts to tie down and secure the movement of the cosmos, Adams had not even approached history in the first place! History for James was essentially a human affair; if the cosmos were ultimately running out of energy, what concerned men was the question of what happened before the energy sustaining human life—true history—expired. The *Letter* had not given compelling evidence that human life had in fact degenerated, only that it occurred within a system, part of which seemed to be dissipating. That

everything in the system was equally affected simply
had not been proved. And that thought was the most
advanced form of degradation followed only from the
unproved assumption that everything in the cosmos
obeyed equally the law of entropy. Adams's conclusions
were hardly warranted by the evidence.

But more than this, James was suggesting an
approach to historical understanding so different in
conception from that of Adams as to put him in a
totally different philosophical camp. The notion of history implicit in the *Letter* was absolutistic: history was
the lawful totality of all that transpired within the universe. About this, James confessed he had little to say.
His view was much more modest and circumspect: history was what one could know about the past that had
significance in terms of human experience. Adams was
reading history through his own particular lenses, but
they were lenses which refracted in a traditional way
and read history as the story of some great design that
finally determined all that was within. James, on the
other hand, read history as a pragmatist: history was
the sense, the experience of the past as it bore upon
the present and flowed into the future.

Defined in James's way, history took on value connotations according to what any generation or culture or
individual historian regarded as valuable. Historical
value did not inhere in the mere passage of time
but in what was assessed to be the significance of
what occurred, or what people understood to have occurred, in history. The basis of this assessment, James
implied, was up to the inquirer, and his criteria might
well change according to the purpose of the inquiry.
Man's sense of value, then, was *added to* the world
he experienced; it did not just passively reflect that
world. "I think," James wrote to a friend the year before he read Adams's *Letter*, "the center of my whole

*Anschauung* . . . has been the belief that something is doing in the universe, and that *novelty* is real."[37] James's sense of history, as his reaction to the *Letter* indicates, was that it was anything but necessary degeneration.

Since history was what came before "that terminal minimum of energy level" and since *"novelty* is real," James was able to hold out for the possibility that human beings could improve their circumstances in time, that historical progress was real. While human thought and action may have transpired in a universe ultimately degenerating, within the limits of human time and time sense they had real meaning and effect. Man's brain, as James put it, made history. And it did so on a double level of meaning: it caused action, and, second, it perceived, comprehended, and evaluated those actions. James accordingly put "progress" and "decay" in quotation marks in the first postscript to his letter of June 17 to show that the words were qualitative designations ascribed to occurrences in time by men whose interests or expectations were either being met or not by their assessment of and participation in those occurrences. The hands of the clock moved over the dial, but men read the clock according to their interests; and they also helped the hands to move. Similarly, as he noted in the second postscript, the value of the work done by the ram depended on "the uses to which the water is put in the house which the ram serves." In each case, James was insisting that history did not by its very nature determine what time was to signify or mean; the designation was up to man. Progress or decay might be real, but their reality was imputed. History did not necessarily mean one or the other.

History did mean, however, the possibility that human effort and will might be real causal factors in the course of events. Ever since *The Will to Believe* was

published in 1897, James had been elaborating on what
he called "the lawfulness of voluntarily adopted faith,"
on the right of individuals to select from experience
ideas possibly true and choose to act upon them, hence
helping by action to create their verity. There were
instances, James contended, in which the course of
events could not be predetermined, in which believing
in the possibility of a truth permitted actions that made
that truth come true; there were times when *"faith in
a fact [could] help create the fact."*[38] The flow of time,
James thought, allowed for the insertion of human
choice and belief in such a way as to change the future
in a morally satisfying way. While James carefully
pointed out that there were real limitations to what
reasonable men were at liberty to believe ("living
options"), within those limitations there was room to
choose and act and hence to create new, desired truths.
History could be changed and made more satisfying
to men by thought, will, and action.

Even more fundamentally, James's understanding of
the nature and function of thought and the conceptualizing process itself was at odds with Adams's scientism. James agreed that thought, like any other physical effort, could be regarded as a form of energy
expenditure, but he denied vehemently that thought
proceeded according to such determinate laws as to be
analogous to the law of gravity or some other formula
derived from physics. Even before *The Principles of
Psychology* (1890) put his arguments into systematic
form, James had held for the creative efficacy of
thought in time. Thought was much more than simply
the pale cast of external, historical reality; it was the
dynamic engagement of the mind with the perceived
past and the as-yet-to-be-created future, a future that
might in substantial but unpredictable ways be modified by the reality of ideas. To the extent that history

was altered by the thoughts of men, it could not be the deterministic sequence of events that Adams suggested.

Thus the lines were drawn. Adams, acting the role of cosmic historical scientist, projected a conception of history as a grand, lawful, dissipating totality that embraced the infinite and, incidentally, dwarfed and negated human desire and effort. James, the pragmatist, suggested that history was less grandiose and a great deal more accessible to finite man. For each, history had a vastly different scale and hence a vastly different meaning. Yet each was making an act of faith in rendering his definition. Adams in the curve of degradation found, at last, a unity in history that suited his temperament; James, in viewing history as the leap and flow of options perceived and acted upon, found a pluralism that suited his. At bottom, they wound up disputing whether the idea of progress meant anything.

*ii*

That Henry Adams and William James should have come to disagree so fundamentally over the nature of history and the question of progress was not at all surprising. On perhaps no other contemporary philosophical question was there more discussion and less agreement than that of progress. The very rush of history in the years bracketing 1900—the heady pace of social change, the dazzling innovations of science and technology, the multiplicity of philosophical and ethical opinions—produced a cacophony that yielded any number of historical interpretations. Ever since the 1890s, when the approach of the twentieth century seized men's imagination as the irresistible symbol of changing times, there had been a torrent of conjecture in America about whether accomplishments of the past and prospects for the future constituted progress. Articles and essays in newspapers, magazines, and journals abounded; the advent of the new century seemed to strike a speculative chord in every literate sensibility. In 1910, the speculation was still rampant, and the question of progress was still unresolved. Perhaps more than they knew, Adams and James reflected the times in which they lived; although their disagreement sprang from a metaphysical rift having profound philosophical significance, their concern with the question of progress was a reflection on a lofty level of a debate that filled the popular media and helped define the intellectual climate of the turn of the century.

As Americans around 1900 evaluated their place in history, they were, on the whole, well satisfied. That they were parties to progress was, as it had been for a century and a half, a primary article of the American faith, and the majority of stocktakings as the century turned assumed that such was still the case. A favorite device of journalists, one that yielded undeniably impressive results and that generously indulged the American proclivity for facts and figures, was to compare America in 1900 with the America of Jefferson's day. In both territory and population, the changes were spectacular.

The *New York Herald* of December 30, 1900, pointed out that during the nineteenth century the United States had grown from a provincial, seaboard country of some 5,308,483 souls and some 830,000 square miles to a gigantic continental leviathan with a population of over ninety million and a territorial domain of 3,714,711 square miles; if the newly acquired American trophies of the Spanish-American War were thrown in, the statistics were even higher. In commerce, the *Herald* noted, the United States had grown from a diminutive, one-ocean carrier of less than 800,000 tons annually to a two-ocean giant carrying nearly five million tons each year; the value of this commerce had leaped from $200 million in 1801 to over $2 billion in 1901. Citing Bureau of the Treasury statistics, the *Herald* estimated that, on this basis, American commerce in the year 2000 would be valued at $22 billion. The population held promise of similar growth: Director of Census W. H. Merriam predicted an America of four hundred million people by the end of the twentieth century. "Shades of Malthus," exclaimed a writer in *The World's Work* in December 1900. "What a mass of humanity that will be!"

In science and technology, similar progress was observed, and glowing, if sometimes exotic, prospects were forecast. The nineteenth century, C. K. Adams wrote in the *Atlantic* in September 1899, was above all a "century of invention" during which one witnessed the "abolition of time and space and delay." Through science, economy and efficiency of effort were reaching new heights in all areas of human activity. The *New York Herald* of December 30, 1900, estimated modestly that "whereas science proves that we get barely two percent out of the real possibilities in the material life about us, it is possible that the generations hence shall get ten or twenty percent." Astounding, lengthy, tedious lists of nineteenth-century inventions were compiled, and sometimes the possibilities for the future seemed to have been preempted. After predicting "ariel" fights in the twentieth century between armed aircraft, H. G. Wells, in the August 1901 *North American Review*, confessed that his imagination failed when it came to submarine warfare: "I must confess that my imagination . . . refuses to see any sort of submarine doing anything but suffocate its crew and founder at sea." Such a failure did not affect O. P. Austin, however, who in the same magazine in November 1900 predicted that in the twentieth century "aerial navigation" would transport "men and mails," that wireless telegraphy would connect "all sections of the world," that electric power would be sent hundreds of miles from its point of origin, and that a canal would soon link the Atlantic and Pacific oceans.

One writer in the December 30, 1900, *New York Herald* predicted that in the coming century science would so perfect posthypnotic suggestion that it would cure St. Vitus's dance and "Americanitis (nervous exhaustion) with its attendant insomnia," as well as prove useful to physicians in "intra-uterine inspiration." Hypnoscience, the writer went on, "is destined to demonstrate immortality on scientific principles, to determine the laws that govern telepathic intercourse, and possibly to extend its investigation into the realm of the dead, establishing communication with spiritual intelligence."

In the optimistic light of the new century, such speculations did not seem farfetched, for who could put limits on the advance of science in the future? "There can be no question," declared an observer in *Living Age* on February 26, 1901, "that the progress of science and the application of science to industry will go on in a geometric ratio, and that eventually every country will benefit by this advance."

In addition to America's growth and its scientific and technological accomplishments, there were numerous other categories in which progress was obvious. Advances in social, biological, physical, and historical knowledge, evidence of a growing sophistication in government, the spread of "civilization" to the "barbarous" regions of the world, expanding economic production and its extension of comparative affluence to the working classes (the *Indianapolis Journal* for January 7, 1900, commented that "no single feature of nineteenth-century progress has been more remarkable or more significant of advancing civilization than the improvement of the working class"), the vistas opened by the application of electric power to all spheres of social activity—all were paraded dutifully and contributed to the general sense of well-being reflected in the journalistic assessments of the day.

But despite the widespread use of the term "progress" in describing these changes, there was equally widespread disagreement over what progress actually meant and, hence, whether it truly prevailed. On one hand, most commentators regarded growth or change in any category as evidence of progress; consequently, the idea attached to nearly every observable variation in American life. On the other, the dominant ballyhoo and self-congratulation notwithstanding, a significant and vocal minority of Americans did not share in the general optimism that greeted the new century. Particularly among intellectuals, lacking as they did the obligation of journalistic uplift, a more sober and often more pessimistic stance was taken. Not all change was necessarily for the better, they noted; the irrefutable evidence of America's emergence as a modern world power did not automatically translate into progress. And though there had always been in the past Cassandras dissenting from the progressive credo of the eighteenth and nineteenth centuries, by 1900 the number of serious and reflective doubters was growing.[39]

Their complaints were both numerous and specific. The imperialistic posture of the country after the Spanish-American War troubled many, although America's acquisition of new territories had been desig-

nated by no less an authority than President William
McKinley himself as the obligation of progress. In a
speech in Boston in 1899, the President had said: "The
Philippines, like Cuba and Porto Rico [*sic*], were
entrusted to our hands by war, and to that great trust,
under the providence of God and in the name of
human progress and civilization we are committed."[40]
Lyman Abbott, among others, accepted the commitment gladly; in an article entitled "The Rights of Man"
in *The Outlook* of June 29, 1901, he wrote: "It is the
function of the Anglo-Saxon race to confer [the] gifts
of civilization . . . on the uncivilized people of the
world. . . . I deny the right of a barbaric people to
retain possession of any quarter of the globe." Such
sentiments challenged even the optimism of William
James, who saw imperialism as a betrayal of America's
heritage. The argument that the United States was
responsible for the spread of civilization was no justification for sheer theft: "Could there be a more damn-
ing indictment of that whole bloated idol termed
'modern civilization' than this amounts to? Civilization
is, then, the big, hollow, resounding, corrupting,
sophisticating, confusing torrent of mere brutal
momentum and irrationality that brings forth fruits
like this?"[41] To the small but vocal band of anti-
imperialists, America, by retaining the territorial spoils
of war, seemed to be departing from its original moral
course, and that departure prevented opponents of
empire from viewing the future in traditional, progressive terms.

Similarly, while the American population had indeed
soared astronomically, especially in the decades since
the Civil War, many saw in the urban sprawl and fester
that accompanied this increase not progress but
degeneration.[42] It was no accident that Henry Adams
began his magnificent autobiography by pointing out

the virtues of rural Quincy and the vices of urban Boston. American intellectuals had traditionally been ambivalent about the values of the city, and by the turn of the century this ambivalence was often blossoming into outright hostility and regret.[43] The influx of non-Anglo-Saxon or even northern European immigrants in the 1880s and 1890s, while swelling the population, seemed to many traditionalists a portent of a disastrous pollution of America's racial purity, and the resulting spate of nativistic outbursts during the 1890s is further evidence of the negative attitude of many Americans toward the future.

Despite the wafting prosperity and productivity that followed the election of 1896 and carried well into the twentieth century, many were troubled by the trend toward corporate consolidation and by the still-growing gap between American haves and have-nots. The disparity was not, critics pointed out repeatedly, merely a question of economic equality; inequitable distribution of the nation's wealth had grave political implications which, if extended, might easily spell the end of America's experiment in democracy. Lyman Abbott, the normally optimistic editor of *The Outlook*, wrote on May 2, 1901, that "as it is the glory of the United States that wealth has never been so widely distributed as it is in the United States today, and employment has never been so much in demand in all the various vocations of life, so it is the peril of the United States that wealth is still too much concentrated in the hands of the few. . . . For we must recognize the fact that . . . this concentration exists, and in forms which are perilous to American institutions."

Ex-Senator George F. Edmunds of Vermont, when asked what he felt was the chief danger of the new century, replied unequivocally in the January 12, 1901, issue of *The Outlook*: "Ignorance, greed, centralization

of wealth and social and political power, and the consequent inequality of position and opportunity without
which liberty and justice cannot exist." Most of these
dissenters agreed with Frederick Harrison, the visiting
Englishman, who saw the end of the century as "a fall
from a higher plane." "The Nineteenth Century," he
said in an article in the *New York Post* in January 1901,
"has left us a terrible legacy of problems—moral, intellectual, political; international rivalries, industrial wars,
metaphysical sophisms, cloudy theosophies, moral can-
cers. . . . Unless the Twentieth Century can recast morality, philosophy, and religion we shall go down a steep
place into the sea like a herd of swine."

Although science was celebrated on many fronts as
the agent of progress, there were those who recognized
that the scientific method itself was corrosive of the
comfortable absolutes that had defined the moral and
physical universe for centuries. The very function of
science, until those turbulent decades after Darwin,
had been to confirm and verify the regularity and harmony of the cosmos. By the turn of the century, many
Americans were coming to share the unsettling conviction that advances in science, exhilarating as they were,
lay directly behind the growing sense of uncertainty
and alienation that was beginning to affect the popular
consciousness. While the noted historian John Fiske, in
surveying the "century's progress in science" in 1896,
could serenely conclude that the "dynamical conception" of the world achieved by Darwin and Spencer
revealed man to be "the child of the universe, the heir
of all the ages, in whose making and perfecting is to
be found the consummation of God's creative work,"[44]
others found in evolutionary science not guaranteed
progress but flux, indeterminacy, and, in Charles S.
Peirce's phrase, a "universe of chance." While his contemporaries were linking and even identifying science

and progress, Peirce was specifically denying that happiness or social improvement had anything to do with science. That which related to improvement, Peirce argued, was not science but some other sort of valuative process.[45]

While popularizations of Darwinian evolutionary theories had crept into every segment of thought, not all were certain that evolution meant progress. This question had been discussed extensively over the preceding decades, and in 1900 no easy, compelling resolution seemed in the offing. On one hand, David J. Brewer, an Associate Justice of the Supreme Court, could write in 1899 that "whether evolution be in all respects scientifically true; whether physiologically we are simply apes—a little higher developed—and in respect to some men whom we see and know we oftimes doubt whether there has been any development—it is true that civilization is progressive. . . . We have a right to expect that this advance will continue, and that it will continue with accelerating speed. The progression is not arithmetical but geometrical."[46] Social Gospeler Washington Gladden found himself in agreement, although he saw the hand of God in the process: "An inexhaustible future beckons a race that feels the energies of God tingling in its nerves. We are part of a growing organism, and human progress is a living experience, therefore there is hope ahead."[47]

On the other hand, there was doubt. Though *The Outlook* of December 1, 1900, had judged Darwin's *Origin of Species* the "most influential book of the century" just passed, H. W. Horwill, for one, did not believe Americans had grasped its significance. Their failure, moreover, prevented them from achieving true progress. "The idea of the supreme importance of selection," he wrote in *Current Opinion* in March 1903, "has not yet laid hold upon the American people. Intellectual or social progress is conceived of as a series of additions. . . . There is little or no understanding of the fact that refinement is not a matter of accumulation."[48] Evolution did not provide a simple answer to the question of progress.

In sum, a vast and pervasive ambivalence toward the idea of progress marked American thought at the turn of the century. Often the very instances that one observer would cite as evidence of progress seemed to another to prove the very opposite. Rapid social and intellectual change was clearly causing some Americans to look with nostalgia on the vanishing order of the past and with foreboding to the future. While hardier—or less perceptive—viewers saw the passage of time in roseate hues, many saw "modernity" as a headlong rush into chaos and destruction.[49] Obviously progress meant different things to different people. Despite the fact that the turn of the twentieth century ushered in what is customarily called the "Progressive" period of American life and politics, few could agree on the freight this defining term should carry. If intellectuals such as Adams and James could not agree over the reality and meaning of progress, neither could their less academic contemporaries.[50]


*iii*


The dispute between Adams and James signified much more than simply another random discrepancy in the turn-of-century assessments of progress. Although their disputation came to focus ultimately on the issue of progress, what was also at stake was the larger problem of the definition of history and the question of what one could know about the past and how that knowledge related to the present. Adams, placing these problems in the context of the dissipating cosmos, was defining history in the tradition of positivism begun by Comte and extended and popularized by Spencer and Fiske. Adams's *Letter* was the final effort by an American historian to produce what so many scholars during the nineteenth century had striven for: a logically induced, all-encompassing historical explanation based on the empirically validated laws of natural science. James's rebuttal was directed not so much at Adams's conclusions as at the whole enterprise represented by this mode of historical philosophizing. The kind of knowledge Adams required of history was, James thought, given only to God; finite men had to be content with less absolute, more experiential varieties of understanding. In disputing as they did, the two friends placed the problem of progress squarely in the intellectual mainstream of the times. James's refutation of Adams's elaborate historical edifice was a classic example of the pragmatic revolt against nineteenth-century formalism.[51]

During the 1880s and 1890s, a profound shift in the intellectual center of gravity in America had prepared the way for what in the opening years of the twentieth century became a concerted assault not only on nineteenth-century definitions of law, history, economics, and philosophy, but on the very conceptual foundations on which those categories of knowledge rested. This revolt challenged the traditional methods of inquiry in these fields; more fundamentally, it charged that the nineteenth-century vision of reality that justified such methods was formalistic: arbitrary, abstract, a priori, and artificially mechanistic. By contrast, the antiformalists' conception of reality, informed as it was by the refinements of Darwinian evolutionism, was dynamic, organic, materialistic, processive, and strongly historical. The legal realism of Oliver Wendell

Holmes, Jr., and Louis Brandeis, the new economics of Thorstein Veblen and Richard T. Ely, the pragmatic philosophizing of William James and John Dewey, the Progressive constitutionalism of Herbert Croly, and the Progressive history of Frederick Jackson Turner, Charles Beard, Carl Becker, Vernon Parrington, and James Harvey Robinson all reflected this shifting sense of reality.[52]

Deeply distressed by the dislocations in American society wrought by industrialization and urbanization, these antiformalists looked to different areas of scholarship to support what were essentially democratic modifications of American education, law, the laissez-faire political economy, and the practice of politics that gave such enormous, unchecked power to party bosses and small cliques of wealthy men. Traditional approaches to law, philosophy, and the social sciences were, they found, too abstract and unyielding to sanction reforms they thought necessary; formalistic renderings of historical and social change, often given in the name of progress, were more often rationalizations of the status quo. If truly substantial reform was to be accomplished, systems of social thought long considered static and autonomous had to be redefined in terms that accurately depicted social conditions and realistically explained how those conditions had evolved and how they could be altered.

In essence, the antiformalists were indicting different spheres of nineteenth-century thought and scholarship with the same crime: overintellectualism. William James's old friend from Harvard, jurist Oliver Wendell Holmes, was one of the first to apply the indictment systematically. Inspired by conversations with James, Charles S. Peirce, and Chauncey Wright during the early 1870s, Holmes in a study entitled *The Common Law* in 1881 challenged the current view that held law to be a body of unchanging principles discovered by judges and applied logically to the case at hand according to the strict traditions of stare decisis. Such a view, Holmes maintained, misconstrued what actually happened in the courtroom and the legislative chambers and gave an artificially abstract and doctrinaire definition of the law itself. Properly, law should be defined as a living process relating intimately to the experiences of people in a specific time and culture. Excessively formalistic conceptions of law had turned it from a regularizing process into a structured, immutable body of legal absolutes. Such a conception was not only prescriptively wrong; it was historically false. As Holmes put it in what has become a classic statement of legal antiformalism, "The life of the law has not been logic: it has been experience." Law and historical change could not be separated, for "the law embodies the story of a nation's development through many centuries. . . . [In] order to know what it is, we must know what it has been, and what it tends to become. Much that has been taken for granted as natural, has been laboriously fought for in the past: the substance of law at any time corresponded fairly well to what was regarded as convenient by those making and interpreting it, but the form and machinery and the degree to which it is able to work out desired results, depended much upon its past."[53] Correctly conceived, law was an instrument for treating problems that changed as society changed; hence its principles could not remain entirely static. Like society, law changed and developed.

This truth had largely been forgotten in America. In the eighteenth century, the founding fathers had bolstered their right to revolution by appeals to the unchanging, higher laws of nature, and thereafter the institutionalization of both natural and common-law concepts in written constitutions helped give to law in America the status of sanctity and permanence. By the end of the nineteenth century, law was still regarded—and taught—as that embodiment of the sacred Newtonian principles elucidated by Blackstone and Americanized by such scholars as James Kent and Joseph Story. Holmes countered this prevailing legal formalism by pointing out that even the most allegedly immutable features of the law (such as contract theory) had evolved in response to specific human and social needs. The law had indeed grown and changed, but it had not done so automatically or by some mysterious process of sanctified accretion. The path of the law followed the needs and interests of men; it changed as they changed, and it changed according to their faith and their predictions about what would serve their interests best. Law could be properly understood only by seeing how in time it had come to be what it was—not by meditation on eternal legal verities. "To gain a liberal view" of the law, one had to "follow the existing body of dogma into its highest generalizations by the help of jurisprudence; next, to discover from history how it has come to be what it is; and, finally, so far as [one] can, to consider the ends which the several rules seek to accomplish, the reasons why those ends are desired, what is given up to gain them, and whether they are worth the price."[54]

Years later, after the Progressive era had reached its zenith, Holmes's lessons were still being taught by such reformers as Herbert Croly, whose *The Promise of American Life* (1909) and *Progressive Democracy* (1914) explored the larger political implications of Holmes's antiformalism. For Croly, the belief that absolute constitutional principles existed was the result of simple historical ignorance and elemental economic greed; conservatives hiding behind the fiction of legal absolutism had turned the Constitution into a prohibition for needed political and economic reforms. Law was not, Croly asserted in *Progressive Democracy*, an absolute existing above and beyond the will of the majority. It was, as Holmes contended, a code of regulations temporary and functional in nature but amenable to the changing needs and desires of the people. Yet law was not so regarded in America, with potentially disastrous consequences for democracy. Like other institutions forming the American system, law had become absolute, private, and, so far as the ordinary citizen was concerned, mysteriously in conflict with his interests. The situation had to change, for nothing less than human freedom was at stake. One of the ways this change could be promoted was by making the intricate workings of the American political and legal system known to all citizens. Croly was optimistic that this could be done; there was too much at stake for it to fail:

> Democracy must risk its success on the integrity of human nature. If among the citizens of a democratic state the intelligence should prove the enemy of the will, if individually and collectively they must purchase enlightenment at the expense of momentum, democracy is doomed to failure. A democratic nation must know all about its own doings, and again be it said, knowledge means a search of values as well as a mastery of facts. The American nation seems to have made up its mind to pursue meanings as well as results. If so, it is certainly by way of attaining a new freedom. Its will is being emancipated from the bondage to immediate practical achievement; and its intelligence is being released from the fascination exercised by a rigid and authoritative creed.[55]

At Harvard in the late 1880s, Croly had been exposed to James's doctrines, which had an abiding effect upon his criticism of American society.[56] Originally, Croly argued, America had stood for the promise "that somehow and sometime something better will happen to good Americans than has happened to men in any other country."[57] This promise, however, was being denied because social and economic conditions, rationalized by "the traditional American patriotic fatalism," had become rigid and inflexible. "The specialized organization of American industry, politics, and labor, and the increasingly severe special discipline imposed upon the individual . . . have their serious and perilous aspects, because no sufficient provision has been made for them in the national democratic tradition."[58] Making such provision was Croly's goal: a "constructive social ideal," at once democratic, cooperative, scientific, and reformist was to become the new promise of American life. Social institutions, political parties, industrial clusters of power had to be redefined and restructured according to their effects upon the lives of private individuals; the quality of life afforded its citizens had to become the criteria for social organization. Although he offered a variety of specific reforms toward this end, Croly was careful not to put his program forth in what might become itself another variety of some doctrinaire formalism. Accordingly, he concluded *The Promise of American Life* with a characteristically antiformalist caveat:

There can be nothing final about the [promise] unless there be something final about the action and purposes of which it is the expression. It must be constantly modified in order to define new experiences and renewed in order to meet unforeseen emergencies. But it should grow, just in so far as the enterprise itself makes new conquests and unfolds new aspects of truth. Democracy is an enterprise of this kind. It may prove to be the most important moral and social enterprise as yet undertaken by mankind; but it is still a very young enterprise, whose meaning and promise is by no means clearly understood. It is continually meeting unforeseen emergencies and gathering an increasing experience. The fundamental duty of a critic in a democracy is to see that the results of these experiences are not misinterpreted and that the best interpretation is embodied in popular doctrinal form.[59]

On a parallel plane, beginning in the 1890s Thorstein Veblen launched a stinging attack on the abstract and hypothetical nature of classical economics as advocated by Adam Smith, Jeremy Bentham, and John Stuart Mill and their successors. Economics, Veblen complained, had not yet become an evolutionary science, since it still treated such archaic fictions as "economic man" and "perfect competition" as realities.[60] Economics still functioned in the subjunctive mood; it asked "what would happen if there were no barriers to exchange" rather than seeking, in the spirit and with the methods of evolutionary science, to discover prevailing market practices.[61] Veblen stressed again and again that economics could not be studied as an isolated, discrete kind of moral essence, for it was in actuality a social process among other social processes and, like law, could be understood only when studied in its social and historical context. That context, as he showed in *The Theory of the Leisure Class* (1899), was a matrix of historically conditioned instincts, habits, psychological imperatives, and institutional practices far too dynamic and labyrinthine to be encompassed by static intellectual conventions. Economics was a complex organic process that could not be made to trot neatly between the traces of some pious formalism, however symmetrically rigged.

For Veblen, to whom so many other antiformalists looked for guidance, economics required the objective, scientific study of not only the production and distribution of goods and services but also of the value systems within which such activities took place. The American value system, he thought, was a relatively simple one: individualism defined by economic consumption and the attendant advertisement of status within a laissez-faire political economy. While disclaiming any ethical reference himself, Veblen's analysis revealed his contempt for both the theory and practice of laissez-faire. The process of exchange based solely on gratifying refined but still vulgar acquisitive instincts had a deleterious effect on the entire social order. The leisure class, that sector of society with such disproportionate power to utilize wealth, led a sheltered, protected existence ideologically reinforced by its own self-evident success. Though cut off by affluence from the rest of society, the leisure class nonetheless still prescribed for everyone the absolute social values it had inherited from the eighteenth century.[62] The result was a dramatic imbalance in the allocation of human and material resources, coupled with a galloping technology that was rapidly making the imbalance critical. Americans needed desperately to renovate the archaic credo that lent to laissez-faire individualism its odor of sanctity. Until their economy was rationalized by a more scientific, progressive value system, Americans would have to suffer the consequences of their habitual adherence to the canons of economic formalism.

Holmes, Croly, and Veblen were all distressed by the

dangerous ignorance practitioners of law and economics displayed about the historical development and dynamics of their fields. This acute sense of historicity also affected, not unsurprisingly, the generation of historians who came of age in the 1890s and shortly thereafter. For such newly minted professionals as Frederick Jackson Turner, Turner's brilliant student, Carl L. Becker, Charles A. Beard, Vernon L. Parrington, and James Harvey Robinson, history had too long been dominated by a Germanic antiquarianism on the one hand and a positivistic preoccupation with "laws" of historical necessity on the other hand. Taking their reference points from Populist and Progressive agitation for reform, as well as from the escalating antiformalism in other fields, these men saw history less as the high road to an all-significant past than as a pathway pointing toward the problems of the present. Acutely conscious of the elusive subject of their craft, as well as of the seminal role the historian played in creating that subject, they turned the writing of history into a pragmatic quest for relating the present and the past in such a way that, as Beard and Robinson put it in their text, *The Development of Modern Europe* (1907), the latter was "consistently subordinated" to the former.[63] The goal of the antiformalist historians was useful historical knowledge; history as they wrote it became the handmaiden of progressive reform.[64]

Beard's notorious *An Economic Interpretation of the Constitution of the United States* (1913) is a case in point. On the surface, Beard's study appeared to be a dispassionate, if somewhat irreverent, inquiry into the economic assets and liabilities of the group of men who gathered in Philadelphia in 1787 to frame a new constitution for the American states. The point of his investigation, Beard said, was to test the possibility that the real explanation for the resulting document lay in the economic interests of the framers, that the Constitution was an economic instrument created at a certain point in history by men with definite self-interests and the sagacity to create a government that would protect them. Beard's conclusion, predictably, confirmed this possibility. In reducing the framers from providentially guided seers of nature's eternal verities to calculating investors out to cover their bets, however, Beard accomplished much more than simple historical iconoclasm. Although his scholarship brought forth howls of outrage and instant denials, Beard, like Croly, was successful in taking the Constitution down from its formalistic pedestal and thrusting it into the vortex of Progressive reform thought. Even if Beard's research was biased and his conclusions foregone, as his critics charged, his message was nonetheless clear: the Constitution, unlike the decalogue, was not divinely prescribed. It was created to meet certain historical needs by real men blessed with wisdom and favored with property. It was not sacrosanct and inviolable; it could hence be freely and deliberately amended by later generations to suit their needs. Beard's study fulfilled Turner's charge that history should "hold the lamp for conservative reform."[65]

There were others, too, after the turn of the century whose thought took a sharply antiformalistic tack, men whose dynamic, evolutionary world view combined with their confidence that through organized, rational effort human society could be progressively improved and reformed. Arthur Bentley, J. Allen Smith, and Charles E. Merriam were prominent in transforming political philosophy into political science, into a modern instrument for reform. Political formalism, these men could agree with young Walter Lippmann, was bankrupt. "It is our desperate adherence to an old method," Lippmann wrote in 1913 in his *Preface to Poli-*

*tics*, "that has produced the confusion of political life. Because we have insisted upon looking at government as a frame and governing as a routine, because in short we have been static in our theories, politics has such an unreal relation to actual conditions. Feckless—that is what our politics is. It is literally eccentric: it has been centered mechanically instead of vitally. We have been seduced by a fictitious analogy: we have hoped for machine regularity when we needed human initiative and leadership, when life was crying out that its inventive abilities should be freed."[66] Albion Small in sociology, John R. Commons in political economy, Roscoe Pound and Louis Brandeis in law, and of course—especially—John Dewey in education and philosophy—all found causes for a similar indictment of their respective fields. Their solutions, too, followed the antiformalist line: if social thought was to furnish an adequate basis for progressive reform, it had to be recast in dynamic, pragmatic terms.

There was, of course, a good reason for this, for in pragmatism the antiformalists found a conception of progress that met their special needs. Many nineteenth-century formalists had also been devotees of the idea of progress. Archformalists such as Herbert Spencer and John Fiske had in fact grounded their conception of social change on a progressive interpretation of the natural laws of evolution, and William Graham Sumner, the bête noire of such antiformalists as Veblen and Croly, was also a firm believer in progress. Yet by definition, formalistic conceptions of progress gave little or no efficacy to human will as an agent of historical improvement. Whereas Sumner believed in progress as the necessary concomitant of evolution, he regarded the deliberate, conscious manipulation of social arrangements as contrary to the laws controlling both. Progress derived in Sumner's view from absolute, natural laws of competition that admitted no interference by individuals; if the competition prescribed by nature as the dynamic of change was unimpeded, progress would slowly, inexorably ensue. This mechanical view was scant comfort to a reformer who found, ironically, a formalistic conception of progress used to prevent a needed, progressive reform! Formalistic versions of progress were too deterministic to satisfy the requirements of the antiformalists. What antiformalism needed was a conception of progress that rendered human will and intelligence effective within the historical process but did not absolutely link human endeavor to some a priori, ironclad causal sequence in time.

The pragmatic definition of progress met this requirement and thus gave antiformalists an alternative to the counterfeit progressivism of the formalists. Although not all of the leaders of the revolt against formalism became orthodox, technical pragmatists, they did share pragmatism's sense of experience as an ongoing process and its belief that thought and knowledge were experientially forged weapons for controlling and improving upon the future. They shared, too, pragmatism's rejection of the formalistic conception of the universe as a finished, closed system—what James called the "block universe"—as well as its optimism that each advance in knowledge created the further likelihood that deliberate improvements in life were possible. Itself a reaction against preexisting modes of philosophical formalism, pragmatism furnished antiformalists with conceptual tools that were at once progressive and voluntaristic, and in this way it came to supply the philosophic heart of antiformalism.

The marriage of pragmatism and antiformalism, though happy, was essentially one of convenience. The two were well suited on several levels, but few antiformalist reformers marched willingly with pragmatism to the altar of relativity. Holmes, for example, though originally influenced by James and Peirce, later denied he was a pragmatist, and Croly, whose thought was cast explicitly in the pragmatic mold, remained to the end a believer in certain Christian absolutes.[67] Most of the reformers who made use of pragmatic arguments on behalf of favorite reforms still remained within an ethical framework that, pushed to its logical extreme, would have conflicted with pragmatism's ultimate commitment to ethical and historical relativism.[68] Nevertheless, pragmatism did serve as a willing partner in the revolt against formalism. To the extent that the revolt involved a rejection of earlier, formalistic notions of progress and the substitution of a more vital, activistic conception, pragmatism's contribution was well nigh definitive.

The pragmatism defined by William James did not contain a fully rendered philosophy of history or progress, for James's preoccupations were essentially with other matters; the varieties of formalism at which he tilted were not primarily philosophies of history. James's philosophy, however, did contain interpretations of experience, will, and truth that were radically moral and that, as his reply to Adams's *Letter* revealed, supported in very definite ways an open and progressive philosophy of historical change. His pragmatism was sufficiently historical in its thrust to provide a mature conceptual basis for refuting so egregious a bit of formalism as the *Letter* and sufficiently progressive and vitalistic to suggest a way out of Adams's dilemma of degradation. But James's conception of progress, though vital, was insufficiently developed to meet the larger needs of social thought in the twentieth century. It was left to others—notably John Dewey and Charles Beard—to amplify and extend the progressive implications of pragmatism and to make of what were largely

Jamesean beginnings a philosophy more socially and
historically informed and a doctrine of progress more
manifest and less implicit.

Defining the social and historical dimensions of the
pragmatic doctrine of progress occupied Dewey and
Beard long after James had died and the revolt against
formalism had lost its revolutionary character. The
impulse for reform of the Progressive era waned during World War I and the decade of the 1920s, only
to wax again with renewed urgency during the depression. By the New Deal years, the pragmatic doctrine
of progress had become orthodoxy among reform-
oriented liberals who, though seeking basic changes in
the American system of capitalism and free enterprise,
wished to stop short of Marxist collectivism. Most
clearly articulated during the 1930s and 1940s, this
latter-day conception of progress acquired under
Dewey and Beard certain attributes that would have
seemed strange or unwarranted to James, but basically
it was identical to the conception he had sketched in
his reply to Adams's *Letter*.

Seen in this light, then, the Adams-James exchange
of 1910 was a microcosm of that disjunction which, on
a larger canvas, separated the formalistic contours of
nineteenth-century social thought from the more
instrumental, antiformalistic constructs of the twentieth
century. The issue was the old one of historical determinism versus free will, a familiar dispute in the
American house of intellect. But by enlisting pragmatism on behalf of the will, James offered both a fresh
escape from the logic of determinism and a new
philosophical and psychological basis for the traditional
American faith in the idea of progress. James's reply
to the *Letter* took a stance that increasing numbers of
Americans found attractive, for the pragmatic explanation of historical progress not only gave proper credit

to individuals for past efforts for social improvement; it also gave assurance that such efforts in the future might be rewarded. Such assurance was increasingly welcome as the complexities of twentieth-century living became apparent.

# 2

# *The Heritage of Progress*

The revolt against formalism signaled a major turning point in the protracted debate over the idea of
progress that had raged on both sides of the Atlantic
since the eighteenth century. Particularly in the United
States, progress found rich soil, for there the newness
of the land and the excitement of creating a new civilization furnished a fund of historical experiences
uniquely appropriate to a progressive interpretation.
In succeeding years, the idea took on the coloration
of shifting climates of opinion. By the time Henry
Adams and William James gave their interpretations,
progress had gone through at least three fairly distinct
phases: rationalist (1750-1815), romantic (1815-1860),
and evolutionist (1860-1900).[1]

The idea of progress that dominated early American
thought directly reflected the demythologized, mechanistic, natural-law universe projected by Enlightenment rationalists in the century after the appearance
of Descartes' *Discourse on Method* in 1637 and Newton's
*Principia Mathematica* in 1687.[2] Newton's discovery that
the laws governing the behavior of natural bodies

could be stated in mathematical form helped convince the educated class of his day that all nature was rationally comprehensible, an assumption that more than any other shaped the idea of progress as it first came to be defined. Popularized uncritically, this Newtonian certitude fired the eighteenth-century imagination with a vision of the possibility of progress to human and social perfection, a vision that Americans seized with special alacrity. The coming of the American Revolution, too, did much to spread progressive notions across the land, for the revolutionary generation found in the rationalist idea of progress a convenient intellectual fulcrum for moving the existing order.

Rationalism is a generic term referring to certain commonly held assumptions about the nature of the universe shared by many thinkers during the eighteenth century. The rationalistic universe, in the familiar analogy of William Paley's *View of the Evidences of Christianity* (1794), was similar to a great watch whose every cog and spindle served an appointed purpose and operated in harmony with the larger regularity of the whole machine. Each component was specially created, unique, and defined by the specific function assigned to it by God, the original cosmic watchmaker. God's intentions and the designated purpose of each part of the watch were one and the same; the properties of every entity within the created order conveyed its nature and suggested its limitations. Thus, man's reasoning capacities were a God-given attribute designed to expedite the intended conduct of man and that part of the machine with which man interacted. Since the entire machine was affected by the operations of smaller constituencies, man's activities had cosmic moral significance. In turn, each of man's faculties for apprehending the universe about him became a channel for the acquisition of moral knowledge.

Rationalism stressed the sufficiency of human reason to comprehend the universe and allowed men to adjust gracefully to nature and to exploit the natural environment for their increased happiness. Nature, it was assumed, had deliberately been organized by God so that men might comprehend and use it rationally for their own greater well-being. Human reason was sufficient to the task of learning and harmonizing with nature's laws and moral principles. These laws and principles in turn gave men their natural identity as well as their natural rights. God's intentions were thus to be read in the structure of nature. These assumptions furnished the basis for the faith in progress that was shared by the majority of America's intellectual community in the formative years, including such philosophers, publicists, politicians, and scientists as Thomas Jefferson, Benjamin Franklin, John Adams, George Washington, Joel Barlow, Tom Paine, Timothy Dwight, Joseph Priestley, David Rittenhouse, Philip Freneau, Benjamin Rush, James Wilson, Richard Henry Lee, David Ramsey, Benjamin Barton, and Charles Willson Peale.

The rationalist conception of progress rested on the premise that the laws of nature were stable, uniform, and discoverable by applying empirical science and right reason to the study of the natural environment and natural history. Human nature was assumed to be once given and constant.[3] What changed, and what furnished the dynamic for progress, was man's growing understanding of himself, his society, and his universe. It was assumed that by studying nature, by untangling its intricacies and discovering its laws of causation, knowledge of human nature grew correspondingly.[4] As such knowledge increased, man's ability to construct moral, social, and political forms in harmony with the order he discovered in nature became greater. What stood between man and perfection was ignorance, outmoded custom, and institutions based on the irrational and the unnatural. History was the story of man's gradual discovery of the laws of nature; translating that discovery into the harmonious ordering of human life was progress.

The structure of nature did not vary. Each category and each entity in creation had its origin in the divine blueprint used to construct the universe. That blueprint was infinitely complex, highly integrated, and rigidly economical. Nature allowed no redundancies or duplications. The variety of types within creation was deliberate, sufficient, and constant. Each entity's characteristics bore the indelible imprimitur of the creator, which located it in the so-called great chain of being, the familiar eighteenth-century metaphor for nature's organization of life. The possibility of a species of plant or animal becoming extinct or evolving out of earlier forms conflicted with the assumption of special creation underlying the great chain of being, and consequently an evolutionary view of nature eluded eighteenth-century thinkers.[5] Change in time was real, but it was developmental, not structural. Sports and mutants were known to have occurred and survived, but they did not imply continuing, creative evolution. Nature was hierarchical, not organic: "the generally accepted idea of a Great Chain of Being implied that anything which did not form part of an existing species would find no room for itself on a ladder of nature, all of whose rungs were already occupied."[6]

Such staticism within nature did not, however, preclude a progressive view of history. On the contrary, the rationalist conception of nature gave the idea of progress a meaning that blended nicely with both contemporary American political needs and the developing ideals of bourgeois liberalism. Progress as defined by Americans during and after the Revolution meant primarily the fulfillment of human nature unfettered by the bonds of feudalism and colonialism. Jefferson stated the case succinctly in the Declaration of Independence, where the "self-evident" ideals of "life, liberty, and the pursuit of happiness" became translated into a rationalist prescription for history. Jefferson's statement furnished a clear summary of the moral criteria by which progress was measured by men in his time. Years later, Jefferson looked back on the writing of the Declaration as his attempt to set forth truths that were neither new nor startling, but simply expressed "the common sense of the subject, in terms so plain and firm as to command their assent. . . . Neither aiming at originality of principles or sentiments, nor yet copied from any particular and previous writing, [the Declaration] was intended as an expression of the American mind. . . . All its authority rests then on the harmonizing sentiments of the day, whether expressed in conversation, in letters, printed essays, or the elementary books of public right, as Aristotle, Cicero, Locke, Sidney, etc."[7]

Jefferson was right, for while not all of his contemporaries agreed with the necessity of revolution, they did agree generally with the principles he used to justify separation from Great Britain. Those Americans who expressed faith in progress—and their number included nearly every major thinker of the day —agreed that progress ultimately meant the approximation of human happiness.[8] Happiness, however, was given a rationalistic definition; it was not simple physical pleasure or psychic euphoria. Happiness was the rational perception of the fitness of the human condition within the order of nature.[9] Happiness, and hence progress, derived from man's achievement of the creator's intention and design. Although the specifics of this design and the question of whether happiness was being truly achieved could be vigorously argued, there was scant dissent from the central proposition that progress, measured by happiness, meant the fulfillment of God-given faculties rather than the creation of some new human dimension.

In turn, the fulfillment of human nature meant that nature's laws regarding humanity had to be obeyed. By their common natural origin, men had certain rights or sanctions for conduct that could not be abrogated by another human or by the community. Best articulated by Jefferson and Thomas Paine, the American version of natural rights was essentially negative; the Revolutionaries were more concerned with prohibiting certain kinds of institutional infringements—arbitrary taxation, for example—than prescribing the specific duties and obligations of individual citizens. This very negativism, however, provides an important clue to the rationalist conception of progress: progress would, it was assumed, follow naturally from the establishment of political and social institutions whose form and function gave individuals the greatest freedom to exercise their foreordained natural rights. Seen in this light, history was the story of man's slow, progressive recognition of his own humanity, and progress thus became the special intention of the author of nature.

Confirmation of a special progressive intent for America was seen in the peculiar conditions of nature in the New World. When several of Europe's leading philosophers and naturalists in the mid-eighteenth century charged that nature had endowed the New World with an inferior climate, flora, and fauna, America's intellectuals, finding their habitat and culture under attack, reexamined the American environment. Not only did America have singular political advantages that accrued from its three-thousand mile separation from Europe's atrophied, unnatural feudalism, they concluded, but its very ecological composition contained evidence of the beneficent purposes of the creator. Nature in Europe and America was indeed different, but Americans found in the difference the natural foundation for an American, republican version of progress.

The attacks came. principally from three French philosophers—Buffon, Abbé Raynal, and Montesquieu—and from the Swedish traveler and scientist Peter Kalm; their criticisms were collected and popularized by the French publicist, Corneille de Pauw.[10] All commented upon the sparse population of North America before colonization, the comparative lowness of the American Indian, physically and morally, compared to European whites (Indians had less hair, they noted too, suggesting immaturity and sexual incapacity), the harshness and coldness of the climate, and the small stature of America's animal life; and all except Montesquieu extended their observations to include the possible harmful effects of this environment on American society. Buffon especially, in his *Theory of the Earth* (1749) and *Epochs of Nature* (1779), indicted America and Americans as uncivilized and backward, although he did concede that some improvements in American society were taking place. But Buffon, compounding biological and social criticism, still found the American climate, animal life, and culture distinctly inferior to that of Europe.

Such attacks, of course, were anathema to the highly self-conscious Americans, and their spirited rejoinders suggest how rationalists read progressive intentions in the composition of nature. The charges of America's natural inferiority were met principally by Franklin, Jefferson, Benjamin Rush, John Bartram, William Barton, and John Adams, who threw into the fray an awesome array of talent, knowledge, and outrage. Far from being inferior to Europe, they argued, nature in America was new and youthful. It was, moreover, highly supportive of what would undoubtedly become a flourishing republican civilization in the future. Franklin, in his *Observations Concerning the Increase of Mankind*, noted these portents in 1755, showing how the population growth rate in the colonies had already surpassed that of Europe and suggesting that a future world power was being born in North America.

In *Notes on the State of Virginia* (1785), Jefferson challenged directly Buffon's assertion that nature in America was degenerative by drawing up an elaborate chart showing the superior size and weight of American animals when compared with their European counterparts. Assuming that "man here is no exception to the general rule," Jefferson went on to affirm the equality, if not the superiority, of native Americans, both red and white, to men in Europe. America, he argued, was producing its full share of geniuses in science and culture, and its population was growing at an astonishing rate: Virginia alone would have some six or seven million inhabitants in another century. And as the recent war for independence revealed, the energies for civilization seemed to be shifting toward the United States. With unmistakable satisfaction, Jefferson noted that Britain seemed to have lost much of its vigor: "The spirit in which she wages war is the only sample before our eyes, and that does not seem the legitimate offspring of either science or of civilization. The sum of her glory is fast descending to the horizon. Her philosophy has crossed the Channel, her freedom the Atlantic, and herself seems passing to that awful dissolution, whose issue is not given human foresight to scan."[11]

Both Franklin's *Observations* and Jefferson's *Notes on*

*Virginia* were written to counter the accusations of America's natural inferiority, as were portions of Adams's *Defence of the Constitutions of Government of the United States of America* (1787), Benjamin Rush's *Account of the Climate of Pennsylvania* (1790), and numerous articles published in the *Transactions of the American Philosophical Society* during the 1790s by William Barton, David Rittenhouse, Nicholas Collin and others. These writers all agreed with the conclusion of Dr. William Currie, a Philadelphia physician, who in 1792 attempted to show that nature in America was uniquely rich and beneficent and that its climatic and organic advantages had an important and direct social consequence: "*North America* is the only portion of this spacious globe where man can live securely, and enjoy all the privileges to which he has a natural right." Echoing the theme of Hector St. John de Crevecoeur, whose *Letters from an American Farmer* (1782) had been dedicated to the highly critical Raynal, Currie concluded in typical republican fashion: "It is true that none of the nervating [*sic*] refinements of luxury or dissipation are to be found here; but here all the necessaries of life and conveniences abound. . . . Here the dignity of the human species is restored, and man enjoys all the freedom to which he is entitled; for here he is a member of the government he obeys, and a framer of the laws by which he is governed, either in person or by the representatives of his own choice."[12]

The scientifically bolstered idea of progress so prevalent in the thought of rationalists was generally compatible with seventeenth- and eighteenth-century Anglicanism and Puritanism, a compatibility encouraged by the receptivity of American Christians to scientific discoveries.[13] Though many rationalists, particularly those who espoused Deism, chose to reject traditional

Christian doctrines and teleology, such a rejection was not mandated by clerical suspicions of science. Franklin, Jefferson, Rush, and Priestley all espoused a rationalistic conception of progress, but, unlike Paine, they found that science and reason did not require them to reject completely their Christian heritage. Rather, Christianity supplied them with a comfortable ethical system whose telic projections could be made entirely harmonious with the methods and conclusions of science. Combining traditional Christian ethics with modern science, rationalists were able to "read in the peculiar conditions of America the Creator's designation of a special role. . . . Had such a vast and fertile continent not been destined for prosperity and for a special example for mankind, there would have been an unthinkable poverty in the Creator."[14]

How rationalistic science, Christian piety, republican politics, and a genial regard for the American environment and its natural advantages merged in support of the idea of progress can be seen clearly in Benjamin Rush's *Three Lectures upon Animal Life* (1799), one of the most cogent expressions of rationalistic optimism produced in the eighteenth century. Arguing that religions generally excited the sensibilities and "luxated passions" of the human animal, as well as elevated its understanding, Rush found that Christianity was a superior "stimulus" to other religions and that the Christian regions of the world (notably Great Britain and the United States) could be shown scientifically to have benefited from the "salutary operations of its doctrines and percepts upon health and life." Progress and liberty were the natural consequences, as could be seen readily in the case of America:

There is an indissoluble union between moral,

political and physical happiness; and if it be true, that elective and representative governments are most favourable to individual, as well as national prosperity, it follows of course, that they are most favourable to animal life. But this opinion does not rest upon an induction derived from the relation, which truths upon all subjects bear to each other. Many facts prove animal life to exist in a larger quantity and for a longer time, in the enlightened and happy state of Connecticut, in which republican liberty has existed above one hundred and fifty years, than in any other country upon the surface of the globe.[15]

If the natural environment in America was a sign of God's special favor, Rush reasoned, the same held true for nature's response to the institutions and ideology of a region; since God was clearly Christian and republican, animal life flourished best in a Christian, republican country!

That happy circularity of Rush's Christian, republican rationalism supported a faith in America's progressive destiny that was to endure long after the debate over the New World's alleged degeneration was over. In 1824, just two years before his death on the fiftieth anniversary of the signing of the Declaration of Independence, Jefferson repeated the litany of progress of his youth. Anticipating the frontier hypothesis that was later to make Frederick Jackson Turner's reputation as an interpreter of American history, Jefferson wrote:

Let the philosophic observer commence a journey from the savages of the Rocky Mountains, eastwardly towards our seacoast. These he would observe in the earliest stage of association, living under no law but that of nature, subsisting and covering themselves with the flesh and skins of wild beasts. He would next find those on our frontiers, in the pastoral state, raising domestic animals to supply the defects of hunting. Then succeed our own semi-barbarous citizens the pioneers of the advance of civilization, and so in his progress he would meet the gradual shades of improving man until he would reach his, as yet, most improved state in our seaport towns. This, in fact, is equivalent to a survey, in time, of the progress of man from the infancy of creation to the present day. I am eighty-one years of age, born where I now live, in the first range of mountains in the interior of our country. And I have observed this march of civilization advancing from the sea-coast, passing over us like a cloud of light, increasing our knowledge and improving our condition, insomuch as that we are at this time more advanced here than the seaports were when I was a boy. And where this progress will stop no one can say. Barbarism has, in the meantime, been receding before the steady step of amelioration, and will in time, I trust, disappear from the earth.[16]

The progressive reading of history was not, to be sure, an original American construct. The philosophy of historical progress was one of the defining accomplishments of the Enlightenment mind in France and England, and American thinkers were heavily influenced by such diverse progressive theorists from across the Atlantic as John Locke, William Godwin, Adam Smith, Bernard de Fontenelle, the Marquis de

Condorcet, Abbé de Saint Pierre, Francois Jean Chas-
tellux, and Denis Diderot.[17] Americans were aware,
moreover, of variations within the progressive
interpretations and, of course, of the counterprogressive arguments of such spokesmen for historical retrogression as Buffon and Raynal. They were aware, too,
of the writings of David Hume, Edmund Burke, and
Jean Jacques Rousseau, in which the progressive view
of history was only one of a number of different possible interpretations.

Yet for a number of reasons, the idea of progress
was especially congenial to Americans, and, as an
interpretation of history, it won out over competing
views. In the first place, Europeans had for several centuries seen in the New World a field sufficiently vast
and mysterious to sustain myriad fantasies of human
harmony and perfection. Ancient myths and legends
of an earthly paradise, dormant for centuries and
revived by Renaissance scholarship, sprang to imagina-
tive life with the news of Columbus's discoveries. The
legends of Atlantis, Arcadia, Eden, and the Fortunate
Isles, legends that harked back to classical Greek and
Rome, boded fair to becoming a reality. "In 1493 the
New World dawned on the European imagination as
a few small, delectable islands, any one of which was
understandable in terms of a *hortus inclusus*, the walls
of which sheltered the Earthly Paradise, or a bower of
bliss, or the garden of youth and spring, from a dark
wilderness of the world."[18] Sir Thomas More located
his Utopia of 1516 in America as did William Shake-
speare the scene of his moral fable, *The Tempest*. And
countless European adventurers saw the New World
containing such mysteries as El Dorado, the city of
gold, a fountain of youth, or at the very least a passage
to the fabulous riches of India. All these imaginings
wedded the New World to a hopeful, even blissful,

conception of the future. If after three centuries of settlement a more realistic sense of New World possibilities prevailed, doubtless Americans' attitudes toward themselves and their future were strongly affected by the accumulated optimism with which they and their enterprises had long been regarded.

The providential habit of mind of the Puritans was another contributor to the progressive tradition in America. Though deeply conscious of man's basic, original sinfulness, the settlers of Massachusetts Bay believed that God had chosen America to be the stage for the recreation of Zion and had chosen them as the cast for this last act in the long drama of Christian history. On the success of that act hung nothing less than the fulfillment of the will of God. All the eyes of the world, as John Winthrop had lectured his fellow emigrants aboard the *Arabella* in 1630, would follow the Puritans' achievements, which would be as a "city set upon a hill" for the rest of Christendom to emulate. The Massachusetts Bay settlers' original sense of divine mission shaped their understanding of the larger meaning of settling America. If latter-day colonials could no longer share the early Puritans' sense of religious zeal, the idea of the providential significance of America's settlement was nonetheless well established before the end of the seventeenth century, and as a habit of mind it had strength that endured long after the original framers had progressed to their reward.

Another source, too, lent universal significance to the otherwise secular story of settlement. The belief that civilization followed a westward course lay deep in the mythic traditions revitalized by the Renaissance: Arcadia, Atlantis, and the Fortunate Isles all were located vaguely in the West. By the eighteenth century, numerous heralds of this mythic tradition were pro-

claiming America its fulfillment. As Bishop George
Berkeley wrote of America in 1726:

> Westward the course of empire takes its way;
> The four first Acts already past,
> A fifth shall close the Drama with the Day;
> Time's noblest offspring is the last.[19]

By midcentury numerous Americans were also seeing
their civilization in these terms. One traveler through
the middle colonies during the French and Indian War
noted, "An idea, strange as it is visionary, has entered
into the minds of the generality of mankind, that
empire is travelling westward; and every one is looking
forward with eager and impatient expectation to that
destined moment, when America is to give law to the
rest of the world."[20] Undoubtedly such an idea contributed to the colonists' sense of their separate and
unique destiny before the Revolution.

After the Revolution, other progressive imaginings
continued to help Americans identify themselves and
their place in history. Franklin's English friend,
Richard Price, in 1783 saw the Revolution in the following terms: "Perhaps I do not go too far when I say
that, next to the introduction of Christianity among
mankind, the American revolution may prove the most
important step in the progressive course of human
improvement."[21] With parallel grandeur, Timothy
Dwight, one of the so-called Connecticut Wits, rhap-
sodized in his long poem *Greenfield Hill* (1794) on the
intoxicating theme of civilization's inexorable westward
progression and projected a vision of its continuance
in the future:

> All Hail, thou western world! by heaven design'd
> Th' example bright, to renovate mankind.

Soon shall thy sons across the mainland roam;
And claim, on far Pacific shores, their home;
Their rule, religion, manners, arts, convey
And spread their freedom to the Asian sea.[22]

Similarly, Joel Barlow in *The Columbiad* (1807) unfurled a lengthy historical panorama stretching back to Columbus's discovery, forward through the migration of hopeful peoples seeking their dreams in America, to the storms and stresses of the Revolution, onward to its final hymn "to the future glories of America." *The Columbiad* summarized in turgid doggerel the confidence Americans felt about their foremost place in history's progressive march toward perfection.

The rapidity with which the frontier was rolled back and settlement accomplished also made the idea of progress apposite to America's history. The hundred years between 1700 and Thomas Jefferson's inauguration as third President of the United States in 1801 saw the transformation of a cluster of fragile colonial communities huddled on North America's eastern seaboard into a thriving, independent nation of over five million people on the threshold of a gigantic continental empire. In the intervening years, the growth of America's cities, the development of intracontinental trade and transportation, the steady rise in the standard of living, the accelerating pace of social change, and the sudden emergence of a sense of American nationalism occasioned by the war for independence became defining elements of the American experience. Consequently, a progressive view of history seemed merely, as Jefferson had said of the Declaration, "the common sense of the subject." If one learned the moral meaning of history from studying the natural environment and the changes men wrought upon it, American history seemed the very model of progress.

Finally, the achievement of independence and the successful establishment of a new government did much to turn the rationalist conception of progress into a veritable orthodoxy among the new nation's intellectuals. Independence itself had originally been justified in progressive terms. As Tom Paine put it, America by the 1770s was the "only spot in the political world where the principles of universal reformation could begin."[23] The central argument of his notorious broadside, *Common Sense*—and one of the reasons it was so effective as revolutionary propaganda—was that separation from Britain was imperative because without independence the American people could not progress at their "natural" rate:

> We [Americans] have it in our power to begin the world over again. A situation, similar to the present, hath not happened since the days of Noah until now. The birthday of a new world is at hand. . . . America doth not yet know what opulence is; and although the progress which she hath made stands unparalleled in the history of other nations, it is but childhood compared with what she could be capable of arriving at had she, as she ought to have, the legislative powers in her own hands.[24]

The American Constitution, as its preamble stated, was compacted "in order to form a more perfect union" of its constitutents; while there was no guarantee that such perfection would ensue, adoption of the Constitution by the states was a hopeful portent. As Benjamin Franklin wrote to an English correspondent on the eve of the Constitution's framing and adoption,

> You seem desirous of knowing what Progress we

make here in improving our Governments. We are, I think, in the right Road of Improvement, for we are making experiments. I do not oppose all that seem wrong, for the Multitude are more effectually set right by experience, than kept from going wrong by Reasoning with them. And I think we are daily more and more enlightened; so that I have no doubt of our obtaining in a few years as much public Felicity, as good government is capable of affording.[25]

Three decades later, after America's independence had once again been secured and after Europe had finally emerged from the convulsions of the Napoleonic wars, Thomas Jefferson could write to his new friend and old rival John Adams that "we are destined to be a barrier against the returns of ignorance and barbarism. Old Europe will have to lean on our shoulders, and to hobble along by our side, under the monkish trammels of priests and kings, as she can. What a colossus shall we be, when the southern continent comes up to our mark! What a stand will it secure as a ralliance for the reason and freedom of the globe!"[26]

*ii*

Although the excesses of the Napoleonic period sounded the death knell of the philosophy of rationalism upon which the Revolutionaries' view of progress was based, its passing did nothing to undermine the American faith in either the principles of the Declaration or the idea of progress. On the contrary, the romantic revolt against Enlightenment rationalism offered a new and broad-based foundation for the

American progressive faith, a faith that became widely popularized and democratized in the half-century after 1815. By 1860, progress was not merely the refraction of the cloistered theorist or the intellectual; it was the faith of the average American, reflecting his confident, if sometimes incoherent, assessment of history and its meaning. As it became popularized and diffused, however, the idea of progress took on connotations that departed significantly from the earlier rationalist version.[27]

A number of factors brought about the change. America's transformation into a continental and proto-industrial giant during the middle period furnished both compelling new statistics and new ideological encouragement for progressive theorists; it furnished, too, a new tension between traditional agrarian, arcadian conceptions of the good life and new industrial and commercial definitions. The spread of political democracy through extension of the franchise and the accompanying spate of social reform movements changed significantly the lives and expectations of ordinary folk, and progress accordingly took on a variety of democratic connotations. The expansion of the frontier provided a psychological, as well as an economic, safety valve for the growing tensions of urban life in the East. The rise of an acute sense of American nationalism linked intimately developments in the nation at large with each individual's perception of himself and his destiny. Advances in public education and communications technology put detailed news of the day's events in everyone's hands, thus raising the general level of awareness of historical change. All of this militated toward the spread and modification of the idea of progress, enabling Arthur Ekirch, the leading historian of that idea, to conclude that by 1860 "the idea of progress was the most popular American philosophy, thoroughly congenial to the ideas and interests of the age."[28]

The forward thrust of these various national experiences after 1815 produced two new corollaries to the inherited idea of progress that in the end helped destroy its rationalist underpinnings. First, Americans in the middle period experienced a collective revolt against certain aspects of the pre-Revolutionary and European past. An integral part of the rise of nationalism, this revolt had many dimensions, yet fundamentally it signified Americans' impatience with social conventions or intellectual constraints not rooted in native American soil. To be acceptable, literary forms, philosophical perspectives, religious dogma, artistic modes, political practices and social mores all had to be consistent with the national sense of a unique democratic destiny. This requirement produced such a virulent hostility to certain forms of tradition that Henry James, Sr., was led to observe in 1851 that "the Democratic idea . . . is revolutionary, not formative. It is born of denial. It comes into existence in the way of denying established institutions. Its office is rather to destroy the old world, than fully to reveal the new." James recognized, however, the positive, progressive aspects of this rejection of tradition; for pre-Civil War Americans, the test of progress was its reflection of uniquely American needs and aspirations. Versions of progress that bore the stamp of European authorship were inappropriate, and hence rejected or ignored. Progress for Americans became less the realization of traditional, a priori cultural norms than the satisfaction of some immediately perceived humanitarian need or requirement. Hence James concluded his essay in a fashion typical of his time: "I am entirely persuaded that nothing but the persistent and enlarging operation of the Democratic principle . . . is requisite to inaugurate the divine life on earth, to bring about that great prophetic period to which all history from the beginning has tended, that everlasting Sabbath or rest which is to close in and glorify the brief but toilsome week of man's past experience."[29]

The second corollary to the romantic view of progress derived from and complemented the first: progress was at bottom an individual, not a species-wide, class, or institutional phenomenon. The single individual was the key to historical betterment. Any progressive possibility began with the quickening of solitary spirits and the uplifting of individual moral sensibilities. In an egalitarian society, the individual might, as Alexis de Tocqueville observed, be isolated and cut off from his peers and hence need a congregation of fellow believers to produce social change, but the initial step was always taken by individuals in the privacy of their minds and hearts.[30] Although the principle of individualism could result in the extravagant privatism of the transcendentalists, which in its most extreme form became antisocial and retrogressive —Emerson's negative reaction to reformers is a case in point—most Americans concurred that progress began and ended at home in the life and mind of the individual citizen. And since the old Calvinistic notion of original sin was finally being laid to rest in the Unitarian boneyard, the most important traditional limitation to individual aspiration no longer seemed absolute to increasing numbers of educated Americans.

Although these two corollaries had their roots in the historical and social circumstances of the American middle period, they took their most coherent form from American adaptations of the romantic revolution in Germany, France, England, and, to a lesser extent, Italy. For despite the nationalistic rejection of European models and standards, American thinkers were inevitably influenced by a wide variety of post-Napoleonic currents of thought. While numerous Americans from Timothy Dwight to Emerson and William Ellery Channing issued urgent pleas for a national literature and intellectual life, the most important innovations in the period in philosophy, history, religion, and science—those categories of knowledge most directly bearing on the question of progress—were linked closely with Continental and English developments.[31]

In Europe, the Enlightenment conception of history, while cognizant of change and progress, had emphasized the mechanical, clocklike features of civilization's advance through a number of stages from barbarism to the present. The causes of this progression were vaguely ascribed to the automatic, unchanging operations of the laws of nature. As a result, Enlightenment thinkers tended to take a condescending attitude toward certain previous stages of history. Since nature's laws were constant, there was no possibility that the dynamics of history might themselves change from stage to stage. Consequently, the Enlightenment view of history was developmental or two-dimensional. Beginning with Rousseau in France, Samuel Coleridge and Percy Shelley in Great Britain, and Immanuel Kant, Johann von Goethe, and Johann von Herder in Germany, by the early nineteenth century, Europeans were assuming a new stance toward history. The past was regarded more sympathetically. As it became accepted that previous ages were peopled by real human beings with problems and motivations similar to those of the present, a new toleration toward history emerged. By 1860, the notion that the past and present were linked in a dynamic process more evolutionary than mechanical had become widespread, as the immediate success of Henry Buckle's *History of*

*Civilisation in England* (1857, 1861) proved. A new kinship with the past had become one of the defining features of European historicism in the first half of the
nineteenth century.[32]

In the United States, partly because of European
trends, a similar kinship for history developed, but it
assumed a somewhat different cast from the European
version. Americans in the middle period had little need
to jettison the historicism of the Enlightenment, for
their revolution had not betrayed the rationalist confidence in progress. History for Americans was short,
homogeneous, and palatably triumphant. Accordingly,
Americans were less concerned with disputing past historical interpretations than with celebrating the present
and future. Since the past was so eminently satisfactory, it could be regarded complacently while national
intellectual energies focused on other tasks; there was
no need to reconstruct the past in order to live comfortably in the present. Hence, the conception of progress emerging from antebellum historical accounts was
less retrospective than earlier views and more given to
the notion that America was starting history afresh.
History as written by George Bancroft, William Prescott, Francis Parkman, or John Motley was less an
encumbrance to be painfully divested or revised than
a clean slate on which the drama of man's providential,
honorific struggle with the New World environment
could be written. For the Revolutionaries, progress had
been the inexorable movement of history toward the
triumph of their cause; for a later generation, progress
was what would ensue from the present. As Bancroft,
the best-known of America's historians of the middle
period, put the matter in his essay, "The Necessity, the
Reality, and the Promise of the Progress of the Human
Race" (1854): "The course of civilization flows on like
a mighty river through a boundless valley, calling to

the streams from every side to swell its current, which is always growing wider, and deeper, and clearer, as it rolls along. . . . Since the progress of the race appears to be the great purpose of Providence, it becomes us all to venerate the future. We must be ready to sacrifice ourselves for our successors, as they in turn must live for their posterity."[33]

Bancroft's metaphor of the "mighty river [flowing] through a boundless valley, . . . always growing wider, and deeper, and clearer," was particularly revealing of the romantic view of progress. The metaphor suggested that history flowed rather than ticked, that it was continuous, and that it accumulated and accrued to itself all the results of each individual tributary, however small or on whatever side. Always growing wider and deeper, the river was also providentially becoming clearer, suggesting that the flow of time was irreversibly evolving toward some sort of moral purity or perfection. Finally, that the river flowed through a "boundless valley" suggested that history moved through limitless natural vistas unbounded by stages or limited by mechanical design. Progress was thus described in terms evoking nature's sublimity, bounty, and organic interrelatedness—all dominant characteristics of the romantic historical outlook.

This, however, was more than mere metaphor. Bancroft, as his monumental, multivolume *History of the United States* (1834-1874) revealed, saw history as an organic process culminating in a rebirth of human opportunity in America. Making extensive use of the imagery of the garden and the Edenic symbolism so prevalent among romantics in the nineteenth century, Bancroft's *History* depicted the American landscape as the source of democratic energies and republican virtues. From the land itself, Bancroft affirmed, in what was as much a literal interpretation as a figurative convention, came both the mysterious animus of progress and the enduring values that transcended temporal change. Human history moved progressively in time, but the values that transformed temporal flux into a progression were inherently and unchangeably embedded in nature. Comparing the virgin land first spied by the early explorers with the America of 1837, Bancroft preferred the latter:

> The earth [in 1837] glows with the colors of civilization. . . . The yeoman, living like a good neighbor near the fields he cultivates, glories in the fruitfulness of the valleys, and counts with honest exultation in the flocks and herds that browse in safety on the hills. The thorn has given way to the rosebush; the cultivated vine clambers over the rocks where the brood of serpents used to nestle; while industry smiles at the changes she has wrought, and inhales the bland air which now has health on its wings.[34]

Bancroft saw American history as progressive and heroic because of the unique relationship American civilization enjoyed with nature.

Bancroft's perspective is especially revealing, for the romantics departed most radically from the rationalist milieu by their attitude toward nature, and this departure bore directly on the changing definition of progress. For rationalists, nature was a vast complexity to be approached empirically, its moral message logically deduced from the design such empirical examination revealed. Understanding nature's intention, then, was essentially a matter of observation, classification, and logical inference, all carried on within a generalized Christian—or at any rate, a theistic—frame of reference. The result, as Daniel Boorstin has shown so convincingly, was that the group of archrationalists comprising "the Jeffersonian circle" saw "morality" and "nature" as a vast tautology: "By admiring the universe as the complete and perfected work of divine artifice, by idealizing process and activity as themselves the end of life, the Jeffersonian was insisting that the values by which the universe was to be assessed were somehow implicit in nature. All facts were endowed with an ambiguous quality: they became normative as well as descriptive."[35] The moral standard by which change could be accounted progress resided as a given within the framework of nature itself: progress for the rationalist became nature, only more so.

While romantics, like rationalists, looked to nature for moral instruction, they looked through different lenses and for different lessons. From the German idealists—Kant, Fichte, Herder, Lessing, Goethe, Hegel—as well as from Coleridge, Carlyle, Wordsworth, and Shelley in Great Britain, and Lamartine, Cousin, Rousseau, Jouffroy, and Chateaubriand in France (Comte's influence coincided with later American attempts to grapple with the implications of Darwinism),[36] Americans learned that while nature provided the sensory stimulus for acquiring knowledge, the human mind was so constructed that it could directly apprehend the true essence of things, that it could penetrate, by empathy and intuition, the reality that lay behind things perceived through sensory perception. Enlightenment rationalists had generally been suspicious of the emotions; now the romantics were liberating men's feelings and relying on them for knowledge. Against the inspiring background of nature, directly apprehended in its God-given splendor, all things became possible for the individual who would but predispose himself to discover the inner moral truth.[37]

Romantics assumed a conception of nature lying

midway between Newton and Darwin, a conception
more vitalistic than that of the rationalists but one that
fell short of Darwin's vision of a created order determined by environmental flux and natural selection.
Labeled by Howard Mumford Jones "the dynamic conception of nature," this view saw the universe in terms
of creative energy rather than mechanical movement,
or organicism rather than rigid hierarchy, as an entity
vitally alive rather than as a construct originally
animated by a now remote creator.[38] The secrets of
nature and its immanent God could be broached by
subjective as well as objective means, and such secrets
yielded readily to the sympathetic, emancipated
individual. For those from whose eyes the scales of
mere reason had been lifted, God and nature gave the
same traditional, progressive reassurance. In the words
of William Henry Channing, nephew of the famous
Unitarian     minister,     William    Ellery    Channing,
"Therefore, in every sphere, however small, let each
of us declare, that Love is the Law of Liberty, that
Faith is forever a Free Inquirer, that Doubt of enlarging Good is virtual Atheism, and Fear of Progress the
unpardonable Sin. Let us attest the truth, that the
Heavenly Father recreates his universe and regenerates
his children, by causing their perennial growth."[39]
Nature's observable changes could still be regarded as
stages of necessary development, but their animus
seemed to come less from some primal mathematical
formulae than from the immediate infusion of divine
energy and spirit.

Spokesmen for the dynamic conception of nature
assumed natural science and revealed religion to be but
different routes to the same cosmic truth; the scientist
of the middle period thought of himself as "one who
thinks God's thoughts after him."[40] Scientific inquiry
was widely assumed merely to confirm that progress

through organic growth was God's law and plan. Professor James Dwight Dana of Yale, the leading geologist of the mid-nineteenth century, found evidence for this faith in the fossil remains of successive geological strata. The progression of organic forms, culminating in man as the highest order of creation, revealed God's planned, ordered dynamism. There was nothing in this scientific approach to unsettle progressive, theistic assumptions, Professor Dana avowed in 1865: "Science should not be feared. Her progress is upward as well as onward, to clearer and clearer visions of infinite beneficence."[41] And from Harvard's even more prominent Louis Agassiz came the parallel assurance that "all organized things exhibit in themselves all those categories of structure and existence upon which a natural system may be founded, in such a manner that in tracing it, the human mind is only translating into human language the Divine thoughts expressed in nature in living realities."[42] Agassiz, who held out to the end against the Darwinian apostasy, regarded nature as a divine process containing an "invisible thread" that "unwinds itself throughout all time, across this immense diversity, and presents to us a definite result, a continual progress in the development of which man is the term."[43]

Scientific and religious authorities found themselves largely in agreement that the natural order was still in the process of creation, still achieving according to God's plan newer and more perfect forms of existence. "But this progressive development does not end with us," Theodore Parker remarked after surveying man's rise in history. "We have seen only the beginning; the future triumphs of the race must be vastly greater than all accomplished yet."[44] Though the records of natural history showed numerous stages through which the created order had passed, nearly all of America's lead-

ing scientists of the 1840s and 1850s believed that
recent scientific findings squared with scriptural
accounts of creation. Both Dana and his famous
teacher, Yale's Benjamin Silliman (who had founded
the influential *American Journal of Science and Arts* in
1818), found the biblical story of the earth's origin consistent with the latest geological discoveries, and the
Reverend Edward Hitchcock, geographer and president of Amherst College, argued in his well-known *The
Religion of Geology and Its Connected Sciences* (1852) that
the principles of science were a more-or-less exact
transcript of nature's "Divine Character." Man was an
organic part of a structured, progressive creation,
Hitchcock said, animating the traditional chain-
of-being concept with a dynamism that came directly
from God.

> *What a centre of influence does man occupy!* . . . It
> is just as if the universe were a tremendous mass
> of jelly which every movement of his made to vi-
> brate from the centre to the circumference. It is
> as if each man had his foot upon the point where
> ten thousand telegraph wires meet from every
> part of the universe, and where he is able, with
> each volition, to send abroad an influence along
> these wires, so as to reach every created being in
> heaven and on earth. . . . It is as if we had the
> more than Gorgon power of transmuting every
> object around us into forms beautiful or hideous,
> and of sending that transmuting process forward
> through time and through eternity.[45]

The comfortable admixture of science and scripture
was possible primarily because the various scientific
tributaries that eventually converged in Darwin's
evolutionary synthesis had not yet gathered sufficient
cohesion to support a totally naturalistic interpretation

of geological and biological change. During the century from 1750 to 1850, a fund of scientific data was brought to light which demonstrated clearly that the earth was much more ancient than it had once appeared to be, that there had been numerous pre-Noachian epochs containing their own unified, discrete ecosystems, that more varied life systems previously and currently existed than could possibly fit into the old Linnaean hierarchy, and that man was unquestionably a latecomer in the great paleo-pageant slowly emerging from scientific inquiry.[46] Yet partly because of traditional religious inhibitions and partly because of the fragmentary nature of scientific findings, it was still possible to see natural change in traditional, theistic terms that allowed science and religion to come together in mutual support of a dynamic view of progress.

Such a view found its most prestigious authority in the figure of Louis Agassiz, whose traditionalistic *Essay on Classification* (1857) set forth what he hoped would be the last word on the unsettled question of organic creation and evolution. Appearing only two years before *Origin of Species*, the *Essay* depicted a natural order characterized by special creation, divine intervention (through floods, glaciers, and disease), and a system of taxonomy that reflected the symmetry and balance of its author, the "Supreme Intelligence." Each species was an "ideal entity," and each individual was the bearer of the "specific characteristics" of his species, genus, family, order, and class. God prescribed the ideal pattern for each species and the "specific characteristics" of its membership, as well as any variations within the species that might have taken place over time. In these prescriptions resided the "natural limits" of individual and group development, which negated the possibility that any "sterotyped order of succession," such as the "idea of a progress from a more general typical organization to its ultimate specialization," had occurred. Life progressed, Agassiz held, but it did so on an individual basis within the framework of God's plan and purpose; empirical investigation revealed no changes in the order of nature that did not reflect intercession by a power external to its laws and limitations. The author of the plan of creation was still immanent; he acted as consistently in the present as he did in the beginning. Change and progress were both reflections of "the thoughts of the Creator of the Universe, as manifested in the animal and vegetable kingdoms, as well as in the inorganic world."[47]

How Agassiz's vision of nature and progress harmonized with contemporary theological opinion was illustrated by Henry James, Sr., in his lengthy essay, "The Scientific Accord of Natural and Revealed Religion" (1852). James, too, believed there was no basic difference between truths experienced by science and/or religion; both were encompassed by nature and referred back to history. The experience of natural phenomena only served as a bridge between it and "pure being," and the human mind, though rooted in temporality and nature, was so wrought by God as to empower men to comprehend the unity and progressive force behind nature's apparently random contradictions. Man's "natural experience" led directly to "the conception of a power superior to nature" and that conception led reciprocally back to human deliverance and perfection in time. This progression from the natural to the spiritual to the social, James concluded, held true both for individuals and for history.

Human history—the history of man in the aggregate—is a portrait in large of the same substantial facts which individual history, the history of any well-developed man, gives us in miniature. . . . Hence the history of the race, like that of the individual, presents a certain order of progress, presents first an infantile stage, then a puerile or transitory stage, then a mature stage. . . . Now creation has actually shaped itself according to this obligation from the beginning. View it geologically even, and you see a continuous progress from grosser, cruder, and chaotic conditions into subtler, more orderly, definite actions. . . .

Science is not a record or aggregation of simple facts. It is a perception of the harmony which embeds all facts, of the unity which subtends all variety. . . .

Science is the pure red blood of the mind. As in natural physiology, the blood is first generated of the food taken in the stomach, and thence after undergoing a slight discipline in the liver and the lower intestines, is taken up into the lungs to be finally purified of all earthiness, and is *then for the first time delivered over to the heart,* to be sent forth in streams of copious refreshment to the whole body: so precisely is it with our spiritual physiology. For the knowledge which we take in at our senses at first undergoes a process of digestion or assimilation in the memory, which is the stomach of the mind: and is thence sublimated into the logical understanding, which is the lungs of the mind, where after being stripped of its local and accidental clothing, it becomes generalized into law or science, and so adapted to the use of the passions or affections, which are the heart of the mind, and which consequently send forth their perpetual streams of renewal and refreshment, through all the channels of practical life.[48]

James's essay reflected the dominant romantic faith that empirical and spiritual modes of knowing were united, coordinate guarantors of progress.

Yet the results of this mode of thinking, as far as the idea of progress is concerned, were sometimes contradictory. Part of the romantic outlook stressed the inward vision, the sufficiency of knowledge and truth gained from intuition, subjectivity, reflection, and self-scrutiny. Pushed to its logical extreme, this sometimes had the effect of negating time, of making distinctions between past and present irrelevant if not unreal. One of Walt Whitman's observations in his epic journey into selfhood, "Song of Myself" (1855), illustrates the point:

> I have heard what the talkers were talking, the
>    talk of the beginning and the end;
> But I do not talk of the beginning or the end.
> There was never any more inception than there
>    is now,
> Nor any more youth or age than there is now,
> Nor any more heaven or hell than there is now.[49]

For Whitman, the deepest perceptions of the self obviated historical progress or even movement; in the vistas contained within the self, past and future merged in the sufficiency of the present. Thoreau suggested the same theme when he observed that "the characteristics of various ages and races of men are always existing in epitome in every neighborhood."[50] And Emerson on occasion reached similar conclusions, as in the famous section of his essay "Self-reliance" in which he denied at length that society advanced in time, his point being that each age and each individual had to discover anew whatever truths the world had to offer.

The romantic emphasis on the need to simplify life, to shift man's primary allegiance from material things to those essentials that sustained life spiritually, also carried an antiprogressive connotation. Thoreau's introspection raised a monumental question mark behind his generation's too easy equation of material change and innovation with the idea of progress. "Modern improvements" such as the railroad tended in Thoreau's eyes to be merely "improved means to an unimproved end"; while they accelerated the pace of life, it was doubtful whether they enhanced its quality. Though the telegraph linked Massachusetts and Texas in electronic communion, Thoreau suspected the two states had little of enduring value to say to one another.[51] And Emerson, though he subscribed generally to the notion of individual improvement, was also skeptical that technological or scientific advance signified progress in either knowledge or in society. The measure of a civilization's progress was the moral quality of men it produced, and Emerson to the last was uncertain that the modern age had in this regard made progress over the past.[52]

The theme of the constancy and sublimity of nature, also a defining feature of romanticism, similarly militated against certain aspects of the idea of progress. While the sublime power of nature might be perceived by men directly and intuitively, it could not be countered or mastered by civilization, which, by comparison, was transitory and frail. The most graphic illustration of this kind of antiprogressive romanticism was Thomas Cole's epic suite of paintings depicting *The Course of Empire* (circa 1836). Commencing with a landscape revealing nature in its most savage and original stage, the suite traced the rise, triumph, and destruction by barbarians of a monumental, classical city and the city's eventual return to a natural woodland amid the ruins. The romantic theme of the futility and fragile character of the works of men, set against the backdrop of nature and the cycle of eternal return, dramatically countered the dominant progressivism of the day.[53]

Despite these threads, however, the main thrust of romanticism in its American guise was undeniably progressive. While in Europe romanticism was strongly marked by neo-Catholicism, the political radicalism of a Paris in 1830 or a Berlin in 1848, the murky gothicism of a Horace Walpole or the Brontës, and the heavy aetheticism of the Erste Romantische Schule and the early pre-Raphaelites, in America romanticism generally took a highly personal and ethical course, stressing the limitlessness of individual possibilities and the faith that society's ills could be progressively reformed by men of goodwill. All men, as Emerson wrote, contained the consciousness of "infinitely versatile resources" within upon which they might call to improve their condition.[54] Though nature was the context for human endeavor and though human institutions often seemed obstructions to individual and social betterment, the option for improvement remained open to those who chose to exercise it. As Charles Sumner of Massachusetts put it in an essay entitled "The Law of Human Progress" in 1849: "Man, as an individual, is capable of indefinite improvement. Societies and nations which are but aggregations of men, and, finally, the Human Race, or collective Humanity, are capable of indefinite improvement. And this is the Destiny of man, of societies, of nations, and of the Human Race."[55]

Romanticism challenged traditional forms and customs and put the burden of proof upon the past. Its mood in America was optimistic, open, and oriented toward the future, reflecting the pervasive sense of security and well-being of the mid-nineteenth century.[56] This did not mean, of course, that romantics failed to engage in criticism of American culture; rarely has a civilization produced a generation of thinkers so conscious of and vocal about its shortcomings. William Ellery Channing, Theodore Parker, Margaret Fuller, Bronson Alcott, Charles Eliot Norton, Wendell Phillips, Orestes Brownson, Emerson, and Thoreau all achieved note as thinkers substantially by the intellectual distance they put between themselves and the America of the 1830s, 1840s, and 1850s. Yet their criticisms were intended primarily to galvanize Americans to renewed exertions on behalf of individual and social improvement and were offered in the spirit of encouragement rather than despair. Improvement was possible, romantics affirmed, and if they chastised their culture freely it was because they felt Americans had not achieved the things of which they were so easily capable. Again and again, the theme of social uplift through individual renovation was emphasized: if each man would but work the vein of his own resources, untold progress would follow. As William Ellery Channing remarked in his famous address, "Self-culture": "Be true to your own highest convictions. Intimations from our own souls of something more perfect than others teach, if faithfully followed, give us a consciousness of spiritual force and progress, never experienced by the vulgar of high life or low life, who march, as they are drilled, to the step of their own times."[57]

Whitman's message to antebellum America in "Song of Myself" was similarly optimistic and individualistic. Conceived as an epic rendering of the American identity, the poem projected an archetypal, limitless self confined by none of the ordinary limits of experience. Whitman's self—and by implication every American self—enjoyed a cosmic freedom unbound by traditional parameters of human existence: age, sex, customs, language, institutions, sympathies, accepted truths—all of which were outmoded, transcended, and ultimately denied as barriers to the fulfillment of individuality. Though perhaps not a perfectionist in the sense of some romantic reformers, Whitman nonetheless asserted that there was an immanent, indwelling perfection in men, which needed only to be evoked (by such a poet as he) to commence the radical uplifting of men and society.

Given his mystical, apocalyptic vision of the self and its possibilities, the traditional institutional processes of reform became largely superfluous. Writing in "The Eighteenth President," an unpublished pamphlet of 1856, Whitman stated, "We want no *reforms*, no *institutions*, no *parties*—We want a living principle such as nature has, under which nothing can go wrong." That principle was the transcendent, democratic self, the basic component of the romantic view of progress.[58] Whitman's anti-institutional, highly individualistic attitude toward progress was echoed in many quarters but never so succinctly as by the anarchistic economist, Stephen Pearl Andrews, who declared in 1852: "I assert that the law of genuine progress in human affairs is identical with the tendency to individualize."[59]

The romantic preoccupation with the limitless potential of the individual, however, did not blind Americans of the middle period to the need for community and the achievement of a social structure necessary for individual fulfillment. Emerson, the most consistent celebrator of atomistic individualism in antebellum America, had an acute sense of the reciprocal benefits individual and community afforded each other.[60] Numerous reformers who shared Emerson's essentially religious conception of the individual as the reservoir of progressive possibilities also shared his concern that society, as it became urbanized and industrialized, be so transformed as to preserve the humaneness upon which democracy and progress depended. Popular democracy, social reform, and the romantic view of progress were usually thus linked, as in the prophetic oration delivered by George Bancroft at Williams College in 1835:

> The public happiness is the true object of legislation, and can be secured only by the masses of mankind themselves awakening to the knowledge and the care of their own interests. Our free institutions have reversed the false and ignoble distinctions of men, and refusing to gratify the pride of caste, have acknowledged the common mind to be the true material for a commonwealth.
>
> The exact measure of the progress of a civilization is the degree in which the intelligence of the common mind has prevailed over wealth and brute force; in other words, the measure of the progress of a civilization is the progress of the people.[61]

Reformers in this perfectionist tradition, however, often saw social progress as the result of an educational crusade in which sufficient numbers of individual conversions took place to solve society's problems in a democratic, majoritarian way. "In the opinion of the romantic reformers the regeneration of American society began not in legislative enactments or political manipulation, but in a calculated appeal to the American urge for individual self-improvement."[62] This was the faith of such diverse reformers as William Lloyd Garrison, Samuel Gridley Howe, George Ripley, Dorothea Dix, Charles Loring Brace, Albert Brisbane, and Charles Sumner, whose causes, all in the name of progress and perfection, ranged from antislavery to chil-

drens' aid and prison reform. So pervasive did the idea
of progress become in these connections that Stow Persons has concluded that "public discussions of every
topic of general interest to the early nineteenth century
was framed in some characteristic way by the assumption of progress—whether it be politics and international relations, economics, education, or peace."[63]

It was on this level—the translation of the idea of
progress into an instrument for or, occasionally,
against social change and reform—that the idea
became so pervasive in America before 1860. From the
rostrums of the lyceum, from the broadsides of moral
and religious crusaders, from the pulpit, political
stump, and from popular journals and the penny
press, Americans were treated to appeals on behalf of
educational reform, support for the war with Mexico
and manifest destiny, temperance, women's rights,
extension of the franchise, the abolition of slavery—all
in the service of progress. Though diffuse and ambiguous, the idea clearly enjoyed a unique status in the
American consciousness. Its frequent usage in support
of conflicting causes and divergent ends suggests how
fully Americans in the antebellum period had
assimilated the notion that their individual destinies
were linked, or could be linked, to the progressive
movement of history. If the precise nature of the linkage was not very clear, the prospect of contributing significantly to historical betterment was enticing enough
to make Americans feel that appeals to action made
in the name of progress would bring favorable results.

The romantic idea of progress, however, was in certain respects surprisingly conservative. Most Americans
during the middle period were basically satisfied with
their lives and their society, and they saw progress
essentially as an extension of certain dimensions of the
present. The establishment of republican institutions,

the spread of political and social democracy, the relative openness and prosperity of the capitalist economy, and the existence of the frontier all reinforced the belief that progress was essentially the perfection of existing American circumstances and that it could be best realized within the framework of the existing social order.[64] That order might be modified in limited ways, but extreme programs that would abruptly alter it—as certain forms of socialism, anarchism, or abolitionism threatened to do, for example—evoked widely negative responses. Like the dynamic conception of nature on which it rested, the romantic idea of progress was essentially an evolutionary, not a revolutionary, construct. Though sometimes couched in radical language, the romantic idea of progress was radical primarily in the sense that it called for dramatic individual reconstruction. The social changes that would presumably follow such individual uplift would, it was assumed, evolve naturally over the course of time.

Though pervasive, recurring, and often clichéd, the American idea of progress in the pre-Darwinian years lacked a generally accepted conceptual framework. No eminent progressive theorist emerged to give an orthodox rendering of the national progressive faith. The idea cropped up in virtually every reference to social or historical change, but it remained loose, unstructured, and often inconsistent; America produced no Comte or Buckle to give it systematic meaning. Publication of Darwin's *Origin of Species* in 1859 and *The Descent of Man* in 1871 helped meet this need by advancing both a cogent biohistorical theory of development and a scientific method and vocabulary for assessing its meaning. But Darwin's hypotheses, while making it possible for Americans to approach the question of progress in a systematic way, threatened ominously the neat compatibility between science and the traditional moral and religious teleology both rationalist and romantic versions of progress had enjoyed. With the advent of Darwinism, American discussions of the idea of progress became at once more coherent and more critical; evolutionism afforded progress a new historical mechanism and raised sharp new questions about what the idea meant for the individual and society.

# The Evolutionary Dialogue

Charles Darwin did not, of course, invent the idea of evolution. For a full century before *Origin of Species* appeared (its complete title was *On the Origin of Species by Means of Natural Selection, or the Preservation of Favoured Races in the Struggle for Life*), the inadequacies of special creation and the fixed hierarchy of the great chain of being had slowly been forcing themselves on reluctant scientists. Even Linnaeus, whose elaborate system of taxonomy attempted to flesh out the chain-of-being concept in its remotest particular, had by the end of his life recognized that its staticism was inadequate to the bewildering variety of nature's morphological forms. Gradually, the possibility that species ebbed and flowed in some evolutionary fashion—or at least that they varied significantly in differing geological periods—became widely accepted. George Louis Buffon, Jean Baptiste Lamarck, Erasmus Darwin (Charles's grandfather), Baron George Cuvier, and Sir Charles Lyell had all affirmed a qualified evolutionism, though each for different reasons stopped short of Charles Darwin's conclusions. By the time *Origin of Species* appeared in 1859, the likelihood that species were not totally immutable had become a familiar and respectable opinion, though it was still unclear precisely how mutable species actually were and what constituted the forces and mechanics of their mutability.

Darwin confronted these questions directly, and his answers had such momentous consequences for all realms of knowledge that it is impossible to underestimate their significance. Both Darwin's conclusions and his methodology had an impact that vastly transcended the rather circumscribed biological scope of his investigations; as John Dewey later wrote, Darwin did nothing less than conquer "the phenomena of life for the principle of transition."[1] Although the mutability of species and the processes of natural and sexual selection implied different things to different people, during the last quarter of the nineteenth century, Darwinism and its variants left their deep impress on all areas of knowledge and thought. Familiar assumptions about change, emergence, and becoming all had to be reexamined, and this reexamination affected every walk of intellectual life. For many, the results were devastating. The easy orchestration of chance, design, logic, and progress, so harmoniously accomplished by rationalists and romantics alike, was no longer possible after Darwin.

The reasons for this lay primarily in "natural selection," the mechanism by which Darwin said species evolved. In a massive, careful presentation based on empirical observation, Darwin concluded that species were not unified entities in any permanent sense, but rather they were "only strongly defined varieties" of organic groupings whose dominant characteristics changed almost imperceptibly over time.[2] Each organism had unique, minute, chance variations in its composition, and these variations, in response to environmental changes and to the natural struggle for survival, allowed certain organisms to survive while others less well endowed died out. Those organisms that survived transmitted their traits to their offspring, who in turn either survived or did not according to their genetically received characteristics and how successfully those characteristics interacted with the environment. Since nature lavishly overproduced and could sustain only a fraction of its progeny, a fierce, brutal process of genetic selection took place. Over countless eons of time, those groups of organisms that adapted best survived; as they did so, their cumulative variations accreted and produced, ultimately, new species. The process took billions of variations and enormous spans of time, and it was not yet finished; *Origin of Species* ineluctably involved man in the processes it described and hence redefined man's relationship to nature.

In addition to the crude machinery of natural selection, in *The Descent of Man* Darwin identified a second force—sexual selection—affecting the development of man and certain higher forms of life. In the case of organisms in which the sexes were highly differentiated, the deliberate selection of a mate possessing desirable qualities added a dimension of consciousness to reproduction and the changes it wrought in species. Sexual selection, Darwin maintained, like natural selection, was a wholly naturalistic process tending "towards the general welfare of the species" but one that accelerated its changes. Sexual selection had historically worked to the greatest benefit for man, whose intellectual powers and socializing instincts, evolving through time, accounted for his dominance over other life forms. Man's higher, selected capacities sometimes led him to take actions contrary to what the laws of natural selection might dictate; cooperation and the conscious choosing of alternatives sometimes obviated the struggle for existence and made civilization and society possible. "Progress is no invariable rule," Darwin observed; often it seemed to depend on negating the laws of natural selection in the higher interest of individual and group survival.[3] In the course of history, this negation took place rarely and only among the higher forms of life. And even then it was uncertain and sporadic, a small tributary in the current of history. Yet on that negation, Darwin implied, hung the prospects for progress.

Thus, while man might point with pride to his progressive achievements, he and his destiny were still linked to nature's laws, processes, and forms. Strive as he might to convince himself of his uniqueness and divinity, man and the other anthropoids shared a common ancestry (what Darwin called our "ape-like progenitor"); for all of man's marvelous moral, social, and intellectual accomplishments, his very "bodily frame" bore the "indelible stamp of his lowly origin." Although Darwin acknowledged that man was "the most dominant animal that has ever appeared on this earth," his naturalistic interpretation of man's history divested it of its special character.[4] By breaking down the barriers between man and the animal kingdom, Darwin implied that history was not exclusively homocentric and that the scientific method (not divine mythologies or analogies) was the proper implement for discovering the cause-and-effect sequences that made man what he was—or what he had become—in time.

On at least three counts then, Darwin's works were revolutionary. Disdaining philosophical disputation, ignoring Plato, Descartes, Locke, Kant, and Hegel, Darwin in one scientific stroke altered the Western concept of the universe and man's position in it. Without engaging in metaphysical combat, Darwin challenged the remnants of Platonism by denying that nature gave obeisance to original types or essences of any kind. Moreover, neither *Origin* nor *Descent* paid the traditional deference of scientists to the niceties of scripture; Darwin offended traditionalists by failing to attempt to reconcile his findings with the accepted pieties of divine intervention in the processes of natural development. He rejected unapologetically special creation and catastrophic intercession by God, so dear to such traditionalists as Agassiz and his followers, as well as any "law of necessary development" guiding the course of evolution.[5] Evolution was a natural process, wholly contained by the energies and forces of this world.

Furthermore, Darwin refrained from putting evolution in any ethical or teleological context. Although on occasion he found it necessary to use words such as "higher," "more advanced," "progress," or "improvement" in discussing evolution, he did so only in a relative and restricted biological fashion.[6] Darwin specifically avoided the shoals of design, eschatology, and perfectionism; as he warned his readers, "Natural selection will not produce perfection."[7] Thus, Darwin's well-documented view of man and his descent raised large questions about the familiar assumptions of cosmic intentionality and progress by design that had become so dear to American sensibilities.

It was not so much Darwin's proofs that evolution had occurred that caused controversy and consternation, but rather his elaboration of natural and sexual selection as nature's evolutionary agencies. These agencies were largely random, chance mechanisms for change; if the evolution of species did take place as Darwin described, chance, not design or some overriding purposefulness in nature, produced the immense variety of life forms as well as governed their development. If species changed by accident rather than

according to divine purpose, traditional concepts of
man's nature and destiny were obsolete. And if chance
and transition were the new laws of nature, then all
aspects of human life—physical, mental, and
spiritual—were subject to those laws. Before Darwin,
human nature and universal morality seemed constant
and inviolable, but now they too were threatened by
evolutionary relativism. Consequently, Darwinism
jeopardized—if not destroyed—the basic assumptions
that had hitherto lent the idea of progress its credibil-
ity.

Or so it might have seemed. But Darwin's refusal to
expand upon the philosophical implications of his findings left others free to, and none did so with more
ebullience and abandon than the English savant, Herbert Spencer. Originally a civil engineer, Spencer had
been speculating about evolution long before *Origin*
appeared, and in Darwin's thorough researches he
found the firm scientific foundation he needed for his
ambitious "synthetic philosophy." Elaborating on certain features of Darwin's theory, Spencer set forth a
series of cosmic generalizations about the laws of
growth controlling all facets of life—biological, social,
historical, psychological, and political. Though based
on what was at best a highly questionable analogy
between biological and social development, Spencer's
theories attained such widespread currency in the
United States in the last quarter of the nineteenth century that Perry Miller was led to observe: "It would
hardly be too much to say that the bulk of American
'thought' in this period, measured solely by the weight
of printed paper, was not thought at all but only a
recapitulation of Spencer."[8] Comparatively few Americans read Darwin in the original; most readers
absorbed their Darwinism from such popularizations of
evolutionary ideas as Spencer's. By 1903, Americans

had purchased some 368,755 volumes of Spencer's works alone.[9]

Spencer's version of evolution was crucial to the history of the idea of progress in America. He softened somewhat the "entangled bank" image of nature that concluded *Origin*, an image depicting a "struggle for life" and a "war of nature," by projecting a reassuring theory of necessary progress based on biological evolution. Spencer drew two fundamental conclusions from his study of science and society, conclusions that Americans found especially congenial: first, social development followed the same general laws that governed biological evolution; second, the laws of social evolution produced the law of progress. Society, like any biological organism, necessarily evolved in time and hence progressed according to natural law: "Evolution is an integration of matter and concomitant dissipation of motion; during which the matter passes from an indefinite, incoherent homogeneity to a definite, coherent heterogeneity; and during which the retained motion undergoes a parallel transformation."[10]

Several consequences followed from the operation of this law of social differentiation. With increasing social heterogeneity and harmony, "evil tends perpetually to disappear." Through increasingly adequate adaptation to the environment, public morality advanced. Finally,

> all excesses and all deficiency must disappear; that is, all unfitness and all deficiency must disappear; that is, all imperfection must disappear. Thus the ultimate development of the ideal man is logically certain—as certain as any conclusion in which we place the most explicit faith; for instance, that all men will die. . . . Progress, therefore, is not an accident, but a necessity. . . . The modifications

> mankind have undergone, are still undergoing,
> result from a law underlying the whole organic
> creation; and provided the human race continues,
> and the constitution of things remains the same,
> those modifications must end in completeness.[11]

Whether he liked it or not, man was slowly evolving toward moral and social perfection through reflexive adaptation to the conditions of his environment. In guaranteeing that progress derived from the acceptance of existing conditions, Spencer formulated a philosophy of optimism and quietism that appealed strongly to traditional American laissez-faire attitudes.

For although evolution for Spencer meant progress toward a guaranteed perfection, such progress was achieved through individual stress and social differentiation. Departing from Darwin's brief suggestion that cooperation (Darwin's term was "cohesion") produced and accelerated improvements in social structures, Spencer interpreted natural selection in such a way as to lend the support of natural law to radical individualism and competition, to the struggle for "the survival of the fittest." Conflict itself, according to Spencer, was the agent of evolution and hence progress. Spencer's philosophy contributed the prestige of the new evolutionary science to the already existing American belief in foreordained progress through individual effort.

Spencer achieved a further reconciliation that helped make evolution even more palatable to Americans. His systematic philosophy, uniting all forms of life from the simplest protozoa to the most civilized polity under the monolithic rubric of progress, seemed to resurrect in scientific garb the familiar notion of cosmic design so threatened by natural selection. Whereas Darwin had made allowance for the operations of a deity only in the earliest stages of creation, Spencer posited a mysterious "Unknowable" force, constant and eternal, acting behind and regulating the development of the cosmos. Such a concession was just enough for those who respected and were tempted by modern science but who still clung to conventional theistical beliefs; if one but read "God" for the "Unknowable," the idea of evolution became infinitely more reassuring and acceptable. Spencer's philosophy thus provided an important middle ground between the evolutionary findings of empirical science and the theistical longings of the devout, a middle ground that renewed the possibility of commerce between science and religion in the interest of progress.

Not all were persuaded, however. Despite the assurances of Spencer that evolution equaled progress, for those who took their Darwin straight, the issue was not that easily resolved. Although it was certainly possible to interpret the mutability of species through natural selection in customary, theistical terms (as Princeton theologian James McCosh put it glibly, "Supernatural design produces natural selection"),[12] it was undeniably true that, in Asa Gray's words, "the theory [of *Origin*] is perfectly compatible with an atheistic view of the universe."[13] While evolution and natural selection could be tailored to fit a framework of theistical design, it was equally possible—and closer to Darwin's intentions —to argue that natural selection made intercession by the deity in history irrelevant and superfluous. The less contrived interpretation of Darwin saw the laws of evolution as long-term, statistical aggregates of accumulated, chance occurrences rather than the fulfillment of some original deific intention. While it was possible for many to agree with McCosh and Henry Ward Beecher, the popular clergyman, that natural selection was merely the device God had chosen for

achieving perfection, it was easier to view the laws of
nature descriptively as a set of random, accrued tendencies and not as a rigid, theistical prescription. Part
of Darwin's significance was that he forced men to
choose between the logic of historical design and the
paradoxical new logic of historical chance.

The wrenchings caused by this necessity for choosing
were a central theme in the history of evolutionism in
American thought. Its story has been told many times
and need not be here repeated.[14] What is important,
however, is how the resulting kinds of evolutionary
theorizing affected the development of the idea of
progress. While progress and evolution had almost as
many meanings as there were theorists, in the decades
after *Origin* and *Descent* appeared three fairly specific
attitudes toward the idea of progress emerged. These
attitudes—which for convenience shall be designated
"soft," "hard," and "telic"—can be viewed as voices in
the American dialogue over progress and evolution.[15]
Each voice represented a distinct, separate interpretation of evolution and progress; each was a polar
extreme of one generation's attempt to understand
how the methods and findings of empirical science
related to received notions of historical change and
meaning. Taken collectively, the soft, hard, and telic
interpretations of evolution and progress furnished the
immediate context from which the pragmatic doctrine
of progress was to emerge.

*ii*

Those maintaining a soft attitude toward the idea of
progress saw in evolution the hand of God, and in the
"laws" of evolution the certainty of progress. Evolution
and progress were the same—divinely ordained, pre-

determined, and inevitable. Advocates of the soft view interpreted Darwin's theory of the mutability of species as the lawful means by which necessary, godly progress occurred. Even though natural selection gave the appearance that chance and not design ruled the evolution of life to higher and higher levels, viewed "correctly" natural selection was simply the regular process by which God, or the "Unknowable," intended the world to reach perfection. The soft view deemphasized the harsh implications of natural selection and held that progress, design, and evolution were the essential historical realities discovered—or confirmed—by empirical science. Spencer's elaboration of Darwin's ideas into a "scientific" guarantee of social and historical progress was the most important early expression of this view. Most Americans who accepted evolutionism accepted the Spencerian interpretation; it was a comfortable conception of history's movement, which did little violence to pre-Darwinian notions of historical change.

Both the scientifically oriented and the theologically inclined, with only minor adjustments, accommodated to the soft view of evolution and progress. Asa Gray, one of the earliest and most respected American scientists to accept Darwin's theories, maintained throughout his life a belief in theistic, progressive design, as did Joseph LeConte, John William Draper, Jeffries Wyman, Alexander Winchell, and numerous other prominent scientific figures. From the religionist side, McCosh, Beecher, Lyman Abbott, George Frederick Wright, Minot Savage, Washington Gladden, and John Bascom also found it possible to conjoin their diverse theisms with evolution and progress. McCosh, perhaps the most prestigious of the accommodationists (he was president of Princeton), compounded these elements into a godly theory of "progressive progression," and

Beecher, the best-known minister of his day, maintained that while "God does not change," civilization was still "progressive, an unfolding process that is carrying creation up to higher planes and upon higher lines, reaching more complicated conditions in structure, in function, in adaptation, with systematic and harmonious results, so that the whole physical creation is organizing itself for a sublime march toward perfectness."[16]

Yet without doubt, the most prominent American spokesman for the soft view of evolution and progress was neither a scientist nor a theologian. He was John Fiske, the popular historian, philosopher, linguist, essayist, and lecturer, whose name in the 1870s, 1880s, and 1890s became synonymous with a benign, evolutionary optimism blending science and religion in a confection called "cosmic philosophy." Fiske's aim, like Spencer's, was to unify all knowledge, to postulate a cosmology "which would subsume physical, biological, psychological, and social phenomena under one system of laws, and at the same time guarantee human progress."[17] His writings manifested a serene, reassuring faith in the necessity and direction of change within the entire created order. Essentially a religionist, Fiske believed that traditional religions could survive only by accepting and assimilating the conclusions of modern science. Accordingly, his cosmic philosophy aimed at destroying finally the antipathy between science and religion; in the process, he synthesized the ingredients for an absolutistic, all-embracing conception of divinely ordained evolutionary progress.[18]

Fiske was raised in Middletown, Connecticut, and graduated from Harvard in 1863. From his early youth, he was an omnivorous reader of science, philosophy, and theology. After graduating from college and flirting briefly with the practice of law, Fiske maintained himself principally by his skill at popularizing the complicated, swirling intellectual currents of the post-Civil War world. A sometime lecturer and librarian at Harvard and a nonresident professor at Washington University in St. Louis (Fiske lost a permanent appointment in history at Harvard in 1870 to his friend Henry Adams, whose father then happened to be chairman of the board of overseers), Fiske wrote voluminously for popular journals, periodicals, and newspapers. He lectured widely, wrote countless book reviews, and finally made a name for himself in the 1880s and 1890s as a writer of interpretive books on American history. By the time of his death on July 4, 1901, he had become the most widely read historian in America, a fact testifying more to his stylistic verve and grace than to his originality or diligence as a researcher.[19]

Despite his preoccupation with popular historical writing, Fiske throughout his life was also absorbed by the large questions of his times: questions of man's origin, nature, evolution, and destiny and of the heroic attempts of philosophers, scientists, and godly theorists to grapple with these issues in an orderly, systematic way. His early reading of Comte, Buckle, Spencer, Friedrich von Humboldt, Theodore Parker, and Horace Bushnell had a profound and continuing influence on his intellectual development; his central obsession was with the patterned lawfulness of historical change and its manifestation in religious and scientific evidence. Such a concern was stimulated by his many friendships with the leading figures of the period: Darwin, Spencer, Huxley, William James, Chauncey Wright, Edward Youmans, Henry Ward Beecher, and Charles S. Peirce. Although his writings ranged from a polemic on the beneficial uses of tobacco and alcohol to a disquisition on myths and superstitions, apart from his historical studies the titles of his most important works—*Outlines of Cosmic Philosophy* (1874), *Darwinism and Other Essays* (1879), *The Destiny of Man Viewed in the Light of His Origin* (1884), *The Idea of God as Affected by Modern Knowledge* (1885), and *Through Nature to God* (1899)—reflected his abiding concern with religious and metaphysical issues. *Outlines of Cosmic Philosophy*, his magnum opus, was his attempt to subsume all modern scientific and religious knowledge under one comprehensive system of thought.

For Fiske, all of the phenomena of nature moved in a certain direction and were harmoniously animated by God.[20] Progress inhered in change itself, and change took place along regular, discernible lines for which natural selection was the *"vera causa."*[21] The law of progress was the law of history.[22] Since change was regular and subject to knowable laws, its pace and ultimate direction could be predicted. Far from destroying the purposefulness of the universe, Darwinian theory gave to man the basis for understanding his destiny and the means by which human destiny was being forged. Rather than degrading humanity by placing it on the same footing with the animal world as its critics often charged, Darwinian theory showed "distinctly for the first time how the creation and perfecting of Man is the goal toward which Nature's work has all the while been tending."[23] Fiske was confident, too, about the ultimate outcome of the processes of the cosmos; Darwin's theories of evolution revealed "all things working together toward one mighty goal, the evolution of the most exalted spiritual qualities which characterize Humanity."[24] Nor did Fiske shrink from framing the law of this heady course toward perfection:

We obtain the Law of Progress, which may be provisionally stated as follows:—

The Evolution of Society is a continuous establishment of psychical relations within the community, in conformity to physical and psychical
relations arising in the Environment; during
which, both the Community and the Environment
pass from a state of relatively indefinite, incoherent homogeneity to a state of relatively definite,
coherent heterogeneity; and during which, the
constituent Units of the Community become ever
more distinctly individuated.[25]

Fiske believed that Darwin and Spencer had given
scientific proof that the evolution of the created order
was in the hands of God and that he "guaranteed that
all would work out for the best in the end."[26] While
seemingly a "deadly struggle for existence," evolution
was in actuality a process in which dependence on
force and competition was slowly bringing a peaceful,
harmonious, and moral order into being. Man was the
end, the goal, the last stage of this process, and, in the
history of man, the same pattern of progress toward
perfection could be observed. From the savageness of
his primitive beginnings, man had, with divine guidance, progressed to his current heights. "He who has
mastered the Darwinian theory," Fiske insisted, recognizes that "the whole creation has been groaning and
travailing together in order to bring forth that last consummate specimen of God's handiwork, the Human
Soul."[27] The process of evolution had a predetermined
moral purpose by which it was guided and to which
it had always adhered: the creation of a society inspired
by divine love and belief in Christian principles. Christianity was, in fact, the supreme product and necessary
result of evolution.[28]
    Like many other theists, Fiske saw natural selection
as compatible with the Calvinistic notion of election;

the struggle for existence, as he put it, "elects one and damns the ninety and nine." Yet natural selection, for all its wastefulness and seeming cruelty, was not the only force working for the perfection of the species. Evolution was not merely material and natural; it was cosmic and spiritual. Man was, to be sure, an immediate product of natural forces, but Fiske was careful to suggest that those forces had been divinely designed and augmented. At sometime in either the "upper Eocene or lower Miocene" period, nature had taken a great leap forward, and a favored genus of primates, "Homo alalus," had appeared. Fiske denied explicitly that this was divine intervention, but his account left readers with the impression that it was at this juncture that the will of God, the "wondrous Dynamis," began to emerge from the chaos of nature. "Preeminent for sagacity," Homo alalus was characterized by its prolonged infancy and hence its greater intelligence, its capacity for language, its progressiveness, its achievement of the moral sensibility, and finally, its civilization. Although the Homo sapiens into which this genus evolved was, again, a product of natural forces, the hand of God was clearly discernible in its history:

> The story shows us Man becoming more and more clearly the image of God, exercising creative attributes, transforming his physical environment, incarnating his thoughts in visible and tangible shapes all over the world, and extorting from the abysses of space the secrets of vanished ages. From lowly beginnings, without breach of continuity, and through the cumulative action of minute and inconspicuous causes, the resistless momentum of cosmic events has tended toward such kind of consummation; and part and parcel

of the whole process, inseparably wrapped up with every other part, has been the evolution of the sentiments which tend to subordinate mere egoism to unselfish and moral ends.[29]

Like Spencer, Fiske equated progress—he used only the term "evolution" in stating its law—with increasing social differentiation and with the harmony he assumed would accompany it. As society evolved toward greater complexity, human selfishness would somehow become less divisive and more in tune with the social aggregate's general aims. The petty passions and willfulness of individuals had little effect upon the grand movement of history, for historical development took place largely apart from conscious human desires and intelligence. The laws of God and nature determined the course of history. Only in this light could historical progress be correctly interpreted: "To write history on any method furnished by the free-will doctrine, would be utterly impossible."[30] The outcome of historical progress was comfortably in God's hands, and Fiske had an almost mystical faith in its consummation:

"When the kindly earth shall slumber, lapt in a universal law," and when the desires of each individual shall be in proximate equilibrium with the . . . desires of all surrounding individuals. Such a state implies at once the highest possible . . . integration among the units of the community; and it is the ideal goal of intellectual and moral progress.[31]

Thus, man was the final consummation of the vast historical process that was evolution. His progress had not, however, been the random, capricious affair that

some evolutionists perceived. And it was not merely
man the animal, the natural phenomenon, that history
had been straining to produce. Rather, the supreme
product of the heaving cosmos was a being made by
God in his own image, a being whose completion would
be signified at some unspecified time in the future by
the emergence of a spiritual dimension that would
make him a closer approximation of his creator and,
by extension, turn his society into a secular counterpart
of the kingdom of heaven.

The evidence for this blissful portent was implicit in
natural, human, and religious history, in the geological
and biological record, in man's ontogenetic and
phylogenetic experiences, and in the long and checkered story of man's attempts to know and heed his
creator. The very evolution of human consciousness,
in Fiske's view, suggested that man was intended,
finally, to know the mysterious processes and forces
behind his being and becoming. The logic of evolution
dictated that all of the distinguishing features of each
organism survived and developed because they had
some compelling, requisite function to perform. Man's
capacity for moral knowledge, then, was not a capricious, chance occurrence, a spin-off of the evolutionary
processes. Rather, it was central to his nature and, like
the prehensile hand, furnished a clue to his ascendancy
and purpose. Man's intelligence and moral sensibilities
revealed his gradual movement toward the wholly
intelligent and the wholly moral—toward the image of
God. Evolution, Fiske maintained, had given man the
capacity to understand his moral destiny and thus
restored him to "his old position of headship in the
universe."[32]

The most important explanation for man's unique
progressive trajectory lay in the fact that human
infancy was so comparatively prolonged.[33] Though

there was little documentation for Fiske's theory, he argued repeatedly that the greatly extended period of infancy in humans allowed the brain to mature and become more complex, giving man a greater range of thought and action. Since his brain had become more highly developed than that of other primates, man eventually achieved a more permanent family structure, a sophisticated social sense, and, finally, a moral perspective that allowed him to subordinate his personal desires to the needs and best interests of the community. His prolonged infancy thus made it possible for him to evolve from egotism to altruism, and in altruism Fiske perceived the moral course of future progress. Because of man's large, highly developed brain and his complex neurological structure, "The capacity for progress begins to come in, and you begin to get at one of the great points in which man is distinguished from the lower animals, for one of those points is undoubtedly his progressiveness; and I think that any one will say, with very little hesitation, that if it were not for our period of infancy we should not be progressive."[34]

Human will, however, played only a circumscribed role in history's movement. The will was indeed a real force in the shaping of events, but it was conditioned and encompassed by a weighty set of complex social, biological, and psychological factors that were themselves historical products subject to general laws of development.[35] Such laws bracketed and overarched the strivings of even heroic individual figures; all societies necessarily passed through various stages of development, and their movement and general characteristics could not be altered by an individual's will. The will was simply one of a large number of forces acting to effect change, and thus it had no special, determining significance that justified its elevation into the essential cause of historical change. When his friend William James attacked Spencer's determinism as a dehumanizing, mechanical conception of history, Fiske quickly responded that Spencer had not disallowed the cumulative effects of individual variations and acts but simply put them within the framework of a general evolutionary law, a position with which Fiske agreed.[36]

Human consciousness, though a functional derivative of the evolutionary process, was simply another part of the larger cosmology of progress.[37] This was the essential metaphysical cargo of Fiske's evolutionary progressivism. Though he did acknowledge that there was in history a rhythm, a cosmically contained ebb and flow of energies that different branches of science had revealed, the main thrust of the cosmos was evolutionary, lawful, and progressive, and its greatest achievement was the human moral sensibility. Though social progress was not the absolute and necessary condition of all times and places, Fiske still insisted that progress, "the all important phenomenon to be investigated," was the fundamental law of history and that the "prime features of social progress are the prime features of evolution in general."[38] Both progress and man's moral sense derived from the continual process of adjustment between the individual, the community, and the environment, and this process, too, with its constant progression from homogeneity to heterogeneity, was governed by the old, familiar laws of evolution.

Fiske's vision of the end of evolutionary progress was a vague, Christianized version of Spencer's notion of "equilibration," a condition of biological, social, and moral stasis, heterogeneity, and harmony. The laws of social differentiation, following the larger dictates of the cosmos, necessarily led toward the triumph of personal altruism and social reconciliation, toward a social order that smacked more of the eschatology of the Social Gospelers than anything else. Theism and science wedded, earthly strife would cease, man would become fully the image of God, anthropomorphism would evolve into "cosmism." The laws of progress and evolution, Fiske concluded,

> placed Humanity on a higher pinnacle than ever. The future is lighted for us with the radiant colors of hope. Peace and love shall reign supreme . . . and as we gird ourselves up for the work of life we may look forward to the time when in the truest sense the kingdoms of this world shall become the kingdom of Christ, and he shall reign for ever and ever, king of kings and lord of lords.[39]

If this hallelujah chorus to progress strikes the modern ear as a strident, operatic travesty on evolutionary science, it must be remembered that nearly all of Fiske's published writings were originally lectures presented to various audiences for profit. This fact enhances Fiske's value as a spokesman for his times; even had he been so inclined, Fiske literally could not have afforded to present unpopular opinions about the weighty matters on which he spoke. Invariably, Fiske ended up telling his listeners what they wanted to hear. His message was authoritative, comfortingly scientific in its terminology, and agreeable to all save the most rock-ribbed fundamentalist or the most tough-minded skeptic. Again and again in the 1880s and 1890s, Fiske was invited to lecture in halls from Boston to St. Louis, from Bangor to Milwaukee. Harvard awarded him an honorary Doctor of Laws degree in 1894, and Yale invited him to accept the same degree at its two hundredth anniversary celebration in 1901.

By this, the year of his death, Fiske was one of the most widely acclaimed popular authorities on historical, scientific, and philosophical matters in America. His enormous success as an interpreter of the meaning of evolution reveals the significance of his views for the idea of progress in the years before the turn of the century.

Fiske's cosmic speculations, however, were riddled with unproved assumptions and fallacious logic. That all of nature throbbed to a single progressive mandate from its creator, that man's moral sense derived from a uniquely extended infancy peculiar to humans, that Christianity was the purpose of creation—these basic elements of his thought were but unverified and unverifiable tenets of a preexistent faith. That the human intellect in some fundamental way aided in the processes of evolution, yet that the human will did not alter the course of history, was a glaring, unresolved logical gaff. And that in the efflorescence of the spirit of altruism lay man's progressive destiny was the fondest hope of a tender-minded traditionalist. Apart from his evolutionary rhetoric, Fiske's mode of theorizing had little to do with Darwinian science.

Yet unquestionably, Fiske's soft view of progress was shared by most Americans of his time. As such, it represents an important example of how one version of evolutionism was used to bolster prior assumptions about the meaning of history and the destiny of man. In Fiske's writings, the traditional faith of nineteenth-century Americans in God, progress, and the moral law found its most optimistic, eloquent, and unified post-Darwinian expression. If his thought was a salmagundi of religious hopes, empirical observations, and shopworn evolutionary clichés, it still reflected accurately the problems and the needs of his age. That the times were out of joint was not Fiske's fault; his cosmic synthesis did its best to heal the dislocation in a manner acceptable to the majority of his contemporaries.

*iii*

In its November 1893 issue, *The Popular Science Monthly* reprinted Thomas H. Huxley's "Evolution and Ethics," the Romanes lecture recently given at Oxford University. Huxley, Darwin's friend, staunch supporter, and self-styled "Bulldog," argued in the lecture that although the notion of evolution was centuries old, having roots in the intellectual and moral traditions of both East and West, the evolutionary process as it was currently known, the so-called struggle for existence, could not be reconciled with "sound ethical principles." The cosmos moved and heaved, its energies shifted and became transformed, but its natural processes produced no consistent ethical imperatives. The most "obvious attribute" of the cosmos was its "impermanence." There could be no "ethics of evolution," Huxley asserted; there was only the "evolution of ethics," the deliberate but unplanned countering by sentient creatures of nature's mechanisms. Whatever ethical improvements the cosmos contained were achieved at the expense of its natural, lawful processes; civilization depended not on the laws of nature but on men's combat with them. Huxley's conclusion was bleak and inescapable: "The theory of evolution encourages no millennial anticipations."[40]

As might be expected, Huxley's remarks caused American readers considerable distress, and succeeding issues of the journal contained several respectful but firm rebuttals.[41] Huxley's insistence on the separation of ethics and morals from nature's laws implied a skepticism—possibly an agnosticism—that flew in the face of that dominant American faith articulated so fluently by Fiske. Huxley's position, however, did reflect another way of looking at the question of evolution and progress. This perspective, distinctly a minority view, had been cogently if tersely expressed in America some twenty years earlier by a close friend of John Fiske, the highly respected but little-known philosophic gadfly of Cambridge, Chauncey Wright. Overlooked by intellectual historians until relatively recently, Wright exerted a strong, early influence on his close friends, Charles S. Peirce and William James. Consequently, his interpretation of the meaning of evolution for the idea of progress, though not a popular one, is highly important: Chauncey Wright was the most consistent American spokesman for the hard view of evolution and progress.

Like Fiske, Wright came from a small New England town—Northampton, Massachusetts—and went to Harvard, graduating in 1852. Supporting himself modestly as a computer for the *Nautical Almanac*, Wright remained in Cambridge after graduation, writing occasional book reviews and philosophical essays, chatting interminably with a large circle of philosophically inclined friends, and teaching from time to time, twice at Harvard for short periods in the 1870s. In 1860 he was elected Fellow of the American Academy of Arts and Sciences, serving as the academy's secretary during the 1860s when the controversy over Darwinism raged fiercest. Not an ambitious man, Wright lived more for his philosophical conversations with friends than anything else. An amiable bachelor, he was welcome in many Cambridge parlors, where his pleasant manner and keen mind made him a most agreeable guest, and his premature death in 1875 elicited many expressions of loss and admiration. Fiske, who had once boarded in the same house with Wright and who belonged to his close circle of intimates, wrote in the *Harvard Advocate* that "to have had him pass away, leaving so scanty a record of what he had it in him to utter, is nothing less than a great public calamity."[42]

Wright did indeed leave a scanty record, for unlike the prolix, publicity-conscious Fiske, he had no desire to leave his intellectual mark upon his times. Curiously phlegmatic, Wright had, in Fiske's words, a kind of "mental inertness" that diverted him from sustained effort of any kind. Consequently, his views, so important for the influence they had over other influential men, are sketchily outlined in a dozen or so essays and reviews collected in 1877 as *Philosophical Discussions* and in a volume of letters privately published in 1878. Wright's significance, however, extends far beyond this meager productivity, for his innumerable conversations with a generation of America's leading thinkers congregating in Cambridge in the 1860s and 1870s deeply affected all of them.

Wright was the key figure of Peirce's so-called Metaphysical Club, which met from time to time in the early 1870s to discuss contemporary philosophy and science and their relationships. The group included James, Peirce, Fiske, Holmes, Nicholas St. John, Green, and Joseph B. Warner, and from its discussions emerged, according to Peirce, the outlines of the philosophy of pragmatism.[43] In the group's deliberations, Wright's voice was predominant. As James observed upon his death, "His best work has been done in conversation; and in the acts and writings of many friends he influenced his spirit will, in one way or another as the years roll on, be more operative than it ever was in direct production."[44] Peirce later estimated that Wright had a mind "about on the level of J. S. Mill."[45]

It was appropriate that Peirce should have compared

Wright to Mill, for the distinguishing features of Wright's thought were its firm adherence to a rigid, extraordinarily refined and consistent empiricism and an equally firm rejection of metaphysical flight. The nominalism of Bacon, Hume, Mill, and Whewell became in Wright a stringent aversion to abstraction. When he read *Origin of Species* in 1860, he became an immediate convert, not so much because he agreed with Darwin's conclusions as because he appreciated the deeper philosophical significance of Darwin's disciplined, a posteriori method. Wright's affinity was for the truly scientific, and truly scientific minds adhered strictly to the limits of the observed; they imputed no causation beyond the immediate reaches of the data. As Wright once wrote to his friend Grace Norton, "It may be, or doubtless is, true that Paris has brought destruction on itself because it was not Christian; but this is as little pertinent to a practical view of the matter as is the fact that its palaces were burned because they were not fireproof."[46] Wright's commitment was to the practical view, and his aversion to arguments from extension and analogy became more marked as he grew older, until, as Ephraim Gurney recalled after Wright's death, he had so ruthlessly used Occam's razor that "nothing was left standing in the mind that was not rooted in experience. Experience of phenomena gave both the content and the form of knowledge; the ground and the sanction of moral judgments; the limits of the universe in its intelligible, credible relations with man."[47]

Wright was singularly unmoved by the large questions of life's meaning and movement that had galvanized philosophers since time began. As James wrote of him, "When mere actuality of phenomena will suffice to describe them he held it pure excess and superstition to speak of a metaphysical whence and whither, of a substance, or meaning, or an end."[48] On questions for which he felt there were no conclusive answers —does God exist? why are men as they are? does fate chart human destiny?—Wright's avowed position was agnostic, or, as he liked to call it, "nihilistic." By this term, which James found so repugnant, Wright meant "an exorcism of the vague; a criticism of questions which by habit have passed beyond the real practical grounds of causes of questions."[49] This intellectual parsimoniousness, sustained with such aplomb on matters of metaphysical conjecture, was to Wright but common sense; he saw no reason to speculate about things that in no way could ever be rooted in experience as he defined it. The elements of experience were externally unrelated, and behind them lay no universal adhesive or animus: things were as they were, and there was no need to anguish over why or why they were not otherwise. Wright's nihilistic world was unified by nothing, leading James once to refer to it contemptuously as a "nulliverse."[50]

One result of Wright's dogged insistence that conclusions be empirically warranted was his rejection, his exorcism, of teleological projections from scientific inquiry. The establishment of certain cause-and-effect probabilities in psychology and biology had invited less critical minds to leap ahead to historical conclusions Wright simply could not endorse. Wright's interpretation of evolution, contrasting starkly with Fiske's, is a case in point. For Fiske, evolution guaranteed progress toward definite moral ends; for Wright, it indicated changes in specific forms of life. Fiske believed Darwin had disclosed the laws of cosmic progress; Wright thought Darwin had demonstrated the efficacy of the inductive, empirical method when applied to natural history, biology, and certain aspects of the development of language and consciousness. Fiske swallowed whole, and extended into the sphere of theology, Spencer's allegedly "scientific" analogy of society to a biological organism; Wright thought Spencer's claims to scientific warrantability were fraudulent and pernicious. As he wrote in his essay, "German Darwinism," in which he criticized sharply Spencer's translation of the evolutionary hypothesis into a first principle of metaphysics:

> The essential error of metaphysics, or "realism," is not merely in attributing to an abstraction a truly individual, thinglike existence, or making it a "realized abstraction," but in treating it *as if* it had such an existence—in other words, *as if* it had a meaning independently of the things which ought to determine the true limits and precision of its meaning. Thus, to apply the mechanical law of the conservation of force, which, as a scientific truth, has no meaning beyond the nature and conditions of material movements (whether these are within or outside of an organism)—to apply this law analogically to all sorts of changes—to the "movements" of society, for example—is, in effect, metaphysics, and strips the law of all the merits of truth it has in the minds and judgments of physical philosophers, or of those through whose experimental and mathematical researches it came to have the clear, distinct, precise, though technical meanings in science that constitute its only real merits.[51]

Far from regarding evolution as the law of progress, Wright characterized it as a limited "abstract statement of the order which the intellect expects to find in the phenomena of nature."[52] Doubtless some forms of animal and plant life had evolved from a lower order of complexity to a higher; and, within the limits of the evidence, Wright had no quarrel with the theory of evolution. It did not follow, however, that evolution necessarily applied to all phases of life and history. Consequently, it was folly to speak of evolution as absolutely guaranteeing historical and social progress. Such thinkers as Fiske and Spencer were in Wright's estimate "speculative" rather than "scientific" philosophers whose proper province was metaphysics, not history or science.[53] An evolutionary design in history had not been proved by Darwin's or Spencer's evidence. Fiske's saccharine, progressive teleology was based on dreams and hopes, not upon evidence, and there was no evidence that men could experience to justify the cosmic maxims Fiske advanced so positively. As Wright argued, "It is possible that laws exist absolutely universal, binding fate and infinite power as well as speech and the intelligible use of words; but it is not possible that the analytical processes of any finite intellect should discover what particular laws there are."[54]

Wright's skepticism of metaphysical extensions of cause-and-effect inferences, perhaps derived from his training as a mathematician and logician, led him to apply scrupulously empirical criteria to all questions of sequence. The results, sometimes startlingly matter-of-fact and mundane, were often discordant to his less cautious auditors. Shrinking always from the "mysticism" inherent in metaphysics, Wright observed in his essay, "A Fragment on Cause and Effect":

> Scientific doctrines and investigations are exclusively concerned with connections in phenomena which are susceptible of demonstration by inductive observation, and independent of diversities or resemblances in their hidden natures, or of any

like questions about their metaphysical derivation
or independence. That like produces like, and
that an effect must resemble its cause are shallow,
scholastic conceptions, hasty blunders of generalization, which science repudiates, and with them it
repudiates the scholastic classification or distinction between material and spiritual which
depended on these classifications.[55]

Hence the "cause" and meaning of consciousness, for
Fiske a question of momentous teleological significance, was for Wright a matter of careful, scientific
inquiry conducted along narrowly empirical lines. In
his 1873 essay, "Evolution of Self-Consciousness,"
Wright rejected the procrustean theism into which
thinkers like Fiske put the fact of human consciousness. Self-consciousness, Wright alleged, could be
accounted for by the wholly natural processes of evolution, whose cosmic meaning, if there was one, did not
yield to scientific scrutiny. The capacity for language,
for cognition, for designation, and for knowing and
abstracting, amounting to a unique *kind* of capability
separating man from the other animals, did not imply
a unique set of laws governing human development.
The power to experience shared by all sentient beings
had in man gradually been put to new and extraordinary uses. Intelligent self-consciousness was the eventual result, but in no way did this warrant the
metaphysical conclusion that humans possessed a
unique, "latent" nature or power that raised them
above other natural creatures and signified their
unique destiny. Science could not support the inference that self-consciousness had any particular
metaphysical significance.
      Wright insisted that science and metaphysics were
fundamentally separate concerns. Science, a neutral,

empirical method of observation and verification, could not possibly be marshaled to support any particular conception of morality. Allying himself with the scientific school of "utilitarian reascn," Wright held that the real enemy of the progress of knowledge was "a priori conviction, or prejudice asserting itself as its own justification, or sentiment born of strife and narrowness, and sanctioned only by custom and traditional religious authority."[56] The insistence of such people as Asa Gray, Louis Agassiz, Spencer, and Fiske of molding scientific inquiry to fit predetermined, essentially theological conclusions was not merely a departure from the scientific method but an affront to critical intelligence. Wright's position on matters of moral law was agnostic; for him, the evidence simply did not exist to support the kind of generalizations in which Fiske trafficked. The clusters of ideas that developed around the "great religious doctrines" of "supernatural causes" and "the future life" Wright viewed as essentially "of the nature of diseases . . . [as] distortions of development."[57]

For these reasons, Wright thought Fiske's elaboration of evolutionary postulates into a comprehensive philosophy of universal progress to be idle speculation. To speak of universal progress required, as Fiske acknowledged, faith in some universal moral law governing all phases of life, singular and collective, at each stage of development. Such an absolutistic view could not, Wright maintained, be documented by the scientific method. Wright's commitment to empiricism was too thoroughgoing to allow him to accept the extension of partial, fragmentary signs of evolution into a universal law of progress. If anything, evolution seemed to him the exception rather than the rule of history: "We strongly suspect that the law of 'evolution' will fail to appear in phenomena not connected, either directly or remotely, with the life of the individual organism, of the growth of which this law is an abstract statement."[58]

Unquestionably there was movement in history, but Wright saw little reason to believe that the movement was progressive. Certainly such change as there was could not be amplified into a grand, monolithic teleology. Simply because the universe could be shown to exist and to change did not necessarily mean that it had a knowable beginning or end; on what empirical grounds could one reveal the origins of eternity or the limits of infinity? Furthermore, for every instance of progressive development the believers in progress identified, numerous examples of retrogression could be shown. Rather than developing along regular lines, the movement of the universe seemed an irregular series of fluctuations in which development and disintegration were mixed and mingled.

Wright's term for this universal flux was "cosmical weather"; it implied his dissent from the view that equated evolution with progress or even directionality. As set forth in his essay "A Physical Theory of the Universe," cosmical weather suggested an analogy between ordinary weather, with its mixture of logical causation and apparent capriciousness, and the constitution of the solar system. Wright assumed that in nature all movement produced or was followed by "countermovement," a principle he found basic to science and physics. The principle of the conservation of energy gave Wright his point of departure, from which he elaborated a theory of nondevelopmental cosmology in which action and reaction, energy and matter, were constantly converting and reversing themselves without moving in any concerted direction apparent to the human observer. Thus Wright came to feel that the teleological interpretation of the cosmos was merely wishful thinking, if not a subtle kind of intellectual dishonesty.[59]

Wright believed that the idea of progress, like the idea of God, was unaffected by evolution. Beyond empirical verification, it remained an idea held or rejected on faith. It represented an a priori ordering of events read into history, a "reflex" of hopes and moral attitudes held at a given time. Empirical science, the only source of true knowledge, could not be concerned with moral judgments and thus could not comment one way or another on progress. As Wright concluded:

> Progress is a grand idea,—Universal Progress is a still grander idea. It strikes the keynote of modern civilization. . . . What the ideas God, the One and the All, the Infinite First Cause, were to an earlier generation, such are Progress and Universal Progress to the modern world,—a reflex of moral ideas and feelings. . . . Theories of society and the character and origin of social progress . . . are all liable to the taint of teleological and cosmological conceptions,—to spring from the order which the mind imposes upon what it imperfectly observes. . . .[60]

Though Chauncey Wright cast a critical eye on his generation's easy assumptions about design and evolution, he did not decree absolutely that progress had no meaning. Nor did he conclude that the scientific method disproved design and progress in history, for to have done so would have made him guilty of a priorism, the same charge he hurled at the speculative metaphysicians. The evidence of evolution neither confirmed nor denied Fiske's progressive cosmology, about which science could have nothing to say. There was, as Wright pointed out, evidence that simply did not fit into a cosmic, progressive framework, and thus Wright's inclinations, expressed very tentatively, leaned toward his theory of cosmic weather. But this too was largely conjecture, for there could be no middle ground between scientific empiricism, which dealt with observable facts, and Spencerian metaphysics, a combination of poetry, speculation, and theology.[61]

There was room in the universe for utilitarian improvement, Wright periodically suggested, though it had no necessary, knowable mandate. As he put it in a letter to Francis Abbott, "No *real* fate or necessity is indeed manifested anywhere in the universe,—only a phenomenal regularity."[62] The regularity had no cause; it simply existed as a condition of the nature of things. To maintain that regularity required a cause was to imply that irregularity was somehow a norm; one experienced regularity in phenomena simply because things given in nature *had* regularity as part of their being. To inquire why this was so was pointless. Although one could point to specific human and social advances within the evolutionary circumference, such amelioration gave no evidence of intentions larger than those behind the specific human efforts for change. Offsetting, counterprogressive efforts could also be detected, and the result was something of a stalemate:

Evidence of progress in life through any ever so considerable portion of the earth's stratified materials would not, in our opinion, warrant us in drawing universal cosmical conclusions therefrom. Alternations of progress and regress relatively to any standard of ends or excellence which we might apply, is to us the most probable hypothesis that the general analogy of natural operation warrants.[63]

Wright's empirical approach to the idea of progress was too rigorous and agnostic to be shared by many of his generation. His calm detachment and his skepticism on moral matters ran counter to the general nineteenth-century American faith in progress and the moral law. His empiricism, an extension of Mill's piecemeal, pluralistic logic applied to the implications of evolution, was at direct odds with the pious conclusions of the Spencerian metaphysicians, and it finally put him at odds with most progressive theorists. Whereas the majority of his contemporaries who dealt with the questions of evolution and progress focused on evolutionary conclusions and their possible historical meaning, Wright's preoccupation remained with empiricism's circumscribed applicability. The hard look he gave to ethical matters and the valuative dimensions of social change followed logically from the limits of his method of inquiry. The result was, often, a kind of moral lassitude that many of his acquaintances—William James especially—found intolerable. Given Wright's empirical premises, however, his agnosticism on the question of progress was difficult to refute. It would take the careful articulation of the radical conception of experience underlying pragmatism and the slow-to-mature doctrine of the will to believe before James created the foundation for such a refutation, and by that time Wright had long since passed from the scene.

Chauncey Wright's insistence that science and metaphysics were unbroachably separate concerns illustrates the extreme effect Darwinian science had on methodologically conscious thinkers. For the few rigor-

ous thinkers who could suspend judgment until the
facts were in and verified, even on moral matters, Darwinism meant a reversal of the order of belief and sub-
stantiation; the true idea was the idea which subsequent testing verified. It was true not by reference
to prior association with some intentional order or system but by reference to its specific, a posteriori consequences and effects. By implication, Wright suggested, only ideas that could be subjected to some form
of empirical scrutiny could lay claim to having meaning
and truth. Wright's separation of science and
metaphysics and his refusal to commit himself to
unverified ideas showed how Darwinism in its most virulent form corroded those large systems of thought
that attempted to reduce the cosmos to some simplistic
formula, even if couched in evolutionary language.
The spirit of Darwin, for a mind like Wright's, was
reductionist, skeptical, and antisystematistic. The result
was that, in Wright's view, science, the most certain
method of knowing, could say nothing very concrete
or positive about the dynamics and meaning of history.

But science could verify the fact that consciousness
and will existed and that, as Wright had shown in
"Evolution of the Self Conscious," the will was a creative agency in time. The laws governing its operations,
if there were any, were obscure and unpredictable.
Wright doubted that the will could be encompassed by
any such glib formula as Fiske and Spencer had invent-
ed; certainly science, though confirming the will's existence, had no legitimate, determining role to play in its
operations. Even though the will's existence implied
some limited telic dimension to those sequences of
events in which the will was operative, science could
not reveal the manner or substance of its operations.

Not everyone who comprehended Darwin and his
method, however, was so rigorous an adherent of

empiricism or so reluctant to lend the cloak of science to considerations of history's course. Between the soft, progressive metaphysics of a Fiske and the hard, empirical neutrality of a Wright lay a middle ground that aspired to be both naturalistic and progressive, both scientific and systematic. Though Wright did not live to see this ground surveyed, and would doubtless have demurred from the telic conception of progress so central to its domain, he would have applauded the efforts of its author, Lester Ward, to extend the methods of science to all realms of human knowledge and inquiry.

*iv*

By any yardstick, Lester Frank Ward was one of the most remarkable intellects of his day. Born in rural Joliet, Illinois, in 1841, he was the tenth child of an uneducated, itinerant mechanic and a talented, resourceful daughter of a minister. Almost single-handedly, Ward pulled himself out of the morass of poverty and the provincialism of the frontier to become, by his death in 1913, one of the most learned, productive, and respected figures in American sociology. Ward's achievements are all the more remarkable when it is remembered that during nearly all his adult life he held routine, lower-level appointments in the federal government in Washington, D.C., and that his enormous intellectual accomplishments and his voluminous writings were largely the products of his spare time. Despite his now-eclipsed reputation, Ward at one time was regarded as the leading American sociologist and was once designated by an enthusiastic biographer "The American Aristotle."[64]
Wounded severely during the battle of Chancellors-

ville in the Civil War, Ward accepted a clerkship in the
Department of the Treasury in 1865 and two years
later began work in the evenings on a bachelor's degree
at George Washington University (then Columbian
College). By 1872, he had completed not only his
bachelor's degree in chemistry but had also won di-
plomas in law and medicine. In addition, he briefly
considered taking up the ministry and accordingly took
courses in Hebrew, Greek, and theology. In—
again—his spare time, he had also become proficient
in five other languages, helped edit and contribute to
a dissenting theological journal, *The Iconoclast*, and
begun publishing assorted essays in the fields of
biology, anthropology, and geology. In 1881, he
entered the United States Geological Survey, and in
1892 he became its chief paleontologist. Not until 1906
did he finally win an academic appointment, the newly
created chair of sociology at Brown University. There,
Ward startled his colleagues and delighted his students
by offering a course entitled "A Survey of All Knowledge," into which he poured the fruits of a lifetime of
phenomenally disciplined and wide-ranging study.

Ward's primary calling was as a scientist, author, and
lecturer. During his various excursions into formal
education—and before completing his bachelor's
degree—he began work on what was to become an
unrecognized classic of its time, the ponderous and
erudite *Dynamic Sociology*, published in two volumes in
1883. The first comprehensive, synthetic sociological
treatise written in America, the book was an instant
failure. Few noticed it and fewer bought it; Ward later
recalled that in its first ten years fewer than five
hundred copies were sold.[65] Discouraged, Ward continued to research, write, and lecture, and, by the
1890s, he began to receive serious attention from the
world of scholarship. *The Psychic Factors of Civilization*,

written in three months while he was on a camping trip, appeared in 1893 and was well received. A second edition of *Dynamic Sociology* was issued in 1897, followed by *Outlines of Sociology* in 1898, *Pure Sociology* in 1903, and *Applied Sociology* in 1906.[66] Ward's writings, if too arcane for popular consumption, could no longer be ignored by academics, and honors began to accrue. In 1897, he was given an honorary LL.D. by his alma mater, and in 1900 he was elected president of the Institut International de Sociologie. In 1906, the year he was called to Brown, he became the first president of the American Sociological Society. Such recognition, if belated, was acknowledgment that Ward himself had been largely responsible for the creation of the discipline of sociology in the United States. As one of his colleagues and collaborators, James Q. Dealey, later wrote, "Lester F. Ward in the field of social science is to the United States what Auguste Comte is to France or Herbert Spencer to England."[67]

If comparing Ward to Comte and Spencer accurately measures his stature, it also describes his approach to sociology. Like the two systematists of whom he thought so highly, Ward saw sociology as the apogee of all laws and principles cognate to the different branches of science. Sociology was monistic, a synthesis of lesser scientific streams that flowed into one consummate, anthropocentric body of knowledge. Both ultimate and reductionist, it was the final distillation of historical and scientific knowledge.[68] As Ward put it, "Sociology is a genetic product, the last term in the genesis of science. . . . Standing at the head of the entire series, [it] is enriched by all of the truths of nature and embraces all truth. It is the *scienta scientarium.*"[69]

Though in agreement with Comte and Spencer as to the location of sociology on the ascending hierarchy of knowledge, Ward departed from them—especially from Spencer—in his conception of sociology's function. For Ward the *scienta scientarium* had one purpose: the synthesis of all knowledge for the deliberate propitiation of human happiness. Science and ethics were not intrinsically separate, as Chauncey Wright had believed. Rather, they were the coordinate keys that human intelligence and feelings had forged over time to unlock the doors of nature's limitations and liberate mankind. Rightly conceived, sociology was a fusion of the best of the scientific method and the loftiest of human ideals wrought together for the conscious improvement of society. Ward's distinctive contribution to the idea of progress in America thus began with the very definition of sociology.

As "dynamic sociology" suggests, Ward's focus in studying society was its dynamics, its impetus for change, and the possibilities for improvement that change created. Implicit in the title was dissent from the assumptions of Spencer's *Social Statics*, in which a naturalistic, gradual evolutionism chained human effort to nature's slow achievement of eventual equilibrium and stasis, a view accepted wholeheartedly by William Graham Sumner and other "biological evolutionists" as scientific sanction for a policy of strict social laissez-faire.[70] Implicit too in the title was a further dissent from Comte and Spencer and their American disciples. For while Ward's notion of sociology was conventionally monistic in the sense that he believed all the sciences to be fundamentally related and methodologically harmonious, running through Ward's view of nature and history was a pervasive dualism that set him apart from most other contemporary sociologists.

The source of this dualism was Ward's recognition of a basic disjunction between biological or natural evolution ("genesis") and social, or conscious, evolution ("telesis"). Genetic evolution referred to the random, mindless, essentially wasteful processes of nature described by Darwin in *Origin of Species*. Telic evolution was the conscious alteration of the natural and social environment through the operation of man's intellect. Genesis and telesis—nature and history—were both natural in that they occurred within the broad framework of creation, but they were nonetheless separate and distinct processes functioning according to coordinate but essentially different laws. Telesis was an "artificial" process in which the human mind interfered with the ordinary workings of haphazard nature, but the interference it wrought was to be preferred over genesis, which was slow, redundant, and atavistic. In Ward's view, the biological sociologists had made a basic error in drawing a specious analogy between biology and society: they did not distinguish between the processes of genesis and telesis and, accordingly, took genetic processes as normative and lawful for all social activity. Genesis became the allegedly scientific warrant for a laissez-faire attitude toward social change, whereas in fact society evolved under the laws of telesis, a process that sanctioned the deliberate manipulation of social arrangements.[71]

Thus, though Ward had great respect for Spencer's intellect and his synthetic philosophy, he believed the Englishman's shopworn, outdated, and combatative social views were predicated on scientific error. Ward criticized William Graham Sumner's equally reactionary *What the Social Classes Owe to Each Other* for perpetuating the same fallacy. Sumner was "not a biologist, as all sociologists should be"; had he been so, he would have recognized the differences between genesis and telesis.[72] The problem with the biological sociologists was that they did not understand even the rudiments of biology. No understanding of social life could be reached by those who failed to understand life itself and its relationship to history and the universe. This was not one of Ward's problems, as he amply demonstrated in the first three hundred pages of *Dynamic Sociology*, through which biological jungle the seeker after sociological knowledge must hack before he is rewarded. Ward liked to begin at the beginning, and he found it thoroughly appropriate to start his study of sociology with a theory of the universe and how life began.

The universe for Ward was basically energy, creative, pulsing, and throbbing motion, always seeking and destroying forms, structures, and equilibriums. Through a process he called "synergy"—a mysterious, essentially dialectical interaction of conflicting and antagonistic forces in nature—the rudiments of first biological and then social organization appeared.[73] Ward gave a wholly naturalistic rendering of the genesis of life out of primordial matter. Organic structures developed as a result of various cosmic forces in the solar system: radiation, temperature changes, atmospheric pressure and gravity, the "molecular impact" of a kind of primitive atomic fission—all operating on certain basic inorganic elements.[74] Through synergy, simple life forms developed, gradually leading to the creation of feeling, of the awareness in matter of sensation (*"the conscious susceptibility of a substance to the impressions made upon it by other substances brought into contact with itself"*).[75]

The development of matter with the capacity for feeling introduced into nature the beginnings of the psychic dimension of evolution. Over the centuries, this capacity, again through synergy, evolved into the faculty among higher forms of animal life for what in man became thought and consciousness. This faculty in turn led man to produce elemental forms of society. As society gradually evolved into more and more complex structures, the role of the psychic factor became larger. Ward's analysis, based as it was on an immense amount of carefully documented and current scientific research, set the stage for a dynamic interpretation of the role of mind and thought in the evolutionary process. For though Ward maintained that "all life is one fact, which only clothes itself in different apparel" (a characteristic bit of monism), his theory of the emergence of the psychic factor in nature underlay his distinction between genesis and telesis and provided the foundation for his voluntaristic, melioristic conception of progress.[76]

Within evolution, then, two broad types of change had developed: out of the haphazard processes of genesis had emerged the capacity for telesis. While genetic progress had indeed been real, it had been unconscious, fortuitous, and highly uneconomical. When set in the context of social change and growth, natural or genetic progress had come to result in harmful conflict, wasted motion, and the survival of a kind of primitivism that in the long run was not progress at all.[77] Thus, modern man's task was to accept the opportunities afforded by his psychic capacities and apply telesis—the deliberate, planned alteration of his environment—to all phases of his existence. This application, despite the caveats of the biological sociologists, was natural and justified; since nature had produced man's reasoning capacity in the first place, how could its exercise be in any way contrary to natural law? Though Spencer and Sumner cited instances of savage competition as the exclusive "law of nature," Ward easily pointed out the superiority of cooperative, symbio-

tic natural relationships. Neither was exclusively nature's prescription; it was now up to man to choose
which way lay true progress.

> Man's progress has been the progress of nature
> (genesis), a secular and cosmical movement, not
> the progress of art (telesis), the result of foresight
> and intelligent direction. In short, man has not yet
> ceased to be an animal, and is still under the con-
> trol of external nature and not under the control
> of his own mind. It is natural selection that has
> created intellect; it is natural selection that has
> developed it to its present condition, and it is
> intellect as a product of natural selection that has
> guided man up to his present position. The prin-
> ciple of artificial selection (telesis) which he has
> been taught by nature, and has applied to other
> creatures, more as an art than as a science, to his
> immense advantage, he has not yet thought of
> applying to himself. Not until he does this can he
> claim any true distinction from the other ani-
> mals.[78]

Ward's entire career can be viewed as an elaboration
of this viewpoint. On all counts, he argued repeatedly,
true progress, dynamic progress, took place when men
asserted their artificial preferences over their natural
circumstances. In every regard, telic progress was
superior to genetic progress. Whatever progress civilization had thus far made (Ward did not think it very
great) derived from the use of telesis, which had
developed late on the evolutionary scale.[79] Indeed,
men generally did not realize how free and powerful
to effect change they actually were; what was needed
was widespread recognition of the distinction between

genesis and telesis. In *Pure Sociology* Ward set forth a graph that summed up the differences:

| *Genetic Progress* | *Telic Progress* |
|---|---|
| in nature: evolution | in man: institution |
| 1. It connotes development. | 1. It connotes dynamic social change. |
| 2. It creates higher and more complex products out of lower and simpler materials. | 2. It has nothing to do with evolution except as a happier state may be said to be an advance over an unhappy one. |
| 3. It has nothing to do with misery or happiness. | 3. Its sole aim is happiness. |
| 4. It is foreign to any values, intelligence or morality. | 4. It connotes values and is based upon reason and morals. |
| 5. As an unconscious growth, it is static, negative, and mechanical—a natural process, automatic and involuntary. | 5. As a planned process, it is dynamic, positive and psychic—a rational process, conscious and voluntary. |
| 6. It applies to nature, and also to man when his actions are unconscious or reflex. | 6. It applies to man alone because only he has rational intelligence [mind].[80] |

Spencer and Sumner and most advocates of "scientifically" sanctioned laissez-faire had not recognized these two types of progress. Ward, however, took great pains in making the distinction clear, for on its clarity hung prospects for the future achievement of conscious, deliberate, true progress.

Ward had, as usual, a special term to convey the precise kind of progress his dynamic sociology advocated. This term was "conation," which signified, generally, "the efforts which organisms put forth in seeking the satisfaction of their desires." The ultimate end of conation for man, Ward believed, was happiness.[81]

> The ends of man . . . are primarily and principally these: 1, the pleasures connected with nutrition; 2, the pleasures connected with reproduction; 3, the pleasures connected with general physical exercise; 4, the pleasures of taste; and, 5, the pleasures of the intellect. These pleasures, taken in connection with those secondary ones derived from them, constitute the immediate incentives to all action, and may be comprehended under the general term happiness.[82]

Direct conation was the simple, instantaneous gratification of only one or two of man's needs. Indirect, or intellectual, conation took into account the entire spectrum of man's needs and attempted to meet them as fully as possible. The desired kind of progress was achieved primarily through indirect conation. This achievement, however, required planning and reflection; thus Ward concluded:

> If a change is to be really made in the conduct of men, it must be brought about by the adoption of some rational scheme which the wisdom of the age shall foresee to be certain to secure this end. . . . The problem of dynamic sociology is the *organization of intelligence.* . . . Knowledge, therefore, is the end to be more directly pursued, since through knowledge comes the entire succession of

desirable objects—right conduct, progress, happiness.[83]

Organizing for happiness, for true progress, required action on both individual and social levels, especially on the latter. Social progress had thus far been the result primarily of individual telesis or conation. With industrialization and urbanization, however, collective telesis had become possible and necessary. Cooperative, intelligent social planning had to be substituted for the intense individual competition of modern society if happiness was to be attained on a broad scale. Collective telesis (or conation) and the resulting planned happiness could be achieved only if society were educated to meeting the task of filling its own needs scientifically. This was to be sociology's vocation.

In many respects anticipating the views of John Dewey, Ward gave primacy to education, not political reform, as the best means of creating the ideal of a cooperative, rational, progressive society. The distribution of knowledge was a prerequisite to reform. Currently, knowledge was too exclusively the property of the privileged classes, and its dissemination among common people was in the long run the necessary condition for progress. Education, the process by which knowledge was diffused, was a crucial component of effective collective telesis; consequently, it had to be scientific, universal, and compulsory. Knowledge was power, power to change the status quo; without education, "the great panacea," the prospects for progress were dim. In closing his first and most important work, Ward saw education deciding

Whether the social system shall always be left to nature, always be genetic and spontaneous and allowed to drift listlessly on, intrusted to the by-no-means always progressive influences which have developed it and brought it to its present condition, or whether it shall be regarded as a proper subject of art, treated as other natural products have been treated by intelligence, and made as much superior to nature in this only proper sense of the word, as other artificial productions are superior to natural ones.[84]

Though Ward was not a socialist, his conception of progress required social planning of a kind and to a degree that can best be described as democratic welfare statism. His humble background provided him with a lifelong sympathy toward ordinary folk, and his sociological views were consistently employed on behalf of broadened opportunities for the average man, to whom Ward looked as the repository of virtue and wisdom. In order for these qualities to fructify and become effective agents of social advance, however, vast changes in society had to occur. Laissez-faire was dominant and stood in the path of progress. It was aristocratic, harmful, archaic, and unscientific; it had to be voided. More than anything else, the laissez-faire philosophy was to blame for "the general paralysis that is creeping over the world."[85] Sociology was to be the antidote; it pointed the way toward the ideal society of the future, toward what Ward called a "sociocracy," a term he borrowed from Comte.

Ward's idealized social order combined the freedom and opportunity for individual expression of a democracy with the scientific, humane planning of a benevolent, merit-oriented socialist state. In his sociocracy, the government would be an active agent for planned social progress. Reflecting the possibilities for positive social action implicit in the idea of telesis, the government would coordinate the psychic energies and potential of men in a responsible, democratic fashion. Legislation would be based on scientific evidence and designed to benefit not merely the moneyed, special interests but the entire social order. Legislators educated in sociology and social science would take the lead in extending social intelligence and applying it to all of society's problems. A national academy of the social sciences would train administrators and public servants and serve as a repository of scientific social knowledge. Based on the ideal of social cooperation rather than individual competition, the sociocracy would produce "attractive legislation" aimed at making "attractive labor," conditions of life and work that the ordinary man would find pleasurable, satisfying, and just.[86]

In an era when government action of any sort was viewed with suspicion, Ward called for a greater extension of governmental activities to combat crime, raise the general standard of living, eliminate disease, advance education, and vastly increase public happiness and welfare. The shibboleths of laissez-faire he discarded as the regressive negativism of advantaged, moneyed groups and individuals standing to lose ground as society as a whole advanced. Far from a utopia after the fashion of Edward Bellamy's *Looking Backward*, Ward's sociocracy attempted to exploit society's already achieved scientific and technological capabilities and apply them within the existing political framework to the problems inherited from the past. Progress, Ward maintained, lay within man's grasp, but it would only be achieved if his capacity for collective telesis was carefully nurtured through the creation of a sociocratic civilization.

Ward's system of thought, founded on empiricism but reaching out for cosmic order, presented many problems. He could achieve the necessary unity behind observed natural and social changes his system required only by inventing the term "synergy," a mysterious force or "principle that explains all organization and created all structures."[87] Sufficiently vague to have been kin to entropy or first cousin to the Unknowable, synergy was a catchall adhesive explaining that regularity which somehow moved creation forward in a unified, lawful manner. Ward's attempts to define synergy led him deep into that metaphysical terrain abandoned earlier by Wright and dismissed as "German Darwinism"; synergy, Ward wrote, echoing Fiske, was a process of "social equilibration" beginning in "collision, conflict, antagonism, and opposition, . . . passing into a *modus vivendi*, ending in collaboration and cooperation. It is the cosmological expression of the Hegelian trilogy."[88] This mode of synthesis had for Wright been the rankest and most flimsy kind of Spencerianism, having no place in a scientific construct. Ward's indiscriminate usage of the abstrusely defined term failed to prove otherwise.

Yet Ward did not, on the other hand, allow synergy to qualify his commitment to naturalism. Life and consciousness, he insisted, were merely organic properties of matter, albeit the highest form of matter in the universe. And matter, he believed, was the only form of reality; the initial energy that coursed through the universe was merely its inherent property. The inorganic and organic, ultimately, were but chemical processes and compounds differing only in degree, not in kind. Life may have been a mystery, but no more so than any other form of matter. Society and progress were real, but they were essentially refinements of those elemental properties of matter that first produced sensation, desire, and, finally, intelligent conation and civilization. It was all lawful, and the laws were all natural processes that referred back to the cabalism of synergy. In the end, Ward's progressive naturalism seemed as arbitrary as Fiske's progressive theism, for one still had to accept the reality of synergy on faith.

But Ward's telic conception of progress, combining the patient minutia of empirical scholarship and the bold sweep of the cosmologist, added a dimension to the definition of progress that departed from both Wright and Fiske. Ward's evangelicism on behalf of scientific social reform was an explicit rejection of the alternatives posed by Fiske's soft, benign Christian quietism and Wright's hard, empirical nihilism. For Ward, the province of science included the whole range of natural and human experience. It was not just the best method of knowing; it was the sum and substance of all that could be known about experience from microscopic study to ethics and values. Its laws of change and growth were unified and holistic, and they encompassed the entire sphere of life. Such a monistic conception of science was itself an act of faith, but it was one that Ward, an acknowledged scientific authority in several fields, felt capable of making. If his reformism would have seemed to Wright scientifically unwarranted by the evidence and to Fiske largely gratuitous in the face of God's progressive intentions, it was for Ward but the extension of that process by which science showed that true progress had been made in the past and could be realized in the future. The telic conception put the burden of progress squarely on man's own shoulders.

Fiske, Wright, and Ward were but three voices in the enormous chorus of fictional imaginings, scientific postulates, sociological systems and theological speculations dealing with the significance of evolutionism for the idea of progress before the turn of the century.

From such myriad sources as anthropologists Sumner and Lewis Henry Morgan, economists Simon Patten and Richard Ely, Social Gospelers George Herron and Walter Rauschenbusch, reformers Henry Demarest Lloyd and Henry George, writers Edward Bellamy and William Dean Howells, and jurists Oliver Wendell Holmes and John William Burgess came programs, analyses, exhortations, and criticisms of progress. Nearly every thinker of the time who addressed himself to evolution and social change (and what social thinker did not?) confronted progress, however obliquely, and commented upon its reality and unreality, its laws and causes, its inevitability and precariousness, its uses and abuses. Yet virtually every theory of progress set forth in their time remained within the philosophical parameters bounded by John Fiske's Christianized evolutionism, Chauncey Wright's skeptical neutrality, and Lester Ward's naturalistic view of telesis.

Few progressive theorists agreed completely with any of the three extremes. Generally, post-Darwinian renditions of progress blended elements of theistical design, ethical nominalism, natural evolutionary processes, empirical observation, and human will together in varying, highly personal, and often contradictory combinations. Simon Patten's progressivism compounded traditional Christianity with the new sophistication of a rigorous, process-oriented economics; on the other extreme, Sumner's view of progress conjoined empiricistic naturalism with a quasireligious commitment to individual competition and laissez-faire as the immutable law of nature. Somewhere in the middle, Walter Rauschenbusch linked Christian ethics to socialistic reform, and Henry George promised to heal the body civil and spiritual with his single tax proposal. While Darwinism may have helped secularize the idea of progress, it did not save it from contention and promiscuity.

But if evolutionism did not resolve the puzzle of progress in any final way, it did illuminate more sharply than ever the need for an explanation of how human will and consciousness related to social change and improvement. This problem, as old as the idea of progress itself, had generally been begged in the pre-Darwinian years by rationalists and romantics alike; indeed, the very definitions of rationalism and romanticism permitted the default. Natural and sexual selection, however, raised anew the old conundrum of the sources of the human mind and its ideas and how they related to change and progress. If intellectual currents as the century turned were drifting toward giving greater credit than ever to human thought, effort, and will as the agencies of social and historical change, the philosophy that would explain how this could be the case had not yet fully emerged. But the psychological basis for such a philosophy, William James's *Principles of Psychology*, had appeared in 1890, and its elaboration and extension into a philosophy of progress would be one of the first intellectual accomplishments of the twentieth century.

# 4

# *William James:*

# *Experience and Meliorism*

More than most men, William James reflected the paradoxes of his society and his times. A reasonable, logical man, trained as a scientist, he deeply mistrusted reason and logic and the pretension that modern science enjoyed exclusive access to truth. Profoundly moralistic and religious, he inveighed against all orthodox moral systems and disdained both organized religion and traditional theisms. Raised as an aristocrat and nurtured in cosmopolitan circumstances in England and on the Continent, James was quintessentially democratic and by preference—unlike his brother Henry, the novelist—an American. Celebrated internationally as a teacher-scholar, he often felt uncomfortable as an academician and had great scorn for pedantry and intellectual affectation. Intolerant of fuzzy-minded, well-intentioned idealisms, James himself was warmly humane and unflinchingly idealistic. He always searched for the deeper meanings of experience, yet he steadfastly denied that experience had any ultimate

146

meaning or that there was any final, ultimate experience. Contemptuous of the idea of necessary progress, he nonetheless framed a philosophy whose cornerstone was the belief that human will and desire might create a future more morally satisfying than the past or the present.

Although a professional philosopher, James did not regard philosophy as a specialized, rarefied undertaking for experts only. All men philosophized, whether they liked it or not, and they philosophized with their entire beings. James did not break philosophy down into neat mental categories allowing mind and body, reason and emotion, thought and action to exist in intrinsic separation. Like any other human process, philosophy was an activity involving many kinds of organically related assumptions, purposes, and actions. However detached and cerebral, no philosophy could be freed from the person and personality that produced it. In the last analysis, a man's philosophy and his autobiography were inseparable, for the distinctive thrust of an individual's thought always carried some revelation of his life. A man's philosophy, James believed, reflected both his character and his experience of the universe. Perhaps it was for this reason that James always tried to secure a photograph of the author of a book he liked or a correspondent he had not yet met. Behind each thought resided a thinker, and James's sympathies reached more toward the living thinker than the verbiage he produced.

Inevitably, James's philosophy bore the stamp of his own history and character. It was open, tolerant, highly individualistic, and resolutely optimistic. It was unorthodox, unsystematic, pluralistic, and too receptive to the expression of spontaneous freedom to fit comfortably into prevailing definitions or schools of philosophy. It was innovative, experimental, practical,

and geared toward investigating the specific consequences of ideas and beliefs. Philosophy for James was
not a luxurious indulgence but a necessary and highly
practical enterprise that could not be avoided by any
self-conscious person. It was an affair of the heart as
well as of the mind, and, to be done well, it required
a certain vitality and hardihood—qualities James possessed in abundance. Both James's life and philosophy
affirmed that the courageous facing up to experience,
whatever its demands and exigencies, afforded the
only sound basis for faith in oneself and for belief in
one's salvation.

The oldest of five children, William James was born
in New York City in 1842. His father, Henry James,
Sr., was a gregarious, eccentric, mystically inclined ex-
seminarian who, because of independent wealth, was
freely able to indulge his unorthodox intellectual interests. Henry James had no vocation in the ordinary
sense, and so, together with his writings on philosophy
and religion, he turned his family's education into his
full-time occupation. The result was a kind of movable
educational feast: William and his three younger
brothers and sister were schooled by a panoply of
teachers and tutors in different schools in the United
States, England, and Europe. William's father was
rarely satisfied with the course of his children's education, and he changed their academy with each season,
the family relocating whenever new schools or tutors
were tried. As a result, William and Henry enjoyed a
varied, highly eclectic early education. They acquired
a greater linguistic competency than most other American youths, as well as a more than superficial familiar-
ity with European thought, letters, and landscape. The
entire family participated in each others' education,
and visitors to the James household were often amazed
by the spirited intellectual disputation and play that

marked each mealtime. Both William and Henry later acknowledged that they had learned more from their father and from each other than from anyone else as they grew up.[1]

Perhaps because of his irregular schooling, William James had a difficult time settling on a field of study leading to a specific vocation. In 1860, the James family moved to Newport, Rhode Island, to allow William to study art in the studio of William M. Hunt; for a time, he seemed sure that art would be his calling. But a year later, partly at his father's urging, he changed his mind and entered Harvard's Lawrence Scientific School to study chemistry with Charles W. Eliot. The James family, of course, moved to Cambridge. At the Lawrence School, James came under the influence of Louis Agassiz and Jeffries Wyman, and his interests shifted toward biology, physiology, and anatomy. In 1864, he resolved to study medicine and entered Harvard Medical School to prepare himself for a teaching career (he never intended to practice medicine). Before finishing his medical degree in 1869, he spent a year with Agassiz in Brazil on a fossil- and specimen-hunting expedition and a year of independent medical study in Germany.

By the time his formal education at Harvard was completed, James found himself suffering acutely from depression, anxiety, back trouble (what he called his "dorsal collapse"), and eyestrain—a cluster of neurotic symptoms diagnosed as neurasthenia from which he would suffer for the rest of his life. This illness and dispiritedness had occurred intermittently before, especially during his year of study in Germany, but never so severely as in the late fall and winter of 1869. By February 1870, he wrote that he had "about touched bottom."[2] Several weeks later, desolated by the premature death of Minnie Temple, his favorite cousin, he experienced a seizure of profound psychic panic that reduced him to a "mass of quivering fear."[3] The seizure and its larger envelope of depression amounted to nothing less than a crisis of the spirit that led James to the brink of suicide. It was several years before he fully recovered his psychological equilibrium.

This spiritual crisis and his subsequent recovery were a turning point in James's life. In his view, the crisis was essentially a moral matter, a deep concern he could neither resolve nor avoid over whether the universe was wholly good or whether it was a mixture of good and evil—and if the latter, was God then the author of evil and, hence, man's damnation? These were, to be sure, momentous matters that, while they occur to most thoughtful youths, do not usually become destructive obsessions. That they nearly did for James reveals a crucial part of his makeup. To him, it mattered greatly if the universe were moral and if his actions bore weight on the scale of good and evil. Scientist though he was, the pervasive religiosity of the James family and his father's abiding influence had left their mark: William was incapable of detachment on the large questions of human morality and their relationship to the universe.

His medical education, with its stress on natural human functions and empirical observation, did not offer consolation. Nor did frequent talks with his friend Chauncey Wright, whose vexing ability to shrug off commitment on moral questions was extremely unsettling to James. Nor did his almost desperate reading of recent developments in psychology and physiology, to which he turned out of a deep desire to discover what was wrong with him. In the end it was not a psychologist but a French philosopher, Charles Renouvier, who held the key to his recovery.

James's diary in the spring of 1870 reveals his perception of the crisis and how he began to resolve it. On February 1, he wrote:

Today I about touched bottom, and perceive plainly that I must face the choice with open eyes: shall I *frankly* throw the moral business overboard, as one unsuited to my innate aptitudes, or shall I follow it and it alone making everything else merely stuff for it? I will give the latter alternative a fair trial. . . .

Can one with full knowledge and sincerity ever bring one's self so to sympathize with the total process of the universe as heartily as to assent to the evil that seems inherent in its details? Is the mind so purely fluid and plastic? If so, optimism is possible. Are, on the other hand, the private interests and sympathies of the individual so essential to his existence that they can never be swallowed up in his feeling for the total process, —and does he nevertheless imperiously crave a reconciliation or unity of some sort. Pessimism must be his portion. But if, as in Homer, a divided universe be a conception possible for his intellect to rest in, and at the same time he have vigor of will enough to look universal death in the face without blinking, he can lead the life of moralism. A militant existence, in which the ego is posited as a monad, with the good as its end, and the final consolation only that of irreconcilable hatred —though evil slay me, she can't subdue me, or make me worship her. The brute force is all at her command, but the final protest of my soul as she squeezes me out of existence gives me still a certain sense of superiority.[4]

In the very framing of this existential dilemma, James hinted at its resolution: only "vigor of will" would suffice to face death and permit one to lead a morally satisfying, if not altogether triumphant, existence. Perhaps, he suggested, morality might reside merely in dying bravely for what one believed in. In any case, human will and morality were somehow linked to the possibility of optimism, though the linkages were not very clear. Even at this early stage, James seemed to foresee that their clarification would occupy the rest of his life.

Several weeks later Minnie Temple died, and for many days thereafter James wrote nothing in his diary; on the day he learned of her death, he simply drew a crude gravestone for an entry. Although the exact date is uncertain, it was probably during this period that he experienced the pathological visitation he later recorded anonymously in *The Varieties of Religious Experience*. This devastating experience, so eerily similar to a psychic "vastation" that terrorized his father when he was a little older than William, left a lasting imprint. In James's words,

> I went one evening into a dressing-room . . . when suddenly there fell upon me without any warning, just as if it came out of the darkness, a horrible fear of my own existence. Simultaneously there arose in my mind the image of an epileptic patient whom I had seen in the asylum, a black-haired youth with greenish skin, entirely idiotic, who used to sit all day on one of the benches, or rather shelves against the wall, with his knees drawn up against his chin, and the coarse grey undershirt, which was his only garment, drawn over them inclosing his entire figure. He sat there like a sort of sculptured Egyptian cat or Peruvian mummy,

moving nothing but his black eyes and looking absolutely non-human. This image and my fear entered into a species of combination with each other. *That shape am I*, I felt, potentially. Nothing that I possess can defend me against that fate, if the hour for it should strike for me as it struck for him. There was such a horror of him, that it was as if something hitherto solid within my breast gave way entirely, and I became a mass of quivering fear. After this the universe was changed for me altogether. I awoke morning after morning with a horrible dread at the pit of my stomach, and with a sense of the insecurity of life that I never knew before, and that I have never felt since. . . . It gradually faded, but for months I was unable to go out into the dark alone.[5]

James regarded this as a religious experience and categorized it as an example of "fear of the universe," of one of the ways "that man's original optimism and self-satisfaction get leveled with the dust."[6]

While James might not have seen himself as a "sinner in the hands of an angry God," his crisis had all the earmarks of the torment many of his Calvinistic forebears had endured. His vigorous assertion of the will as the agent of salvation they would have recognized as a virulent form of the Arminian heresy, the interpretation of the New Testament that found salvation in good works rather than divine grace. Yet James's inspiration came not from scripture; it came from Renouvier. As he wrote in his diary on April 3, 1870:

I think that yesterday was a crisis in my life. I finished the first part of Renouvier's second "Essais" and see no reason why his definition of free will—"the sustaining of a thought *because I choose to* when I might have other thoughts" —need be the definition of an illusion. At any rate, I will assume for the present—until next year—that it is no illusion. My first act of free will shall be to believe in free will. . . . I will . . . voluntarily cultivate the feeling of moral freedom, by reading books favorable to it as well as by acting. . . . Hitherto, when I have felt like taking a free initiative, like daring to act originally . . . suicide seemed the most manly form to put my daring into; now, I will go a step further with my will, not only act with it, but believe as well; believe in my individual reality and creative power. . . . I will posit life (the real, the good) in the self-governing *resistance* of the ego to the world.[7]

Renouvier's free-will tonic was apparently the right prescription, for in the ensuing months James's condition improved markedly. By 1871, he had resumed his studies, and the following year he was well enough to accept with alacrity the offer of a teaching position at Harvard in comparative anatomy and physiology. The crisis, however, had an abiding effect. James knew from painful experience that mental and physical health were intimately connected and that it mattered greatly in life what one chose to believe as true. That in this case the results of choosing were beneficial did not obviate the fact that a man's beliefs inevitably made a difference in the kind of life he led. James was always to keep this knowledge before him.

There was, of course, a certain irony in James's choosing to believe in free will out of psychic necessity: his survival as a human being was at stake. His choice, however, was predictable, for all of his intellectual instincts leaned toward personal freedom and creativity. But belief in the free-will doctrine that helped save him was not easily achieved. As James observed repeatedly, there were limits to what one was free to believe; had his own character and experiences been different, it is doubtful that Renouvier's ideas would have had the effect that they did. Moreover, the concept of free will, like any other assumed moral posture, had to work, to endure as an article of belief according to its consequences and effects in time, before it could in any sense be judged to be true. The rest of James's life was a vindication of his faith.

From 1872 until his retirement in 1907, James taught at Harvard, though he did not remain a teacher of physiology for long. Pursuit of "the moral business" was a deep-seated need, steadily pushing him away from medicine toward philosophy. In 1875, he was urging President Eliot (his former teacher, now president of Harvard) to create a new chair in psychology, one that would allow the appointment of an instructor well grounded in all the elements of "the new science of man now being built up out of the theory of evolution and the facts of archeology, the nervous system and the senses."[8] That same year, he began offering a graduate course entitled "The Relations between Physiology and Psychology"; three years later, his teaching and research interests had led him into the relations between psychology and philosophy. By 1879, he was teaching his first course in philosophy, and in 1885 he was named professor of philosophy. After publication of *The Principles of Psychology* in 1890, he devoted himself primarily to philosophy.

James's progression from physiology through psychology to philosophy recapitulates the main thrust of his thinking and provides the key to the consistency underlying his somewhat disjointed philosophizing. Although pragmatism, pluralism, and the will to believe reached far beyond the boundaries of the *Principles*, James's philosophy was firmly based on his psychology of mind, thought, and experience; always central was the sensate, feeling, acting individual striving to make reason out of sensed data and conceptual order out of the "booming, buzzing" confusion of the world as experienced. As Paul Conkin observed, *"The Principles of Psychology* was his philosophic *Das Capital*; *Pragmatism* was his *Manifesto*."[9]

Like the *Principles*, most of James's books originated as lectures or essays published in such popular magazines as the *Atlantic Monthly, Scribner's*, and the *Nation* or in such professional journals as *Mind* or the *Journal of Speculative Philosophy*. He made highly efficient use of his teaching and lecture materials (from 1880, he was in constant demand as a lecturer), and consequently his published works are exceptionally readable, if at times seemingly loose and simplistic. James devoutly believed that philosophy was every man's vocation, and, like Emerson, he felt a great responsibility to enlighten the public. Philosophy as practiced in his time was full of arcane, monistic bugbears and deterministic tyrannies to be stalked and attacked with common sense, wit, and relish. Hence, much of James's writing has an antiestablishment cast, and a polemical tone always lurks near the surface of his prose.

James was a man of keen curiosity, boundless energy, and great personal warmth. His capacity for friendship was enormous; during his life, he became a friend and correspondent of nearly every major philosopher and psychologist in the United States, England, France, and Germany. He could appreciate, both personally and philosophically, such extremes as Emerson and Freud, Bergson and Spencer, Fiske and Wright, Peirce and Royce. Many influences, often in conflict with one another, were at work in his thinking. His father's Swedenborgian mysticism, with its distinctive transcendental idealism, was an early and pervasive influence, as were his associations with Agassiz, Oliver Wendell Holmes, Chauncey Wright, and Charles Peirce. James was an early convert to Darwinism and was vitally absorbed by the question of the evolution of the brain and the consciousness; thus, he found the works of Wilhelm Wundt, Hermann Helmholtz, and Alexander Bain highly significant. Though generally an empiricist within the tradition of Locke, Hume, and Mill, James found their atomism too dry and fragmented, and his own pragmatic philosophy veered off distinctly from the British empiricists. The logical rigor of Peirce was perhaps the strongest single influence on his thought, although Peirce disclaimed responsibility for James's brand of pragmatism. In the last analysis, James's philosophy was woven from many strands, but it had a pattern and texture that was uniquely his.

While reflecting his own personality and style, James's ideas instantly struck a responsive chord in readers both within and outside the academic community. Like Franklin and Jefferson, James had a gift for expressing sentiments that seemed timely and true to other Americans. *The Principles of Psychology*, for all its massiveness, immediately established him as a scholar and scientist of the first order as well as a graceful, readable interpreter of the new psychology. Succeeding works such as *The Will to Believe* (1897) and, especially, *Pragmatism* (1907) were not only widely read and commented upon, but the shrillness of their critics revealed that James had indeed touched an exposed nerve in the philosophical world. As "absolutely the only philosophy with *no* humbug in it" (James's estimate), pragmatism appealed broadly to literate Americans.[10] By 1910, the year of his death, the pragmatic revolt in American thought was well underway, and James's ideas very much in the vanguard.

*ii*

William James's *Principles of Psychology* almost never appeared, for its publisher, Henry Holt, first approached John Fiske with the assignment in 1878. Fiske, who rarely fumbled an opportunity to appear in print on any subject, with unusual modesty referred Holt to his friend James, whom he said was much better prepared to undertake such a work.[11] James signed the contract for the book in June 1878, estimating that the study would take two years. He was short by ten long years: and, miraculously, Henry Holt waited.

Like all other seminal intellectual works, when the *Principles* finally appeared, it was Janus-faced: it summarized and drew upon existing scholarship, and it gave new shape and direction to the future course of studies of the mind. Its fourteen hundred pages represented the culmination of the most recent innovations in science applied to the ancient questions of thought, mind, sensation, habit, and will, thus furnishing the point of departure for the trends in philosophy' that led to pragmatism, voluntarism, and phenomenology as well as developments in psychology that led to abnormal psychology, behaviorism, and psychoanalysis. The *Principles* also applied evolutionary postulates to the question of consciousness, giving the human mind a naturalistic explanation that undergirded the pragmatic definitions of belief, truth, and progress.

Before 1890, psychology was basically divided into two camps: the old psychology, with its metaphysical, sometimes religious orientation toward "human nature," and the so-called new psychology, based on physiological and behavioral data drawn from anatomic studies and minute laboratory experimentation and observation. The old psychology, exemplified by James McCosh's *Psychology* (1886), clung to its spiritual category of the soul and its definite number of distinct human faculties operating in a quasischolastic moral framework. Generally, this traditional brand of psychology saw itself as a branch of moral philosophy. On the other hand, the new psychology of Helmholtz, Wundt, and Rudolf Lotze redefined the study of the mind as a branch of natural science and natural history. Although James allied himself with the new psychology in treating the mind and its activities in purely functional, physiological terms, his *Principles* was something of a compromise between the two camps; James's definition of mind and thought, though stringently scientific and empirical, made provision for morality and ethics as an integral part of how human mentality functioned. In effecting this compromise, however, James gave a radically experiential twist to the idea of morality.

James believed the mind, like any other prospering biological entity, functioned to facilitate the organism's adaptation to its environment. This attitude, essentially a Darwinian variant, went far toward establishing the legitimate nature and limitations of psychology. At the outset, James rejected the notions of absolute intelligence and unattached psychic states that had hitherto plagued studies of the mind. The true subject of psychological investigation was "the mind of distinct individuals inhabiting definite portions of a real space and a real time."[12] This kind of psychological individualism enabled James to identify mentality as a process governing a discrete organism's responses to its particular environment; in turn, he argued, "the pursuance of further ends and the choice of means for their attainment are thus the work and criterion of the presence of mentality in a phenomenon."[13] The individual self was the experiential constant and the vortex of psychological inquiry, and that self's most effective instrument for adaptation and survival was its capacity for mental activity.

In viewing the mind this way, James was deliberately dissociating himself from the prevailing orthodoxy of the automaton theory of the mind. This mechanical, neo-Lockean notion, offered in varying combinations by such eminent writers as Bain, Spencer, Mill, and Huxley, held that man's mental life functioned somewhat on the order of a piano: each external stimulus pressed a key (or sensory nerve ending), which in turn struck a cluster of specific brain cells, and hence a predictable note—a mental or physical response—was produced. Once the key was struck, the mental consequences inevitably followed. No cerebral volition interfered with this automatic progression of events; consciousness had nothing to do with the process once the initial depression of the key occurred. The mind, then, automatically "copied" the stimuli that affected it, and the appropriate idea emerged.

From James's point of view, there were several things wrong with this conception. First, the brain simply did not function in the passive, mechanical way described by the automatists; it was far more than a mere sounding board to receive the data of external stimuli and automatically discharge the appropriate notes. The exclusion of consciousness and volition from the automaton theory misconstrued the fact that the brain, at least in the upper portions of the cortex, was vitally suffused with consciousness, and hence choice and selection characterized its functioning. The brain was, as James put it, the "organ of consciousness," and by definition "consciousness must everywhere *prefer* some of the sensations which it gets to others."[14] Consciousness, the brain's inseparable functional dimension, had evolved over time through natural selection, a fact that demonstrated the essentially dynamic, selective, preferential nature of mind and thought. The contention of automatists such as Thomas Huxley that men are merely "conscious automata" was a contradiction in terms.

Moreover, the description of the thought process as pianolike took no cognizance of the fact that surrounding the mental perception of specific stimuli was a halo of impressions existing on the fringes and that each perception of a particular thing was itself a deliberate, chosen composite of many subsidiary impressions. A table might be perceived by the mind, but in order for that to happen, its various qualities—hardness, color, size, texture—had to be perceived and distinguished from other objects in the room that were *not* attributes of the table. For the mind to hold the idea of "table," an infinitely complex series of stimuli, perception, and selection had to occur in the consciousness: the consciousness had to guide and direct, for whatever purpose, the different components of external sense and internal intention that eventuated in "table." Clearly, this process involved a great deal more than the working of sensory keys to produce mental melodies.

James's conviction that consciousness permeated all thought processes, however rudimentary, and that consciousness necessarily meant choice and preference led to the conclusion that the mind functioned as a teleological instrument to advance what the human organism felt to be its interests. The consciousness was "an organ, superadded to the other organs which maintain the animal in the struggle for existence," and James treated it throughout the *Principles* as "at all times primarily a *selecting agency*."[15] On every level, from the initial apprehension of sensation through the most sophisticated and abstract moral expressions, consciousness affirmed the human organism's interests and actively manipulated the brain accordingly. This affirmation was fed by both thought and feeling, for the notion of "interests" necessarily included feelings and emotions as well as more considered, abstract, reasoned ideas. Although the will might act as a refinement and guide to the teleological activities of the consciousness, the fact remained that consciousness involved choice and that the basis of the choice was the advancement of the whole organism's well-being.

First explored in an early article, "Are We Automata?" appearing in *Mind* in 1879, this basic postulate became the organizational principle and cardinal tenet of James's psychology and philosophy. It recurred again and again in various guises throughout his writings, but rarely with the pungency and color of the famous passage in chapter 9 of the *Principles*:

> The mind is at every stage a theatre of simultaneous possibilities. Consciousness consists in the comparison of these with each other, the selection of some, and the suppression of the rest by the reinforcing and inhibiting agency of attention. The highest and most elaborated mental products are filtered from the data chosen by the faculty next beneath, out of the mass offered by the faculty below that, which mass in turn was sifted from a still larger amount of yet simpler material, and so on. The mind, in short, works on the data it receives very much as a sculptor works on his block of stone. In a sense the statue stood there from eternity. But there were a thousand different ones beside it, and the sculptor alone is to

thank for having extricated this one from the rest. Just so the world of each of us, howsoever different our several views of it may be, all lay embedded in the primordial chaos of sensations, which gave the mere matter to the thought of all of us indifferently. We may, if we like, by our reasonings unwind things back to that black and white jointless continuity of space and moving clouds of swarming atoms which science calls the only real world. But all the while the world we feel and live in will be that which our ancestors and we, by slowly cumulative strokes of choice, have extricated out of this, like sculptors, by simply rejecting certain portions of the given stuff. Other sculptors, other statues from the same stone! Other minds, other worlds from the same monotonous and inexpressive chaos! My world is but one in a million alike embedded, alike real to those who may abstract them. How different must be the worlds in the consciousness of ant, cuttle-fish, or crab![16]

The teleological interpretation of the mind, made possible by recent discoveries in biology and physiology that revealed how the brain functioned, marked the most significant advance of the new psychology over the old, and it serves as a prime example of James's psychological antiformalism. Under its aegis, thought became transformed from a passive copier of the world as perceived through the senses into an active, discriminating agent for that world's modification in light of the organism's needs and interests. As James put it in "What the Will Effects" (1888), "the thinking and feeling portions of our life seem little more than half-way houses to behavior; and recent Psychology accordingly tends to treat consciousness more and more as if it existed only for the sake of the conduct which it seems to introduce, and tries to explain its peculiarities (so far as they can be explained at all) by their practical utility."[17] For James, each man's consciousness, not some external imperative, became the true locus of history's teleological dynamism.

The consequences of this internalization of teleology reached far beyond the mere question of consciousness; as James's philosophic writings show, they affected vitally his definition of belief, ethics, truth, and history. Since the mind was functionally a *"fighter for ends*, of which many but for its presence would not be ends at all," a new and scientifically supported argument for human freedom and creativity was in the making.[18] If psychology could show that consciousness in some dynamic and original way helped create out of data received new ends toward which will and action might move, the idea of teleology itself took on new meaning, and the individual could rightfully begin to assume a new and more dynamic relationship to purpose in history. Affirming that teleological factors were demonstrably real but denying that their reality confined the individual to some a priori, formalistic determinacy, this new relationship could be open, purposive, and progressive—depending on the felt "interests" and the will of the individual. Thus James's portrayal of the teleological character of consciousness laid the psychological foundation for the pragmatic idea of progress.

The process by which the consciousness operates to select and organize the data it receives is tremendously complex, and in elucidating it James contributed an epochal concept to psychology: the "stream of consciousness." The brain, James maintained, is in a constant process of change and alteration; never in the course of one's life does it cease to receive sensory stimuli and to issue commands to some other part of the body. "We believe the brain to be an organ whose internal equilibrium is always in a state of change,—the change affecting every part."[19] Every stimulus detected by any sense organ, whether above or below the shifting line of conscious mental attention, produces some physiological alteration of the brain's cellular structure, its neurological composition, and its output of brain waves. Respiration, digestion, heartbeat, and so forth continue to take place without one's having to think about them, when one sleeps or wakes, but they are always part of consciousness and are intimately and instantly affected by external stimuli. As James put it, "All we know of submaximal nerve irritations, and of the summation of apparently ineffective stimuli, tends to show that *no* changes in the brain are physiologically ineffective, and that presumably none are bare of psychological result."[20]

Though levels of mental attention and purpose may change, the brain and the consciousness are always flowing and providing the organism with its unique sense of continuity and selfhood. Within this stream of consciousness, many mental activities are simultaneously submerged, but the flowing never ceases nor does the selective emphasizing of certain rivulets that seem to have some special utility for the organism. Though consciousness contains parts that apparently cluster and become intensely discrete, they are never actually cut off from the larger experiential stream; both the "substantive" and "transitive" parts of the stream of thought are organic parts of consciousness, which, "like a bird's life, . . . seems to be made of an alteration of flights and perchings."[21]

At the higher levels of mental activity, where the stream of consciousness "perches" in a substantive way, the mind's teleological nature becomes even more pronounced and significant. Through the process of "selective attention," the mind focuses on certain groupings of experienced sensations ("percepts") and elevates them into "concepts" or rudimentary mental processes leading toward conception, the shaping of a mature idea. When the attention has focused long and singularly enough on a portion of experience to convert it into a conception, the resulting abstraction has been lifted out of the "continuum of felt experience" and "isolated so as to make of it an individual topic of discourse."[22] It can then be manipulated or used in such a way as to benefit the conceiver. The idea has come into being because, willy-nilly, the mind *chose* to concentrate on that portion of experience from whence it came.[23]

Why the mind makes the choices it does cannot be fully explained, but a large part of the choosing derives from the reflexive action of instinctive interests, which prefer certain "effects, forms, and orders" suggested by the flow of experience. Because man has a superior power to associate and discriminate among the data of perception and to manipulate them to his liking, his mental life becomes an elaborate process of planning actions that will satisfy his complex aesthetic, emotional, and instinctual needs. The feeling department of man's nature can never be totally disjoined from the conceiving department; the two work together to advance the interests of the whole. This telic view of the mind explains its central characteristic and function: the "remodeling" of the world in the light of one's interests.

> The conceiving or theorizing faculty works exclusively for the sake of ends that do not exist at all in the world of impressions received by way of our senses, but are set by our emotional and practical

subjectivity. It is a transformer of the world of our impressions into a totally different world, the world of our conception; and the transformation is effected in the interests of our volitional nature, and for no other purpose whatsoever. Destroy the volitional nature, the definite subjective purposes, preferences, fondness for certain effects, forms, orders, and not the slightest motive would remain for the brute order of our experience to be remodelled at all.[24]

But simple reflex action, however incredibly complex it becomes on close scrutiny, still fails to indicate fully the telic cast of the mind. For it is the will, the voluntary, self-conscious determination of mental and physical acts selected from among other possibilities, that finally crowns the human mind. It is the will, the most refined functioning of the volitional process, that leads the mind to use the ideas continually flowing through it. Fed by the subsidiary streams of emotion and memory, the will becomes man's paramount mental feature, directing the effort of attention and ordering the resulting concepts in some idea capable of direct action. The willed employment of an idea is the ultimate end of the psychological process of volition. Using ideas, mobilizing concepts in a directed ideational fashion, is the will's supreme achievement; the will is the coordinator of relations "between the mind and its ideas."[25]

Since every stimulus in the mind, however fleeting and fragmentary, produces some sort of bodily response, how the will plays its relational role is crucial to the body's welfare. It is doubly so when one recognizes that the will must mediate between competing ideas that have germinated in the consciousness, some of which will undoubtedly be in conflict with others relating to the same objects. In this case, the will must select among divergent calls to action, inhibit conflicting ideas, and free the body to act in a concerted way prefigured by that idea upon which the will resolves. The will, then, acts as an internal psychophysical self-regulator, the mind's supreme teleological determinant. Its acts are by no means autonomous, however, since they must be preceded by lower-level stimuli and the other intervening processes of selection eventuating in the concepts and ideas with which the will deals. The will may create new combinations of ideas and formulate new goals for actions, but its choices are conditioned by previous stimuli and especially, by what the different levels of consciousness have done with them. The will, paradoxically, is in reality both physiologically bound and creatively free.

Throughout the *Principles*, James struggled to remain within the legitimate boundaries of psychology. It was a difficult task; James the psychologist could scarcely contain James the philosopher, and when it came to the question of the will the task was virtually impossible. The will, James the psychologist had to conclude, essentially had done its job when it caused the mind to focus on a given subject and hold it fast. The effort of attention being willed, the mind had its directive, and the motor reflexes might then take over. The question of whether the idea willed was right or true—whether it subsequently caused the organism to feel the way it expected to feel when acting on the idea—these were questions that were now out of the will's province. And the still larger questions of the will's efficacy and freedom, questions near and dear to James's concern with psychology in the first place, could not even be raised within its parameters.

Yet the temptation to philosophize was too strong for James not to indulge it, albeit rather briefly in an aside in his chapter on will. Free will was easy enough to define from a psychological point of view. It meant that thought, when the product of effort, was not the fixed and necessary function of its object. Free will meant that even if a thought's object did not change, one was free to make more or less of it as one chose. But could one know whether, in each case, more or less effort or attention might have been given to an idea?

> To tell that, we should have to ascent to the antecedents of the effort, and defining them with mathematical exactitude, prove, by laws of which we have not at present even an inkling, that the only amount of sequent effort which could *possibly* comport with them was the precise amount which actually came. Measurements, whether of psychic or of neural quantities, and deductive reasonings such as this method of proof implies, will surely be forever beyond human reach. No serious psychologist or physiologist will venture even to suggest a notion of how they might be practically made.[26]

Accordingly, James concluded that the question of free will "is insoluble on strictly psychological grounds," and he referred readers of the *Principles* interested in the larger ramifications of the question to his essay of 1884, "The Dilemma of Determinism."[27]

James could not refrain, however, from permitting himself a few words about the "logic" of the question. If all was determined and free will an illusion, "the world must be one unbroken fact, and . . . prediction of all things without exception must be ideally, even if not actually, possible." Free will, on the other hand, was a "*moral* postulate about the Universe . . . that *what ought to be can be, and that bad acts cannot be fated, but that good ones must be possible in their place.*"²⁸ If the sense of freedom and creative inception suffusing conscious- ness and volition was not illusory, then deterministic arguments could not be coercive. The issue was between a fatalism that ultimately claimed all events, even mental ones, as necessary parts of its inexorable tide and the possibility that consciousness and the will might in some degree swim independently of fatalism's predetermined flow. If there was no such thing as free will, all the infinite variables contributing to sensation, perception, and volition had to occur just as they did and the feelings of choice and volition, as well as the description of the entire substructure of consciousness as a genuinely selecting activity, were either a mistake or they took place within a larger a priori framework that existed outside the realm of human experience and hence could never be known in any verifiable way.

James's sketch of the logic of determinism ran diametrically against the grain of the teleological description of mind threading his study. If the *Princi- ples* was correct, determinism was psychologically untenable. Moreover, the logical dimensions of the problem were such that its solution could not be proved conclusively one way or the other, which was, if true, a victory for those who elected to hold for free will. Determinism could not be proved, and since it warred inconclusively with the "moral postulate" of free will, one was left free to take the course of "voluntary choice, for skepticism itself, if systematic, is also a voluntary choice."²⁹ The burden of proof lay with determinism, and all the weight of the *Principles* lay in opposition. Characteristically, after outlining the logic of free will, James left the reader free to decide the case for himself.

This brief excursion into philosophy—there were many others—revealed James's predicament in the *Principles*. On the one hand, he could not probe deeply into questions of meaning without departing from sound scientific procedure, and on the other his analysis of mind as a teleological instrument led him inexorably beyond psychology's limitations. His psychology demonstrated that the end of thought was not just survival and adaptation but survival on terms that satisfied the thinker's diverse emotional, moral, and aesthetic needs. In short, thought did not merely operate in a reflexive way; it operated in a selective or ethical way. James saw his responsibility as a psychologist that of describing the process of thinking, but such a task said nothing about the substance of what was being thought—and James as a man had far too many opinions on that matter to remain silent in the interest of science. The "moral business" always drove him, and after publication of the *Principles* it drove him to attempt to resolve in a more coherent way many of the philosophic issues his psychology had skirted.

James's struggle with the confines of science forecast one of the most important themes of his subsequent thought: the need for science in its quest for truth to leave room for other ways of knowing and experiencing, for faith, for subjectivity, for originality not adumbrated by precedent or simple causal sequences. As a psychologist, James knew well the limits under which science would always labor in attempting to explain so mercurial a phenomenon as the human mind. Consequently, he knew that any system of philosophy worth its salt, even the most rigidly empirical and positivistic variety, had to acknowledge at some point that it was dealing with a mysterious, unstable compound that tended, when too tightly compressed, to explode and shatter its mold. The human mind and its functioning could be minutely analyzed and described, but it could never be contained by any unyielding, formalistic system.

On the other hand, James's careful rendering of the mind as a teleological instrument provided the firm scientific foundation a modern, post-Darwinian philosophy required. His devout belief that the universe was open enough for "good" ideas to be willfully chosen over "bad" ideas, a faith harking back to his psychic crisis and subsequent discovery of free will in the early 1870s, found sanction and support in his psychology. If the discussions of such topics as conception or the will were, from the standpoint of ethics, necessarily truncated and foreshortened in the *Principles*, James's philosophy of pragmatism and his description of the universe as pluralistic still found in them a firm and scientifically respectable footing. And the idea of progress—or "meliorism," as he was later to call it—found in them a new and secure psychological warrant.

*iii*

William James began writing philosophic essays in the late 1870s, but it was not until 1897 that his first book on philosophy, *The Will to Believe*, appeared.[30] And it was not until 1907, three years before his death, that *Pragmatism: A New Name for Some Old Ways of Thinking*, the volume most usually identified with his philosophy, was collected. But while three more collections of his philosophic essays were published in his lifetime, James nevertheless did not live to see his philosophy completed. The possibility that this might be the case bothered him greatly, which partly explains why his last years were marked by such feverish activity. As he wrote to his brother Henry in 1906: "I live in apprehension lest the Avenger should cut me off before I get my message out. It is an aesthetic tragedy to have a bridge begun and stopped in the middle of an arch."[31]

Four posthumous collections of writings still left the arch of James's philosophy incomplete; the metaphysics he planned as the capstone of his career was never written, though portions of *Some Problems of Philosophy* (1911) and, especially, *Essays in Radical Empiricism* (1912) reveal the shape of his thinking in the later years. Essentially an essayist, James flitted agilely from one philosophic problem to the next, crossing and recrossing traditional thematic boundaries with abandon. As a result, the building blocks of his philosophy, many of them only rough-hewn, lie scattered throughout his disparate and deliberately unsystematic writings. The sensitive reader can indeed locate what Ralph Barton Perry called James's "unconscious self-consistency," but he must still finish the arch for himself.

The concept of meliorism was one of those rough-hewn blocks, an idea mentioned briefly toward the conclusion of *Pragmatism*, as an adjunct to the long discussion of novelty that concluded *Some Problems of Philosophy*, and again for several pages in "Faith and the Right to Believe," an unpublished manuscript appended to the latter collection by James's son (it was originally intended to serve as part of the introduction). Taken alone, meliorism was hardly a large or significant part of James's thought. But when the other blocks forming the arch are carefully assembled, meliorism, despite its small size and ragged edges, fits into a vital slot that helps to locate the preferred arrangement of the other blocks and, hence, determines the overall shape of the arch.

James's pragmatism was formulated in response to a dilemma in which modern philosophy found itself. In the years since Descartes invincibly divided mind and body into separate realms, the philosophic world had become riven by two warring camps; the result, in James's view, was philosophic stalemate and attrition. Rationalists, on the one hand, saw the universe as holistic, unified, and finished, as a block complete in itself with a given, predetermined character. The rationalist—John Fiske was one—saw the universe in terms of a priori principles from which particular bits of that universe derived their nature and meaning. The rationalist's universe was monistic or absolutistic, and its discreet parts were defined deductively by their relationship to absolute principle. The thought process of the rationalist began with a fundamental concept or principle and then proceeded to a regard of particulars or percepts. This manner of thinking, which James called variously "tender-mindedness," intellectualism, rationalism, idealism, determinism, monism, or absolutism, constituted one side of the cleavage in modern philosophy.

On the other side was a diametrically opposing way of perceiving the universe. Empiricists—or pluralists, indeterminists, materialists, the "tough-minded"—saw the universe as an agglomeration of things known individually through sense impressions. For the empiricist, the character of the universe was many, not one, and it might well be in the process of growing or becoming; in any event, it was not a predetermined unity. Whereas the rationalist attempted to define a particular thing or idea according to its relationship to some absolute first principle, the empiricist—Chauncey Wright, for example—proceeded inductively, from parts to tentative conclusions about wholes. While the rationalist knew fact from principle, the empiricist knew (or induced) principle from fact.

The split between rationalism and empiricism, "the chief rival attitudes toward life," had been long developing, but during the decades since Mill and Darwin it had begun to reach critical proportions. Rationalists—idealistic, religious, intellectualistic, optimistic, dogmatic—saw the world as a closed, unilinear, finished system. On the other extreme, empiricists—materialistic, skeptical, sensationalistic, pessimistic—saw the world as an open, multilinear system in which chance and spontaneity were real, and perhaps the only, elements. The schism between the two camps was widening alarmingly, as the crucial areas of difference between a Fiske and a Wright revealed. James firmly believed that the philosophy men espoused made a real difference in the kind of lives they led and saw the schism as threatening to limit men's options by preventing any commerce between the two camps: "And this is then your dilemma: you find the two parts of your *quaesitum* hopelessly separated. You find empiricism with inhumanism and irreligion; or else you find a rationalistic philosophy that indeed may call itself religious, but that keeps out of all definite touch with concrete facts and joys and sorrows."[32]

What was making the crisis so acute was the current tendency among believers in both schools toward exclusiveness. Rationalists and empiricists focused, arbitrarily, James thought, on different aspects of man's total experience and then elevated them into the singular sources of philosophic knowledge and truth. Since their criteria of selection were so dissimilar, the discrepancies between the outlook of the rationalist and the empiricist had hardened into a schism that was

manifestly artificial. The "present dilemma in philosophy," as James termed this situation, had arisen
because neither side of the "quaesitum" could, with
consistency, acknowledge the terms of the other in sub-
mitting basic philosophic questions to crucial, mutually
meaningful tests. Each side operated within the epistemological sanctions of its separate metaphysics, and
the result was a gratuitous polarization in philosophy
that threatened to halt man's intellectual progress.

A major part of this dilemma was the fact that both
philosophic tendencies, when taken to their logical
extremes, had the effect of negating moral choice and,
hence, true morality.[33] Rationalism, with its deterministic union of all things into monistic, necessary universal
laws and principles, and empiricism, with its "barren"
fragmentation of all portions of experience into
atomistic, unconnected entities—each side of the
"quaesitum" rendered morality nugatory. Rationalists
held that since the universe's course was predetermined and charted, there could be no real choices or
alternatives on moral questions, while empiricists
denied that there were knowable elements of continuity in experience upon which any viable system of
moral regularity could be based. Believing as he did
that a feeling of moral order was one of man's deepest
human needs, James found this situation intolerable.
His pragmatism was consequently a philosophy that
aimed at revitalizing man's sense of the reality of ethical choice and morality.

Pragmatism did not so much attempt to reconcile
rationalism and empiricism on a metaphysical level as
to shift the grounds of the debate and thus provide
an alternative to the dilemma it posed. In essence,
James diagnosed the conflict more as a "clash of temperaments" than a collision of mutually exclusive
philosophical truths. Giving philosophy a broad and

nontechnical definition ("our individual way of just seeing and feeling the total push and pressure of the cosmos"), James argued that it was natural for men with
different emotional and intellectual makeups to feel
the "push and pressure" in different ways.[34] The
characterological sensibilities of rationalists and empiricists led them in opposing directions. But it did not
follow that truth lay exclusively in one camp or the
other. What was needed was a philosophy that defined
experience broadly enough to encompass the sense of
reality both kinds of temperaments gravitated toward.
Once an adequate definition of experience was
reached, the schism could be healed, and philosophy
could get on with the business of solving men's problems and improving their lives accordingly. In framing
a philosophy that would escape the horns of the
dilemma, James sketched, implicitly but vitally, the outlines of what was to become the dominant position of
American liberals in the first half of the twentieth century on the idea of progress.

In order to demonstrate the inadequacies of rationalism's assumptions about experience, James
focused, as he had in the *Principles*, on the difficulties
involved in the acceptance of determinism. Neither
determinism nor indeterminism could be proved in
any final way by marshaling evidence, he acknowledged, but the implications for believing both views
could be explicated and set against one's sense of the
cosmos's "push and pressure." In the first place, if one
were a determinist one had to accept that

> those parts of the universe already laid down
> absolutely appoint and decree what the other
> parts shall be. The future has no ambiguous pos-
> sibilities present in its womb; the part we call the
> present is compatible with only one totality. Any

other future complement than the one fixed from
eternity is impossible. The whole is in each and
every part, and welds it with the rest into an
absolute unity, an iron block, in which there can
be no equivocation or shadow of turning.[35]

Rationalism projected a monistic "block universe" in
which all change and modification was logically an illusion.

Furthermore, the determinist also had to accept that
the only categories of reality were those of necessity
and impossibility: only those things that have or have
had existence are or ever were possible. The sense
one's mind holds that there might have been alternatives to what has transpired in the world—including
one's own feelings, thoughts, and actions—also is
nothing but an illusion. What has transpired is the only
thing that could have transpired. In the world of the
determinist, there is no chance, no choice, and no possibility that, but for human volition, things might be
different from what they were foreordained to be.
"Determinism denies the ambiguity of future volitions,
because it affirms that nothing future can be
ambiguous."[36]

The consequences of this kind of belief led inexorably to a debilitating, dispiriting pessimism. Even
though one might, for example, instinctively feel
repugnance and regret in contemplating a particularly
bestial murder, such feelings in a monistic world have
no real meaning since the murder must necessarily be
part of the larger course of things. Even though feelings of regret or outrage or absurdity press naturally
on all people, as do the perceptions of certain kinds
of evil in life, the determinist must reconcile these feelings with his knowledge that ultimately there is no
alternative. In effect, the *is* and the *ought* are one and

the same in the determinist's universe: moral judgments based on alternatives that might have been real but for differing exigencies have no meaning. In the last analysis, there *are* no differing exigencies in that world.

When set against the background of the teleological description of the mind's functioning in the *Principles of Psychology*, James's analysis of the logic of determinism paved the way for pragmatism's powerful, commonsensical rebuttal of the rationalist's main argument for unity and monism. James's arguments were especially effective when aimed at the rheumy Spencerian philosophy (James used the term generically) which, like Fiske's, saw history as a series of ironclad causal sequences that guaranteed what evolutionists uncritically called "progress." This kind of rationalism, denying to the individual any important initiatory role in history, paraded an ontology cloaked in facile optimism. Yet despite its superficial appearance of hope, Spencerian evolutionism could not mask its true character of fatalism; James could only regard it with contempt. Systems of thought such as Fiske's were, as speculative metaphysical creeds, obsolete, anachronistic, and unwarranted by any analysis of specific incidents of historical change. They represented a "mood of contemplation, an emotional attitude . . . which is as old as the world; . . . the mood of fatalistic pantheism, with its intuition of the One and All, which was, and is, and ever shall be."[37] And James reserved a special sarcasm for the hypothesized ends of such deterministic progressions: "The white-robed harp-playing heaven of our sabbath-schools, and the ladylike teatable elysium represented in Mr. Spencer's *Data of Ethics*, as the final consummation of progress, are on a par in this respect,—lubberlands, pure and simple, one and all."[38] James's rejection of determinism was based squarely on his belief that experience was the continuous flowing of real alternative possibilities offered to human volition. Since rationalism's deterministic block universe precluded such alternatives, James felt justified in placing his faith elsewhere.

The other horn of the dilemma, empiricism's skepticism and tendency to shatter all elements of experience into disjointed bits and particles, required a more sustained and persuasive argument before it too could be slipped. Both pragmatism and what James called "radical empiricism" contained lengthy attempts to put the Humpty-Dumpty atomism of empiricism back together again while still avoiding the holistic monism of the rationalists. The task was a difficult one, for it required acceptance of the empiricists' notion that the world as experienced was many, not one, while at the same time rejecting the extreme disintegration and discontinuity that this notion frequently produced.

In James's estimate, empiricism separated all things experienced into discreet and isolated entities, projecting a universe made up of parts that could be individually perceived but whose connections or relations could not themselves be verified. In its most virulent form, empiricism eventuated in an intellectual parsimoniousness that could only confine itself to the barest description of observed phenomena. The result was a universe in which no order based on the reality of external connections could exist. For so arch an empiricist as Chauncey Wright, for example, faith, subjectivity, and progressive morality were banished in favor of a strict neutrality on the part of the observer. Wright's toughminded empiricism was so disquietingly nihilistic that, as has been shown, James once charged his friend with denying the reality of the universe in favor of a "nulliverse" in which there was no continuity or phenomenal common ground.[39]

In the absence of warrantable evidence for such continuity, Wright maintained that one must withhold belief and refuse to speculate about cause and effect or the moral dimensions of a given phenomena; his exorcism of teleology from the process of inquiry similarly was based on his refusal to run ahead of observed evidence. He steadfastly denied to the process of knowing any role for subjectivity or emotionality. As a consistent empiricist, Wright refused to defer to any morality beyond that of the most scrupulously neutral, scientific method of observation and reporting. For Wright, things were experienced essentially apart from prior conditions, reflections, or anticipations. For him, as James commented, "The only order which has any objective existence is the elemental order. . . . The elements act and react, pursuing each its private law, while the 'thing' floats out incidentally as it were, exerting no influence on its factors, and ignored by them." James went on to add that "to human nature there is something uncanny, *unheimlich*, in the notion of a universe stripped so stark naked, brought down to its fighting weight so to speak."[40]

Chauncey Wright's brand of empiricism required an olympian detachment no human could attain. Moreover, James pointed out, the decision not to make moral judgments was as real as the decision to make them. Decisions on moral matters continually forced themselves on men, and deliberate failure to respond in no way negated their demands. Morality, the exercise of choice, was an organic part of human experience and will and could not be rendered inoperative by conscious decision. For James, morality existed endemically within human consciousness; it originated whenever the intellect made choices between apparent alternatives and the will resolved to act. Since moral values originated only in the human consciousness, the creative individual was the moral center of the universe, and morality was part of his every discrimination.

The operative word here is "creative," for James insisted that the individual had it within his power to add things totally new to the universe, things whose existence was not adumbrated before the individual's mind and will and acts created them. Since James's view of the world was one in which chance and contingency were realities, the individual was free to create new things (whether ideas or objects) and thus to alter the future. Wright's neutrality not only precluded this possibility; it militated actively against it: "Skepticism in moral matters is an active ally of immorality. Who is not for is against. The universe will have no neutrals in these matters."[41]

> If a thinker had no stake in the unknown, no vital needs, to live or languish according to what the unseen world contained, a philosophical neutrality and refusal to believe either one way or the other would be his wisest cue. But, unfortunately, neutrality is not only inwardly difficult, it is also outwardly unrealizable, where our relations to an alternative are practical and vital. . . . In all such cases strict and consistent neutrality is an unattainable thing.[42]

Wright could banish teleology from inquiry only because he inadequately grasped the purposive nature of thought; and his insistence on the strict neutrality of the observer, when applied to moral matters, resulted in a kind of agnosticism, a "mental nullity," which, like the view of the rationalists, took only a partial account of total human experience. Since man was irrevocably in the universe and moral impulses were structurally part of his experience, it followed that the universe as experienced by man was in some sense moral. In insisting that modern science sanctioned only moral neutrality, Wright overlooked the fact that moral imperatives operate on all men in the world and that they are therefore a part of external reality, compelling recognition and constantly requiring evaluation.

Thus, while James agreed with Wright that the Spencerian philosophy of predetermined progress was mere unscientific speculation and that the universe gave evidence of no singular, unilinear movement, moral or otherwise, he could not accept Wright's agnostic, empirical neutralism. Wright's view ignored the possibility that belief in morality might help create its reality.[43] For James, the empiricist's neutrality on moral matters was based on ignorance of how the will helped to decide the reality of the moral. As he wrote in his essay "Reflex Action and Theism," repeating the metaphor he had used in the *Principles*, "To bid the man's subjective interests be passive till truth express itself from out the environment, is to bid the sculptor's chisel be passive till the statue express itself from out the stone."[44] The whole burden of *The Will to Believe* was that belief in a certain future possibility might help it to become a reality.

Wright's "scientific" indeterminism was for James as tyrannous and arbitrary as Fiske's coercive determinism. His objection to Fiske's block universe and Wright's "nulliverse" was in this sense the same: both denied the existence of meaningful moral choices that individuals could know through experience and act upon in the future. The positions they represented denied the individual the moral freedom necessary for effecting progress. In offering pragmatism expressly as a mediator between tough-mindedness and tender-mindedness, between rationalism and empiricism,

James set forth a conception of experience specifically designed to enable the individual to act efficiently and responsibly in terms of his moral ideals and purposes, and, by insisting that there was always another choice to be made, to escape the horns of the dilemma and make progress a reality.

The pragmatic definition of experience recapitulated the findings of the *Principles of Psychology*. It began at the most fundamental physiological and psychological level: the individual's interaction with his environment. Experience was a streaming sense of personal continuity enveloping external objects, their relationship to each other, and their shifting relationship to a dynamic, purposeful experiencer and thinker. Out of this flowing interaction emerged a state of consciousness or a sense of continuity and movement among the data of experience. These data did not remain random or chaotic but rather, in the very fact of their becoming part of consciousness, they assumed a purposive or intentional structure. They became, in short, ideas or concepts, patterns of percepts arranged so as to allow the individual to respond satisfactorily to his environment and to plan its modification to enhance that satisfaction. The very nature of thought, the evidence and substance of consciousness, implied the ability of the thinker not merely to survive in a complex experiential situation but to survive on his own terms. Consciousness and thought implied an active, purposive, selective stance toward the future. Such a view suggested that experience itself was progressive, that it contained categorically both the possibility of responding to the environment in new ways as well as the standard for evaluating how effectively this was being accomplished.

Clearly, James's definition of experience was broad enough to allow both rationalists and empiricists to accept it. He departed from both extremes, however, by making experience the exclusive source of knowledge and by arguing that experience was both open *and* continuous enough to allow men efficacious choice in shaping a future to their liking. Thought itself, the process of conceptualization, implied the selection of future modes of conduct and the rejection of alternatives, but there was nothing deterministic or necessary about the selection, as the logic of rationalism required. Only in a pluralistic, indeterminate world such as empiricism indicated could pragmatism's view of experience be accurate; pragmatism thus leaned strongly toward empiricism.

But James's pragmatic pluralism too had a logic, and while it denied the coercive fatalism of rationalism's block universe, it also had to show that there was sufficient continuity in the universe for human thought and action to proceed effectively and meaningfully from one object and point in time to another. If morality could be real only in a universe of chance and choice, it could similarly be real only in a universe in which there was a certain amount or quality of continuity in experience. While accepting empiricism's external multiplicity, James had to show that Wright's nihilistic, morally naked universe was inadequate to the larger demands of experienced reality.

The reason why Wright's universe seemed so "uncannily stripped" was, of course, that it separated the subjective and the objective facets of experience in a rigid fashion James knew to be psychologically impossible: percepts and concepts could never be totally sundered. Hence his tactic for slipping the horn of empiricism, one of the central concerns of his unfinished metaphysics, was to argue that the empiricist's conception of experience was insufficiently radical, that it failed to recognize that the relations between objects perceived were themselves as real a part of experience as were the objects themselves. Empiricists such as Wright, much like the associationist psychologists, gave insufficient attention to the fact that experience was never discontinuous and that the objects it contained were organically embedded in the consciousness that perceived them, as were all their external relations. And all was enveloped in the selective, intentional character of consciousness itself. Radical empiricism, James's term for his pragmatic modification of empiricism, projected a world made up of pure experience, a world in which experience was the basic, primal "stuff" of reality.

Consequently, whereas determinism inexorably led toward pessimism, and empiricism led toward disbelief and moral nihilism, pragmatic pluralism meant that there was real cause for optimism. James's pluralism envisioned the world as unfinished and plastic, in which human preferences and purposes might help to create the conditions of human destiny. For the pluralist, the "ordinary unsophisticated view of things" was the true perception of reality: despite the claims of the determinist, pragmatism's universe was open enough to allow the individual a certain leverage on the future. For the pragmatist, the sense of the reality of choice, though eluding any final schema for proof, offered the gift of volition that became real with the taking. Pragmatism could not guarantee that every human purpose would be gratified—that would have involved a lapse back into determinism's logic—but it did hold that a more satisfactory future was possible because individuals might choose to act on its behalf. Avoiding both rationalism's thorny constrictions and empiricism's looseness and discontinuity, James opted for a pluralism whose openness and cohesion jibed with what he knew experience and thought to be.

Deliberately formulated to avoid the "present

dilemma in philosophy," pragmatism made man's will to believe in a better future its philosophical ideal. Quite simply, pragmatism asked what the consequences were of believing this or that idea to be true. Truth was not an inherent property of certain correct ideas but the relationship of an idea to its consequences when acted upon. Ideas that produced the appropriate results—appropriate in terms of the thinker's purpose—were true. True ideas had constant reference to the future and to the consequences of believing a concept to be valid enough to act upon it. No truth was ever final or permanent since experience, the ultimate court of appeal, was ongoing and in flux. The process by which a concept became true, like experience itself, was progressive: "Truth happens to an idea. . . . Its verity is in fact an event, a process: the process namely of its verifying itself, its veri-fication. . . . The connexions and transitions (leading from an idea to factual reality) come to us from point to point as being progressive, harmonious, satisfactory."[45]

Since, from the point of view of James's psychology, human will and purpose played such a predominant role in the construction of ideas in the first place, the validity of the pragmatic criteria of their verification implied a great deal more than a simple epistemological device for estimating an idea's validity. Pragmatism suggested that in a pluralistic, additive world in which novelty was real and the will truly creative, history, as men experienced it, was by nature voluntaristic. When James proclaimed that the value of an idea was to be judged by how effectively it served to "carry us prosperously from one part of our experience to any other part, linking things satisfactorily, working securely, simplifying, saving labor," he revealed how pragmatism assumed and built upon a particular philosophy of history.[46] This philosophy was never worked out in great detail, but in his later writings James did suggest what pragmatism's historical requirements would be. It was at this juncture that he sketched his doctrine of meliorism.

Pragmatic pluralism denied that history was "one unbending unit of fact." It held, on the contrary, that historical "actualities seem to float in a wider sea of possibilities from out of which they are chosen."[47] In the pluralist's view of history, the existence of one set of current conditions did not mean that only one set of subsequent conditions could eventuate. For the pluralist, the concept of the possible had an equal claim on reality with the facts of existence and the idea of the impossible. The pluralism to which James gave his allegiance meant that "some of the conditions of the world's salvation are actually extant," and one of those conditions was the reality of human choice coupled with man's innate drive to improve his moral circumstances.[48] Pluralism meant the chance that a better world might come into being through human effort, "the chance that in moral respects the future may be other and better than the past has been."[49]

From his youth, James's prejudices had run in this direction. His emotional crisis of the early 1870s sprang at least partly from the depression and claustrophobia he felt when he contemplated the coils of a deterministic world in which evil was an undeniable reality; his antidote, as he then put it, had been deliberately to exercise his "individuality and creative power." Only a few years later, in 1880, he was refuting Spencer's contention that the "great man" in history could only be explained by a matrix of antecedent "aggregate conditions" that operated according to natural law. James's point in opposing this assertion was that Spencer and other like-minded evolutionists failed to see that great men, like Darwin's "spontaneous variations," possessed a genius that could modify the environment in "entirely original" and unpredictable ways.[50] While society might condition, it could not determine what the great man might do and what effects his deeds might have on history. The pragmatic doctrine of meliorism was a larger amplification of these early views.

Meliorism was the historical concomitant or extension of pragmatism, pluralism, and the will to believe. Like pragmatism, it wended a middle way between rationalism's determinism and empiricism's neutrality; like pluralism, it was receptive to a variety of future historical trends and possibilities; like the will to believe, it saw the improvement that might lie in these possibilities as contingent upon the faith men placed in their moral ideals. Meliorism made "the world's salvation depend upon the energizing of its several parts, among which we are."[51] It recognized that, as James wrote in the opening sentence of *Some Problems of Philosophy*, "The progress of society is due to the fact that individuals vary from the human average in all sorts of directions" and that their accumulated influences, examples, and initiatives produce change.[52]

In James's historical purview, men stood, or floated, in a broad sea of contingencies and options, and how and where they steered was largely up to them. Since men had the power to affect the course of history, the burden of qualitative change or progress lay squarely on their shoulders. "We build the flux out inevitably. The great question is: does it, with our additions, *rise or fall in value?* . . . In our cognitive as well as in our active life we are creative. We *add* both to the subject and to the predicate part of reality. The world stands really malleable, waiting to receive its final touches at our hands."[53]

Standing midway between the false optimism of

necessary progress and the unnecessary hopelessness
and impotence of extreme empiricism's nihilism,
meliorism held that progress toward selected goals,
toward what men held and hoped to be morally possible, was a true "living option." "Meliorism treats salvation as neither necessary nor impossible. It treats it as
a possibility which becomes more and more of a probability the more numerous the actual conditions of salvation become. It is clear that pragmatism must incline
towards meliorism. . . . [Our acts] create the world's
salvation."[54] Meliorism was the directed manipulation
of those portions of reality that were genuinely
unfinished and could be molded; it assumed that
"work is still doing in the world-process" and that the
"character of the world's results may in part depend
upon our acts."[55] The meliorist maintained that faith
in a better future was "one of the inalienable birth-
rights" of the human mind and that if "*we* do *our* best,
*and* the other powers do *their* best, the world will be
perfected."[56]

James's melioristic, cumulative conception of progress involved a continuing element of risk. Progress
was uncertain, contingent; reduced to its essence, it was
a matter of will and goodwill, of the determination of
individuals to act courageously on behalf of their moral
convictions. The world's "perfection" was by no means
assured, but, given men's power to effect directed
change, it might become actualized. "We can and we
may, as it were, jump with both feet off the ground
into or towards a world of which we trust the other
parts to meet our jump—and *only so* can the *making* of
a perfected world of the pluralistic pattern ever take
place."[57] The genuine pragmatist and meliorist was
"willing to live on a scheme of uncertified possibilities
which he trusts; willing to pay with his own person,
if need be, for the realization of the ideals which he

frames."[58] Meliorism implied a certain ultimate hardihood, for it required that men act without assurances or guarantees. James personally relished the risk, which he thought gave life its savor and significance:

> The significance of human life for communicable and publicly recognized purposes is the offspring of a marriage of two different parents, either of whom alone is barren. . . . And let the orientalists and pessimists say what they will, the thing of deepest . . . significance in life does seem to be its character of *progress*, or that strange union of reality with ideal novelty which it continues from one moment to another to present.[59]

Since the most plausible final purpose of creation (despite his pluralism, James did not withdraw from such speculation) seemed to be the "greatest possible enrichment of our ethical consciousness," James was optimistic about the future: "The ceaseless whisper of the more permanent ideals, the steady tug of truth and justice, give them but time, *must* warp the world in their direction."[60] Because man's impulses were so largely moral and his need to realize his morality so basic a motive for action, the moral influence would be increasingly evident as man came to exert more and more control over his environment. While progress was never guaranteed, man's constant efforts to ameliorate his condition would in all likelihood result in a future better than the past.

This, then, as James formulated it, was the pragmatic idea of progress: individualistic, purposive, relativistic, contingent, both "carrot and stick," both object and process, both end and means. Progress was achieved through the cumulative effect of individuals striving to make their beliefs and hopes come true. Men had the will, sometimes indeed the necessity, to believe that their intelligence could help create a future that would satisfy their changing needs and desires. Whatever improvement in the human condition had occurred in the past had come about through human thought, will, desire, and action. No deus ex machina, whether conceived in theistic or scientific terms, controlled historical development or determined that change would be improvement or decline; no single moral criterion could serve as the yardstick of progress. But this did not mean that the idea of progress was a fiction; it meant that human experience contained a variety of qualitative estimates, purposes, and standards by which to direct and measure those changes men could effect in time.

James's conception of progress did not, however, cohere into anything resembling a consistent social philosophy. His social and political ideas were a hodgepodge of mugwumpism, anti-imperialism, pacifism, internationalism, and nineteenth-century democratic liberalism.[61] He admitted that his early political education derived almost totally from E. L. Godkin's the *Nation*, a staunchly Republican organ, but in the final years of his life he was strongly affected by H. G. Wells's fabian socialism. In his last year, he published a famous essay, "The Moral Equivalent of War," in which he advocated creation of an antimilitarist army of social action and service and stated that he "devoutly believe[d] in the reign of peace and in the gradual advent of some sort of a socialist equilibrium."[62]

James was sufficiently enraged by America's international posture following the Spanish-American War to become a vice president of the Anti-Imperialist League, and he found the militant opinions of Theodore Roosevelt, his former student, highly obnoxious on the subject of American expansion. But the coalescence of the large, organized democratic reform groups that gave the country its Progressive era offended his somewhat yeasty individualism. As he expressed the matter:

> I am against bigness and greatness in all their forms, and with the invisible molecular moral forces that work from individual to individual, stealing in through the crannies of the world like so many soft rootlets, or like the capillary oozing of water, and yet rending the hardest monuments of man's pride, if you give them time. The bigger the unit you deal with, the hollower, the more brutal, the more mendacious is the life displayed. So I am against all big organizations as such, national ones first and foremost; against all big successes and big results; and in favor of the eternal forces of truth which always work in the individual and immediately unsuccessful way, under-dogs always, till history comes, after they are long dead, and puts them on the top.[63]

Progress, James believed, resulted from men of strength and goodwill making individual acts of faith and trust on behalf of "the old confidence in human values." The principal agent of progress was the man of genius, whose vigor and leadership was eventually recognized by his democratic fellows. There was, James implied, a natural aristocracy that made democracy work. James's faith in democracy as "a kind of religion" was firm and unshakable; it was a faith that assumed that democracy progressed because it allowed the "better men" ultimately to take the lead: "Mankind does nothing save through initiatives on the part of inventors, great or small, and imitation by the rest of us—these are the sole factors active in human progress.

Individuals of genius show the way, and set the patterns, which common people then adopt and follow."[64]
The world was ultimately to be saved by the character
and virtue of society's better men.

But while James spoke hopefully of the world's "salvation," and put responsibility for its achievement in
man's own hands, his conception of progress failed to
indicate which way salvation lay. Although his pragmatism strove to make morality real for individuals,
James shrank from formulating any coherent theory
of ethics or from framing a social ideology that sought
their application through organized effort. Fearing the
confines of any closed circuit of ethical "givens," he
affirmed only that every man should have his experience and his say. Pragmatism envisioned as many
statues in the block of stone as there were sculptors,
but the idea of meliorism lacked the apparatus for discriminating among them. James insisted that history
was open and that the individual of genius could alter
its course, but, unlike Lester Ward, whose views in certain regards paralleled his own, he refused to say in
what direction it should be altered.

This fear of dogmatism—or, on the positive side, this
respect for the autonomy and integrity of the
individual's experience—led James to set forth a
philosophy subject to a variety of applications, many
of the consequences of which James himself would
have deplored. While he insisted that pragmatism was
primarily a theory of truth, in James's hands it sanctioned as many truths as there were human purposes;
while meliorism meant that acting on behalf of one's
ideals might help them to come true, it gave no
guidelines as to which ideals might truly be worthy of
the effort. As a psychologist-philosopher, James gave
more attention to the problems of how and why
individuals create and use ideas than to their substance

and effect in history and society. Pragmatism as James defined it was deficient as a social theory, and meliorism was but the bare bones of a conception of historical progress.

Yet when the time came, James's understanding of the nature of experience was sufficiently formed to provide him with an effective refutation of Henry Adams's curve of degradation. An entire lifetime of study and effort leading up to his correspondence with his pessimistic old friend in the summer of 1910 prepared him to reject out of hand the *Letter*'s specious formalism. The unwieldy, monistic abstraction Adams called "history" had all the foibles and inadequacies of any deterministic construct, and implicit in James's rejection were all of his doctrines of pluralism, pragmatism, the will to believe, and meliorism. If as a theory of history these ideas were uncoordinated and inchoate, James nevertheless illustrated how they could be turned into a vitally suggestive idea of progress and, at the same time, a vigorously antiformalistic historical argument.

But this was hardly enough. If James's depiction of philosophy as an enterprise making a difference in the arrangements of men's lives was correct, acute observers after the turn of the century—and there were many —realized that the philosophic dilemma James detected and attempted to escape was being reflected in society at large. Its effect on society, as on philosophy, was a paralysis of the will to act energetically and effectively to alleviate social and moral problems. If James's pragmatism offered a way out of the dilemma for individuals, might not its elaboration and extension as a social philosophy hold out the same hope to society? Such was to be the vocation and achievement of James's pragmatic legatee, John Dewey.

# 5

# John Dewey:
# The Experimentalist
# Criterion

"By the death of William James at the age of sixty-eight," John Dewey wrote in an obituary in *The Independent*, "America loses its most distinguished figure in the field of psychology and philosophy."[1] Dewey could well have added that James's stature was enhanced by his enormous influence on a generation of American thinkers—and on no one more fruitfully than Dewey himself. Ever since 1891, when he first encountered James's *Principles of Psychology*, Dewey had increasingly been affected by the pragmatic interpretation of experience and by the possibilities for a systematic restructuring of philosophy that the *Principles* seemed to require. Though Dewey saw pragmatism in a very different light than James did, his debt to the Harvard professor was immense. In a letter to James dated March 1903, Dewey termed the *Principles* the "spiritual *progenitor* of the whole industry" of pragmatism, and when Dewey's edited *Studies in Logical Theory* appeared in the same year, it bore the following dedication: "For both inspiration and the forging of the tools with which the writers have worked there is a preeminent obligation on the part of all of us to William James, of Harvard University, who, we hope, will accept this acknowledgement and this book as unworthy tokens of a regard and an admiration that are coequal."[2]

James and Dewey began corresponding in 1891, and, as was the case with so many of James's correspondents, their exchanges soon ripened into a warm friendship and a mutually supportive, though not uncritical, collaboration. Both approached pragmatism with a reformer's zeal and saw in the pragmatic movement generally—or, as Dewey preferred to call it "experimentalism"—the seeds of a profound alteration in Western philosophic development. Dewey wrote to James early in their friendship that, after reading the *Principles*, he was convinced "that a tremendous movement is impending, when the intellectual forces that have been gathering since the Renascence and Reformation, shall demand complete free movement, and, by getting their physical leverage in the telegraph and printing press, shall, through free inquiry in a centralized way, demand the authority of all other so-called authorities."[3] James, enthusiastically reviewing *Studies in Logical Theory* some years later, concurred, and saw Dewey and his pragmatic disciples at Chicago creating a "genuine school of thought" deserving of "the title of a new system of philosophy."[4]

Dewey's birth in 1859, the year *Origin of Species* was published, provides an appropriate symbol for intellectual historians looking back over Dewey's life and thought, for Darwinian conceptions of organic growth and of the necessary interdependence of living things came to be reflected in all aspects of Dewey's work. But it would be a mistake to attribute all of Dewey's acute sense of organic social and natural interaction to the Darwinians. Kant and, more particularly, Hegel influenced Dewey's thinking more directly than Darwin and nearly as much as James, and George Sylvester Morris, Dewey's highly regarded teacher at Johns Hopkins University, was an idealist of the first order. Years after Dewey's conversion to experimentalism, he maintained that "there is greater richness and greater variety of insight in Hegel than in any other single systematic philosopher."[5] Nonetheless, it was the Darwinian evolutionist T. H. Huxley who first led Dewey as an undergraduate at the University of Vermont in the late 1870s to an "awakening of a distinctive philosophic interest."[6]

But these intellectual interests came relatively late, for Dewey's evolution into a philosopher could not be predicted from the events or influences of his youth. Born in Burlington, Vermont, Dewey came from middle-class New England stock and enjoyed a pleasant, wholesome, thoroughly unremarkable boyhood. His father was an amiable, uneducated merchant who could recall as a boy listening to the guns of British and American warships during a battle on Lake Champlain in the War of 1812. (The brevity of American history becomes apparent when one considers that Dewey lived to witness the Korean War!) Dewey and his brothers attended the Burlington public schools, where John was an adequate though somewhat perfunctory student. In college he was sufficiently diligent to win election to Phi Beta Kappa, although it was not until his senior year that he discovered Huxley, Plato, and Comte and, under the guidance of Professor H. A. P. Torrey, became profoundly interested in philosophy.

After two years of teaching high school in Pennsylvania, Dewey returned to Burlington to study philosophy privately under Torrey. In 1882, using money borrowed from an aunt, he began formal graduate study in philosophy at Johns Hopkins University, working principally under Morris and G. Stanley Hall and taking a minor in history and political science under Herbert Baxter Adams. Morris's influence was especially evident at this period; under his tutelage, Dewey became an avowed Hegelian. Hegel, as Dewey later recalled, filled his need for a unifying philosophy that overcame the "sense of divisions and separations that were, I suppose, borne in upon me as a consequence of a heritage of New England culture, divisions by way of isolation of self from the world, of soul from body, of nature from God."[7] Dewey's deep-felt need to reconcile these seeming opposites not only explains his affinity for Hegel's idealistic synthesis, but it also suggests why he was later so strongly affected by James's all-encompassing psychology and philosophy of experience.

Dewey was a highly successful graduate student, finishing his doctorate in only two years. In 1884, already having begun his long publishing career, he was offered an instructorship at the University of Michigan, where, save for one year at the University of Minnesota, he remained for the next ten years. In 1894, partly through the efforts of his former colleague at Michigan, James H. Tufts, Dewey was called to the University of Chicago, where President William Rainey Harper was collecting one of the most distinguished and controversial graduate faculties in the country. At Chicago, Dewey played a principal role in building a philosophy department that eventually boasted such notables as Tufts, George H. Mead, James R. Angell, Edward S. Ames, and Addison W. Moore.[8] At Chicago, he also became director of the School of Education and head of the university's experimental school, the so-called Dewey School. A dispute over funding of the school led to his resignation from Chicago in 1904 and a subsequent move to Columbia University, where he remained, happily and productively, until his retirement in 1930. It was during the Columbia years that Dewey rose to international prominence as the inheritor of James's pragmatic mantle, as well as, in his own right, an original and articulate spokesman for the logic of experimentalism and the philosophy of liberal democracy. After an extraordinarily prolific and varied life, Dewey died in New York City in 1952 at the age of ninety-two.

John Dewey was never a "closet philosopher." Personal involvement in public movements and events was the natural extension of both his temperament and his philosophy of instrumentalism, as well as the result of his wife's abiding social concerns. Dewey was a close friend of Jane Addams and an early supporter of her endeavors at Hull House. An instinctive as well as a reflective democrat, he worked tirelessly to make education available to all Americans, for, like Lester Ward, he saw the school and the university as the great ameliorative institutions of a democratic society.

These convictions were reflected in the variety of civic and educational organizations to which he lent leadership and prestige; throughout his life, Dewey tried to bridge the gap between the academic and the social. He was an active supporter of such liberal organizations as the American Civil Liberties Union, the League for Industrial Democracy, and the Committee for Cultural Freedom. In 1917, he helped found the New School for Social Research in New York, and during the 1920s he was a leader of the New York Teachers' Guild. He was the first president of the American Association of University Professors and was voted the lifelong honorary presidency of the National

Education Association. In the 1930s, he became disenchanted with capitalism and became a socialist, although his tough-minded assessment of both Marxism and the Soviet Union helped make him a vigorous anticommunist. He was long active on behalf of women's rights and served as the first president of the reform-oriented Peoples' Lobby. He helped found the League for Independent Political Action in 1929, and in 1937 he served as head of the commission that investigated the charges made against Leon Trotsky at the infamous Moscow trial. All of these activities reflected accurately Dewey's way of thinking; as he once remarked of himself, "My belief in the office of intelligence as a continuously reconstructive agency is at least a faithful report of my own life and experience."[9]

Dewey's ability to sustain both social involvement and intellectual detachment was promoted at least in part by the perspective he gained from his interest in history and his numerous travels abroad. He spent several years teaching in the Orient and lectured and toured extensively in Japan and China, winning honors and making friends in both countries and gaining what might almost be termed an anthropological sense of the cultural differences between East and West. During the 1920's, he also visited and consulted with educators in Mexico, Turkey, and the Soviet Union. These experiences, together with his wide reading in the history of philosophy and his involvement in current social affairs, helped shape his belief that philosophy was conditioned by a matrix of historical and cultural, as well as personal, considerations and that it was inevitably as much the product of a time and a civilization as the achievement of a single individual mind.

Despite an incredibly busy life outside the study and the classroom, Dewey was one of the most prolific scholars America has produced. His first essays appeared in 1882 and his last publication was in 1950. During the interim, he authored at least twenty-five major books, numerous minor ones, and hundreds of essays, articles, and reviews. In his obituary, the *New York Times* estimated his total published works to include well over a thousand items. His most influential books, however, were written during the period that embraced America's entry into World War I, the decade of prosperity of the 1920s, and the depression years leading up to World War II. Taken collectively, these works might well be said to represent the vortex of liberal democratic thought during this period. They include *Democracy and Education* (1916), *Reconstruction in Philosophy* (1920), *Human Nature and Conduct* (1922), *Experience and Nature* (1925), *The Quest for Certainty* (1929), *Individualism—Old and New* (1930), *Liberalism and Social Action* (1935), and *Logic: The Theory of Inquiry* (1938). All of these works were written after Dewey had evolved into a full-fledged pragmatist shortly after the turn of the century.

From 1879, when he left the University of Vermont, to 1891, when he published the *Outlines of a Critical Theory of Ethics* and began his correspondence with William James, might be called Dewey's "absolutist" period.[10] During this time, he was an enthusiastic Hegelian, through Morris's influence devouring the works of T. H. Green and Edward Caird and the young Oxford idealists. His first philosophic essays appeared in the *Journal of Speculative Philosophy*, edited by the Hegelian W. T. Harris of St. Louis, about whom a number of philosophically inclined German exiles of 1848 had gathered. Hegel's dynamic historical treatment of human culture and institutions, with its synthetic dissolution of hard-and-fast distinctions between social and intellectual entities, held a special attraction for Dewey, whose thought from the beginning tended toward a comprehensive, organic view of nature and its constituents. His doctoral dissertation, completed in 1884, was a Hegelian critique of Kant's psychology.

Dewey was already inclined to regard psychology as an integral part of philosophy (he had stated this in 1887 in the preface to his *Psychology*, his first book) before reading James's *Principles*. But James was a galvanizing influence nonetheless; his "discovery" of the stream of consciousness and his treatment of the mind as a selective, teleological instrument for the realization of human preference and purpose particularly stimulated Dewey. James, as Horace Kallen observed, awoke Dewey from his "Hegelian slumbers" and turned his attention from the concept of the mind as spirit to a regard for intelligence and thought as purely natural devices for realizing a better life for mankind.[11]

This movement away from idealism stemmed primarily from Dewey's growing appreciation of the definitive importance of biology and psychology for the study of logic and the problem of knowledge. James's influence here was crucial, but Dewey was also deeply influenced by his associations with Mead and the others who attracted James's approving attention as the "Chicago School." By 1903, Dewey's conversion of naturalism was complete; after publication of *Studies in Logical Theory*, everything he wrote assumed or expressed a naturalistic approach to mind, logic, knowledge, and values. Dewey had found in pragmatism a philosophy that promised to reconcile, without recourse to the contrivance of a dialectical world spirit, the contrapuntal social and intellectual tendencies that had once seemed to require the Hegelian synthesis. Dewey's conversion to pragmatic naturalism was a major part—indeed, a classic example—of the change in intellectual climate so many Americans experienced around the turn of the century. By the early 1900s,

Dewey had become a charter member of the company inhabiting George Santayana's "skyscraper" of the will.

As is frequently the case with converts to a new cause, following his espousal of pragmatism Dewey carried on a lifelong critical debate with the idealist position he had abandoned. This debate gives his writing, like James's, a distinctly polemical tone, for Dewey rarely missed an opportunity to gibe at the incongruities and self-contradictions within idealism. Yet despite his diatribes against idealism as a metaphysic, Dewey consistently battled for idealism in practical morality and ethics. Metaphysical idealism, he felt, made such practical, experiential idealism impossible. Dewey remained a moral idealist while eschewing the traditional metaphysical basis for such idealism. He became, as Morton White remarked, "what an idealist becomes when he incorporates the results of modern biology, psychology, and social science"; he became a pragmatist.[12]

Even though James's writings were, as Dewey's daughter observed in a biographical sketch of her father, "much the greatest single influence in changing the direction of Dewey's thinking," from the beginning Dewey's pragmatism had a markedly different cast from that of James.[13] Each arrived at pragmatism by different routes, James moving from an original affinity for British empiricism and Dewey from long nurture in traditional idealism. Moreover, while each was discontented with the merely theoretical and shared an appetite for action and for concrete effects, their backgrounds and training gave them radically different reference points for assessing the nature and function of philosophy.

Philosophy always remained a personal, highly individual affair for James. So preoccupied was he with the need to demonstrate the personal contribution to the creation of reality, truth, and morality that he rarely paid heed to the larger context in which the individual operated; he almost totally neglected the social and historical dimensions of behavior and the personality. He firmly believed that "the individual, the person in the singular number, is the more fundamental phenomenon, and the social institution, of whatever grade, is but secondary and ministerial."[14] Consequently, his brand of pragmatism assumed that a "social organism is what it is because each member proceeds to do his own duty with a trust that the other members simultaneously do theirs," but it conspicuously failed to show why this should be the case or of what one's "own duty" should consist.[15] The result was a philosophy that opted so vigorously for individual freedom as to border on anarchism. While it opened the door to the possibility of social progress and improvement, James's pragmatism gave few clues as to what the actual experience of progress should be. James's universe was one in which meliorism was truly possible, but its melioristic capabilities depended on the singular goodwill and intelligent resolve of individuals acting independently of one another. And while James explicitly linked pragmatism and pluralism with meliorism, the latter concept was only one of a number of fascinating implications deriving from his basic belief that experience continuously flowed and that the individual mind worked selectively and creatively within its stream.

For Dewey, on the other hand, an individual's ideas and actions were intrinsically part of a dynamic sociohistorical process, and thus philosophy itself was a social activity. While Dewey too opted for a universe in which meliorism was possible, for him such a possibility became the very definition and raison d'être of the entire philosophic enterprise. In Dewey's opinion, human minds, individually and collectively, functioned to improve man's relationship to his natural and social environment; there could be no absolute separation between individual acts and social effects. As a result, the idea of progress constituted the warp and woof of Dewey's interpretation of the history of philosophy, its relationship to cultural and institutional change, the logic of logic, and the values and ethics that philosophers themselves were constantly criticizing and evaluating. Dewey saw clearly what James only partly perceived: that a philosophy stressing consequences and effects as the criteria of truth and value had itself to be assessed by its own extended consequences and, more importantly, that such an assessment at once took philosophy out of the philosopher's study and into the streets of society and the byways of history.

These differing perspectives help explain why James and Dewey regarded the contemporary situation in philosophy in somewhat divergent terms. James's stress on the personal resulted in his characterization of the "present dilemma in philosophy" as a clash of individual temperaments that construed reality in opposing ways. Dewey, who agreed that by the twentieth century Western thought had reached a state of crisis, understood the crisis to be a vastly more complex situation than James's characterization allowed. For Dewey, the crisis in thought was largely the cumulative failure of philosophy to adjust its terms and its logic to changing realities in the external world. While his analysis did not preclude or contradict James's explanation, it went far beyond it to inquire into the social and historical causes impelling rationalists and empiricists to comprehend reality so differently and to describe the disastrous effects upon society of their continued divergence. For James, the crisis was essentially an individual affair to be resolved by revamping the idea of experience, while for Dewey its lineaments reached out into social arrangements, back into history, and forward into the future; consequently, its solution required nothing less than a drastic reconstruction of *both* philosophy *and* society. Thus James saw the crisis in one-dimensional terms; Dewey saw it three-dimensionally. And whereas James refused to prescribe an ideological cure for the social aspects of the crisis, Dewey saw this as the sum and substance of philosophical responsibility.

*ii*

John Dewey believed that philosophy and civilization were intrinsically related processes that evolved interdependently. Developments in science and technology, in social institutions and conventions, in politics and economics, and in class structures and cultural mores directly carried over to condition prevalent philosophical orthodoxies. In turn, those orthodox ideas helped rationalize and explain society's institutional structures, values, and the behavior they required. Hence, from Dewey's viewpoint, the crisis in thought that precipitated the pragmatic revolt had to be explained in long-range historical terms that took account of the accumulated social and intellectual shortcomings of Western culture.

On the level of intellect, Dewey's indictment of traditional philosophy charged the ancient Greeks with a philosophical felony whose effects had plagued Western man for twenty-five hundred years. This Hellenic "original sin" was the separation of the real and the ideal, appearance and reality, into two essentially different universes. The resulting duality had come to pervade all aspects of Western thought, language, and culture, causing men since the time of Plato and Aristotle to ask the wrong questions about themselves and their world and thus to dissipate their energies on chimerical problems having no solutions that men might experience and truly know.

The Grecian separation of the real and the ideal came to produce various subdualities so deeply entrenched in the Western consciousness that they largely defined it. Mind and matter, body and spirit, man and nature, science and morality, subject and object, fact and value, means and ends, the changeless and the changing—all these rigid dichotomies stemmed from the original metaphysical sundering of the real and the ideal. Even such relatively modern dualities as the "individual" and "society" sprang from this traditional, rationalistic divisiveness.

In Dewey's opinion, rationalism's dualism, primarily because of its conception of knowledge and truth as *ab extra* to human experience, had had a paralytic effect on philosophy and on social and intellectual development generally. From the time of the Sophists, rationalism prevented men from going to their own experiences as the source of knowledge of the good and the true. As a result, philosophy had become an exotic, esoteric means of preserving culture's sacred cows, its spirit apologetic rather than exploratory, its purpose retentive and defensive rather than aggressive and inquiring. "It became the work of philosophy to justify on rational grounds the spirit, though not the form, of accepted beliefs and traditional customs."[16]

More specifically, rationalism's dualistic predilections resulted in a hierarchy of values that placed the permanent and changeless ideal above the moving and changeable real, the spiritual above the material, and the past above the present and the future. Practical, usable, mundane knowledge was devalued in favor of

the more aristocratic "quest for certainty," the mission
to seek out and possess an absolute truth that transcended time.[17] Since the ideal was immutable,
philosophers saw their office as the building of ever
larger and more comprehensive ontological systems
whose very stasis gave assurance that they were
approximating the ineffable and leaving behind the
transient glut of common experience. By accepting this
hierarchy of values, "philosophy bound the once erect,
form of human endeavor to the chariot wheels of cosmology and theology."[18] Separated from the timeserv-
ing real, the ideal became a "refuge, an asylum from
effort. Thus the energy that might be spent in transforming present ills [went] into oscillating flights into
a far away perfect world and the tedium of enforced
returns into the necessities of the present evil world."[19]

From the social standpoint, throughout history
absolute truth in one form or another had always
become the special province of some institution or class
in whose defense philosophers manned the ramparts.
The prototype for the resulting division of labor and
virtue was Athenian Greece, where a class of slaves did
everyday, menial labor and a class of thus "freed" citizens, priests, and philosopher-statesmen could pursue
knowledge of the ideal without having to involve themselves too intimately with commonplace concerns. But
whether Greek city-state, the Christian church, feudal-
barony, nation-state, economic interest, or political
party, there always had been in history some exclusive
corporate body claiming privileged access to essential
truth and goodness. By asserting squatters' rights, this
agency marked off some segment or interpretation of
human experience as its private domain and defended
it stoutly against all encroachment. Such social arrangements Dewey saw as the direct result of a philosophical
dualism perpetuating private, inaccessible truth above

the flux and crudity of ordinary experience. By virtue of such an exclusive ownership of truth, institutional oligarchies with an official doctrine of human nature and destiny assumed authority to legislate morality for everyone. Only the orthodox rendering of meanings told men what their diverse experiences could signify.

The result of this kind of elitism was that progress gained by intelligent inquiry into the interaction between human nature and the environment, natural and social, was made infinitely more difficult than need ever have been the case. Inevitably, these elitist institutions, with their private, monopolistic conceptions of the truth, came to regard any intellectual change or innovation as a threat. Because philosophy both served and reflected the traditional values and beliefs of the custodians of the culture, innovators or agnostics had to muffle their voices or suffer dire consequences. Even when the experiences of people brought their inherited beliefs into question, a formidable social and intellectual apparatus was ready to mobilize against advocated change. But in the long run, such inflexibility usually proved futile, even though short-term resistance might have been successful. "All that institutions have ever succeeded in doing by their resistance to change," Dewey wrote in 1936, "has been to dam up social forces until they finally and inevitably manifested themselves in eruptions of great, and usually violent and catastrophic, change."[20]

The scientific revolution of the sixteenth, seventeenth, and eighteenth centuries was one of those great eruptions, a time when the accumulated shocks to European culture brought on by the end of feudalism, the rise of the city and the nation-state, the discovery of the New World, and the Protestant reformation produced a revolutionary new climate of intellectual and scientific opinion. The intellectual origin of this revolution lay in Copernican physics; its prophet was Francis Bacon, whose practical, empirical approach to the question of knowledge, apothesized by his famous dictum that "knowledge is power," exemplified a new and more secular attitude toward man's relationship to nature. Bacon saw the great body of learning inherited from the classical and scholastic past as a useless, unworkable encumbrance perpetuated largely by the weight of tradition and the hoary authority of an unassailable, entrenched class of knowers. For Bacon, "progress [was] the aim and test of genuine knowledge," and progress could only be achieved by applying disciplined methods of inquiry to the problems men faced every day in dealing with nature and with each other.[21] The Baconian view was the forerunner of modern pragmatism, a still newer and more scientific way of looking at experience and nature.

> To Plato, experience meant enslavement to the past, to custom. . . . When we come to Bacon and his successors, we discover a curious reversal. Reason and its bodyguards of general notions is now the conservative, mind-enslaving factor. Experience means the new, that which calls us away from adherence to the past, that which reveals novel facts and truths. Faith in experience produces not devotion to custom, but endeavor for progress.[22]

The upshot of this Baconian refraction, extended by Newton in physics, Descartes in logic, and Locke in political theory and psychology, was to shift the focus of men's reason away from questing after the eternal absolute and toward the discovery of nature's laws as revealed to reason and experience. Science became less concerned with cosmic first causes than with the

immediate causes of particular observable phenomena.
Linked intimately with rapidly changing commercial,
political, and technological innovations, this empirical
revolution "tended to wean men from preoccupation
with the metaphysical and theological, and to turn their
minds with newly awakened interest to the joys of
nature and this life."[23] By regarding the problem of
knowledge as experiential and particularistic and the
sensing individual as an agent vested with power to use
reason and knowledge to attain his own ends,
philosophers in the Baconian tradition helped
inaugurate a new world in which science, democracy,
individualism, and progress were the watchwords, a
world in which man's primary intellectual energies
were directed toward the mastery of the natural environment through the discovery of its laws.

> Hence the conception of progress as a ruling idea;
> the conception of the individual as the source and
> standard of rights; and the problem of knowl-
> edge, were all born together. Given the free
> individual, who feels called upon to create a new
> heaven and a new earth, and who feels himself
> gifted to perform this task to which he is
> called:—the demand for science, for a method of
> discovering and verifying truth, becomes
> imperious.[24]

But despite the drastic alteration in men's attitudes
signified by this revolution, certain forms of absolutism, with their inherited dualisms and their persistent
conception of morality and truth as *ab extra* to human
experience, remained embedded in men's minds and
institutions. While Locke and others in the empirical
tradition eschewed much of the formal scholasticism of
the past they set up their own absolute dichotomies in

its place: sense data and the impressionable human mind, natural and human law, the individual and society. Even though experience was elevated to the threshold of knowledge, it was still assumed merely to give acquaintance with laws of nature that were themselves fixed and absolute. While Locke rejected the old, honorific notion of innate ideas, he retained the immutable laws of nature that allegedly bounded and gave meaning to the reasonable ordering of sense-data. Despite his activities as a knower, man was still assumed to function within fixed laws, which derived from the original design and purpose of the universe's chief architect. Thus, although greater value was given to the practical application of knowledge to modify and control the natural world, many of the prior intellectual habit patterns of the prescientific era remained.

As a result, in spite of the emergence and currency of the idea of progress, men's grasp of the real causes and dynamics of social change lagged behind their growing technological competency in restricted, specialized scientific and commercial undertakings. Although the early empiricists welcomed change, they assumed it inevitably worked in the interests of men because of the fixed laws of nature that governed human events.[25] "The philosophical empiricism initiated by Locke . . . optimistically took for granted that when the burden of blind custom, imposed authority, and accidental associations was removed, progress in science and social organization would spontaneously take place."[26] Yet the unquestioned assumption that there were fixed laws of nature meant that human efforts to effect social and historical change had to occur within exceedingly narrow and relatively unimportant limits. Moreover, according to Dewey's interpretation, "the fixed or necessary law [meant] a future like the past—a dead, an unidealized future."[27]

Before an "idealized future" could be achieved—before
the idea of progress could have true significance and
meaning—a second scientific revolution had to trans-
pire.

The Copernicus of the second scientific revolution
was Charles Darwin and its Bacon was William James
(and, one might add parenthetically, its Locke was
John Dewey). Whereas the first revolution was a reaction against the rationalistic strictures of scholasticism,
the second was an as-yet-incomplete reaction against
the sensationalistic epistemology of empiricism,
together with all the limitations to human aspiration
this view involved. Locke's psychology held a static,
unidirectional conception of experience, which
resulted in a hard-and-fast separation between the
atomistic individual (the knower) and the objects he
sensed (the known). Empiricism's absolute individual
was bound by sense-data that afforded only a partial
glimpse of reality. This kind of empiricism—what
Dewey called "mere empiricsm"—assumed that certain
kinds or sectors of experience were inviolable and
unyielding to rational inquiry (ethics and morality, for
example). Precisely how things experienced (or not
experienced) became "moral" was a continuing embar-
rassment to empirical thinkers. Such, at least, was the
situation until James, proceeding from a Darwinian vision of the world as an evolutionary process, demonstrated that experience was a dynamic, flowing stream
and that within its boundaries consciousness and will
could be truly creative. The second scientific revolution
would not be complete, however, until philosophy and
science had fully assimilated James's insight and
applied it to all problems of knowledge and life.

Staggering in its scope and import, this was nonetheless the task Dewey set for himself. It involved, first,
a reconstruction of philosophy into an instrument for

the conscious, deliberate improvement of men's everyday lives. Instead of a restricted method for solving the problems of philosophers, philosophy was to be transformed into a workable device for taking events that brutally occur and helping men to understand their significance and to infer their probable consequences. As he put it in *Essays in Experimental Logic*, "the chief function of philosophy is not to find out what difference ready-made formulae make, *if true*, but to arrive at and to clarify their *meaning as programs of behavior for modifying the existing world*."[28] Philosophy in all of its aspects—logic, metaphysics, ethics, epistemology, and values—had to culminate in the art of responsible social control and improvement if it was to justify its existence and seize upon the opportunities that modern science afforded it. This meant not only discovering and defending what was of value from the past but assessing the effects of those values when acted upon in terms of present and future needs.

The second aspect of this reconstruction was to insure that philosophy as a modern, experimental instrument actually canalized society's moral aspirations and effectively directed them toward specific goals. However rationally correct, a philosophy that produced no social consequences or changes was moribund and worthless. Dewey's philosophy aimed at clarifying the issues of social conflict in the twentieth century and providing guidelines for their resolution. A merely empirical, descriptive philosophy was impotent to this end. Experimental and pragmatic rather than merely empirical, Dewey's philosophy intended "to carry over into any inquiry into human and moral subjects the kind of method (the method of observation, theory as hypothesis, and experimental test) by which understanding of physical nature has been brought to its present pitch."[29] The current crisis in philosophy and society arose because the methods of modern science had been used primarily to achieve specialized, pecuniary goals formulated while rationalism's values still prevailed; consequently, they were often, in effect, antisocial. "Science," Dewey complained, "has hardly been used to modify men's fundamental acts and attitudes in social matters."[30] Dewey believed that if the experimental method in philosophy and science was systematically applied to the pressing social and political questions of the day, merely gratuitous social change might be converted into consciously wrought and directed social improvement.

> Philosophy thus has a double task: that of criticizing existing aims with respect to the existing state of science, pointing out values which have become obsolete with the command of new resources, showing what values are merely sentimental because there are no means for their realization; and also that of interpreting the results of specialized science in their future social behavior.[31]

The principal obstruction to this recasting of philosophy and society, involving as it did the application of modern science's methods of inquiry and testing to all philosophical and social questions, was the prevailing habit of mind that insisted science and morality be dealt with separately. This divisive habit, harking back to the ancient Greek split between the real and the ideal, was buttressed by such firmly established institutions and customs as the church, the educational system, the values and superstructure of corporate capitalism, and the sacrosanct mystique of the free, autonomous individual whose moral sensibilities and knowledge were allegedly unbroachable by science. If philosophy was to become a method for improving the quality of men's lives, it had to be capable of both criticizing human values and testing scientifically whether those values were satisfactory and effective. Philosophy and the experimental method had to merge, and the outmoded dualism that put fact and value into separate universes had to be rejected. Just as the first scientific revolution with its emphasis on empiricism began to transform men's relationship to the physical world, so the second revolution with its stress on experimentalism and human purpose would complete the transformation by applying the scientific method to all questions of human activity: physical, social, intellectual, and moral. From this transformation would emerge new progressive dimensions to the old human quest for power over its own destiny.

In rendering his interpretation of the crisis, Dewey was careful to show how experimentalism in philosophy was itself a historical achievement, that it derived from the long process of trial and error preceding the discoveries of Copernicus and Newton down to the refined methodology of Darwin and other moderns. There were several advantages to explaining philosophy's crisis in such historical or, as Dewey called it, "genetic" terms. In the first place, Dewey's tactic neatly drew the fangs of traditional rationalists by talking history rather than engaging in metaphysical disputation. Second, his genetic interpretation fatally linked philosophical absolutism to many reactionary and marginally operative values and institutions that by the early twentieth century were becoming, if not patently obsolete, less compelling and vital in men's lives. Finally, Dewey's account showed vividly how the social and economic conditions of a given period helped shape its intellectual issues and how, as those conditions changed, so too did the intellectual climate. His best example was his own times, when the dislocations of the modern industrial world could easily be seen as relating to the crisis in philosophy.

All of these tactics were carefully synchronized so as to put pragmatism generally and experimentalism specifically in the vanguard of intellectual progressivism. Dewey wrote as part of the honorable company of those who, like Bacon and James before him, asserted the power of liberated, free inquiry into all facets of human experience over against the inhibitions and prohibitions of the absolutistic shamans. His disarmingly simple and entirely naturalistic rendering of the history of philosophy made experimentalism seem the only sensible philosophic consequence of modern science and its opponents seem reactionary and self-serving practitioners of the powers of intellectual darkness.[32]

*iii*

Science for John Dewey was quite simply the best way of knowing the world. But knowing the world meant, among other things, the power to bring about desired changes in the knower's relationship with his environment; science became, then, the best method of putting the knower in a satisfactory relationship with the object of his inquiry. In Dewey's view, science was a way of altering, for the better, both the knower and his knowing. In the process, however, the knower, the method, and the known were all changed by the journey that was science, and the end of the journey, the attainment of sought-after knowledge, was but the start of a still newer embarkation. Thus, modern science involved a kind of doubling process, and its end, a certain quality in the experienced relationship between inquiry, the inquirer, and inquiry's object, was itself shifting and on-going rather than static and once-and-for-all-secured. Each subsequent usage of the knowledge that resulted involved a testing of whether that relationship still retained its desired quality.

This, in essence, was what Dewey meant by the experimental method. Its achievements in physics, chemistry, mathematics, and in applied technology and industry were part of everyone's experience in the twentieth century. Yet because of the ancient and entrenched dualism separating science and morality, or "things of experience and things in themselves concealed behind experience," experimentalism was only just beginning to make inroads into philosophy.[33] Its progress was impeded at every step by prejudices and customs whose roots extended back into the preexperimental years of the first scientific revolution. Philosophy's reconstruction required at the outset that experience, logic, and values be approached and interpreted experimentally and that the results of this approach be instrumentally applied to social and political reality.

For Dewey, as for James, the basic category was experience. In true Darwinian fashion, Dewey described experience as the total, reciprocal interaction between an intelligent organism and its environment. Whereas empiricists had seen experience as the passive impressment of discrete properties of the environment upon the senses, for Dewey experience encompassed the entire range of physical and psychical interactions (often called "transactions") between humans and their natural and social worlds. This rendering of experience as a wholly natural process destroyed the dualisms contained in previous philosophies by proclaiming experience to be the foundation and source of *all* knowledge. Since experience was a dynamic, total living process within nature, no hard-and-fast delineation could legitimately be made between cognitive and other modes of knowing, and thus the metaphysical backbone of the traditional dualisms was broken. This perspective, experimentalism's point of departure, opened new vistas for philosophy and society:

> In the first place, the interaction of organism and environment, resulting in some adaptation which secures utilization of the latter, is the primary fact, the basic category. Knowledge . . . is involved in the process by which life is sustained and evolved. The senses lose their place as gateways of knowing to take their rightful place as stimuli to action. . . . The whole controversy between empiricism and rationalism as to the intellectual worth of sensations is rendered strangely obsolete.[34]

Both rationalists and empiricists failed to see that "the function of sensory stimulation and thought is relative to the reorganizing of experience in applying the old to the new, thereby maintaining the continuity or consistency of life."[35] As for James, experience for Dewey was the raw material out of which men built, first by instinct and then, gradually, by conscious thought and intelligence, a world that gave them physical and moral satisfaction. The capacity for intelligent thought had itself evolved out of the need for human survival and the desire to make the terms of that survival increasingly agreeable. What, Dewey asked, was the nature of the relationship of intelligence to experience past, present, and future? The answer was essentially simple and starkly naturalistic: intelligence was a quality of experience that had evolved into a human faculty for facilitating the survival of the species. Throughout history, it had constantly developed and become more effective to this end. By the twentieth century, this evolutionary process had reached the stage where men's intelligence could know the process by which it had come to be.

That is to say, if we look at human history and especially at the historic development of the natural sciences, we find progress made from a crude experience in which beliefs about nature and natural events were very different from those now scientifically authorized. At the same time we find the latter now enable us to frame a theory of experience by which we can tell *how* this development out of gross experience into the highly refined conclusions of science has taken place.[36]

The real burden of that quality of experience called "intelligence" was to insure that continually improving methods for "reorganizing experience" were developed. As a device for this kind of knowing, empirical science in the past had given men considerable control over certain portions of their conduct and their environment. In the post-Darwinian years, however, history had become self-conscious; it had produced a truly intelligent knower whose knowing capacity had the same doubling effect as experimental science. Thanks to experimentalism, men were now able not only to select and test intelligently material from experience which bore on its reorganization, but they were also able to comprehend the process whereby they did so and to apply that process to the selection and verification method itself. This possibility was, in Dewey's eyes, the ultimate philosophical expression of the Darwinian revolution and the center of the new possibilities opened to philosophy by the second scientific revolution. As Dewey put it,

> Intelligence is a quality of some acts, those which are directed; and directed action is an achievement not an original endowment. The history of human progress is the story of the transformation of acts which, like the interactions of inanimate things, take place unknowingly to actions qualified by understanding of what they are about; from actions controlled by external conditions to actions having their guidance in their intent:—their insight into their own consequences.[37]

Defined this way, intelligence meant that philosophy's legitimate concern was no longer with static and ontological questions but rather with conceptions that were dynamic, teleological, and purposefully aimed at qualitative adjustments within the process of living.[38] The time had arrived, Dewey announced, "for a pragmatism which shall be empirically idealistic, proclaiming the essential connexion of intelligence with the unachieved future—with possibilities involving a transformation."[39] A new and more scientific idea of progress was central to this kind of philosophy, for human progress was the goal and measure of experimentalism.

> The change of attitude from conservative reliance on the past, upon routine and custom, to faith and progress through intelligent regulation of existing conditions, is, of course, the reflex of the scientific method of experimentation. . . . By this method the notion of progress secures scientific warrant. . . . The prime necessity for scientific thought is

that thinkers be freed from the tyranny of sense stimulation and habit, and this emancipation is also the necessary condition of progress.[40]

Philosophy in the modern world had to become experimental, and experimentalism applied to the whole range of human activity and experience was the method and "necessary condition" of progress.

This concern of Dewey's to secure for progress a scientific "warrant" determined his approach to a number of specific philosophical topics, particularly questions of logic and value. Traditional philosophies regarded these categories of knowing in terms of their relationship to fixed forms, to the allegedly higher reality of the ideal behind the appearance of changing times. When regarded experimentally, however, logic became disciplined inquiry into the process of inquiry, and value became the process of evaluating that which had authority in human motivation. Both processes referred back, ultimately, to the point at which all intellectual activity began: the thoughtful organism consciously using its intellect to alter and improve its life experiences.

Dewey believed logic had always been a *"progressive discipline,"* resting upon "analysis of the best methods of inquiry (being judged 'best' by their results with respect to continued inquiry) that exist at a given time."[41] As the methods of science gradually improved, corresponding modifications took place in logical theory. Cartesian logic, for example, was a direct reflex of the first scientific revolution. But with Darwin, science had become radically experimental, rendering traditional, formal notions of logic obsolete.

Dewey's quarrel with formal logic, extending from the early *Studies in Logical Theory* (1903) through *Essays in Experimental Logic* (1916) to his most mature exposition, *Logic: The Theory of Inquiry* (1938), was that logic as traditionally practiced aimed at reproducing the eternal forms of ontological principles rather than serving as a corrective to the process of experiential inquiry. Formalistic logic derived from the notion of truth as that which corresponded to some immutable category of things-in-themselves. This kind of logic claimed verity if its forms and sequences corresponded to absolute principles governing induction and deduction. Such a conception, abetting and reflecting the ancient "quest for certainty," Dewey believed profoundly incompatible with the experimental practices of modern science.

By contrast, experimental logic took as its essential feature the instrumental, survival-oriented quality of thought itself and, rather than attempting to mimic some universal constant, aimed at "control of the environment in behalf of human progress and well-being."[42] Rationalistic logic attempted to establish universal principles of discourse independent of specific human inquiry; it proceeded from metaphysical principles that were assumed to antedate the particular problematic situations to which logic could be applied. Such an assumption, Dewey held, claimed more for the nature of thought than modern science, particularly psychology, could allow. Logic arose, Dewey argued, not from the imperative of fixed principles but from the particular requirements of indeterminate or problematic situations and from the kinds of resolutions that would be satisfying to those who inquired into them. Since logic was essentially the best way of resolving indeterminate situations, its claims could legitimately extend only to highly personalized solutions of the problem at hand.

The essential message of experimentalism was that

logical inquiry always had to result in some definite, purposive change in the physical world before the term "logic" applied. For Dewey, if inquiry did not contribute directly to some actual manipulation of some aspect of nature, it was fundamentally meaningless; logic had to result in the indeterminate situation becoming logically determinate in some real, physical sense. The notion of universal logical principles, Dewey felt, fostered intellectual irresponsibility in the face of logical indeterminacies, whereas experimental logic, with its emphasis on the concrete effects of specific inquiry, introduced responsibility into intellectual life: "To idealize and rationalize the universe at large is after all a confession of inability to master the course of things that specifically concern us. As long as mankind suffered from this impotency, it naturally shifted a burden of responsibility that it could not carry over to the more competent shoulders of the transcendent cause."[43]

Thought grounded in human experience, as all thought had to be, was incapable of "assailing" universal ends. Thought was teleological and selective, not cosmic and ontological; its goal was not copying some dimly apprehended *ding an sich* but rather constructing a hypothetically projected "end-in-view" which, when made the basis of certain deliberate actions, might render the problem at hand experientially determinate. There was, to be sure, no guarantee that any given action or end-in-view would produce the desired experiential qualities of resolution. But the end-in-view did constitute a provisional means for action that offered new possibilities for both resolution and for the further inquiry such resolution might occasion.

Thus experimental logic, with its goal of specificity, concreteness, and change, had the same progressive, doubling quality as modern science generally: it aimed at providing a method whereby thought processes resulted *both* in the continuing realization *and* subsequent revision of whatever end-in-view arose from a problematic situation. No formalistic, a priori prescription for this could suffice, for whether an idea was logical could not be ascertained until it was acted upon and had consequences. Those consequences, in turn, renewed the process of inquiry and made experimental logic continuous, "progressive inquiry."[44] As one philosopher put it in summing up "the core of Dewey's way of thinking,"

> Ends vary from situation to situation and every end, when attained, becomes a means to some further end in every new situation in which it can thus function. Human experience is a progressive reconstruction of ends as well as a selection of means for the realization of ends already accepted, and the vital task of moral philosophy is to provide a method by which men may guide their reflection in performing this two-fold task.[45]

Experimentalism emphasized that ideas could be considered logical only in terms of the deliberate actions they precipitated and the particular purposes of the inquirer; accordingly, it required a constant testing of these variables. The result was a relativistic conception of logic whose forms and standards changed from inquiry to inquiry and from time to time. This kind of logical relativism, with its constant reference back to human experience and purpose, led to repeated charges by Dewey's critics that his logic neglected the constancy of mathematics and its symbolic representations. But for Dewey the test of logic was the achieved resolution of some interruption in the flow of experience, not whether a given idea fit neatly into some Aristotelian, procrustean bed. Dewey's thinking about logic was characteristically open and democratic. As he once remarked with the casualness that enraged his more formalistic adversaries,

> Any proposition that serves the purpose for which it is made is logically adequate; the idea that it is inadequate until the whole universe has been included is a consequence of giving judgment a wrong office—an error that has its source in failure to see the domination of every instance of thought by a qualitative whole needing statement in order that it may function.[46]

It was one thing, however, to argue that logic was relative to human experience and purpose and that its goal was the realization of a particular end-in-view as distinct from an end as universal essence, and quite another to establish guidelines for selecting appropriate and beneficial ends-in-view. As was the case with logic, Dewey's experimentalism lent to the study of values the best of recent scientific thinking and turned value theory into yet another facet of man's attempt to improve his transactions with his environment.

Dewey saw value arising from alternatives men contemplated in attempting to survive and progress in the natural world. Man's ability to think and his power to choose between different courses of action introduced a qualitative dimension into what would otherwise have been a merely quantitative world. Men, not God or some other prior ineffable, were the creators of value; value was a wholly natural aspect of certain facets of experience. Value inhered in the self-conscious struggle to control the natural and social environment, and beyond this it had no meaning. Dewey's thoroughgoing naturalism was never more explicit than when he dealt with values and ethics.

Traditional conceptions drew a distinction between intrinsic and extrinsic, or final and instrumental, values. Intrinsic values were those properties or things relating to some prior, eternal set of standards; extrinsic values were of a lower order, having value only insofar as they bore on or advanced the interests of that having intrinsic value. Such a distinction, of course, Dewey saw as but another expression of the ancient preexperimentalist dualism separating essences from instruments or ends from means. Naturally, Dewey rejected this view. On the contrary, he argued, value attached not to ends as essences but to ends-in-view, to conceptualized solutions designed to remedy particular, temporal problems. Value was not intrinsic just as knowledge was not immediate: both were products of a selective or reflective process provoked and guided by an experienced problem and the purposes and goals of the experiencer. Valuation did not pervade the universe at large but it occurred, rather, within a specific existential context. And its nature and function, Dewey insisted, were subject to the same kind of scientific, experimental scrutiny as were other, nonvaluative ideas or things.

In John Dewey's eyes, humans engendered value upon the world whenever they elected one particular course of action over another. The essence of value was the process of choosing a path that led in a desired direction. Ideas were valuable as parts of a selective process; the valuable idea was "progressive, reformatory, reconstructive, synthetic" in expediting human purpose and extending human will.[47] "There are values, goods, actually realized upon a natural basis.

. . . The idealizing imagination seizes upon the most precious things found in the climacteric moments of experience and projects them. We need no external criterion and guarantee for their goodness. They are had, they exist as good, and out of them we frame our ideal ends."[48]

Dewey's theory of value grew out of his conviction that thought functioned to secure imagined goods and to promote their actualization in a real, experiential context. The proper role of value theory, as of all philosophy and logic, was to facilitate this very human quest. If this concern with the mundane process of life adjustment made philosophy seem trivial and ordinary, seem part of the commonplace problem-solving men go through daily, then so much the better. Fact and value could not be sundered, and it was in confronting the facts of ordinary experience that men best knew what in their lives had value. Conceptions of value that attempted to measure man's experiences by remote, immutable standards turned man's attention away from (rather than toward) the concrete realities of value decisions. As Dewey put it in his early *Outlines of a Critical Theory of Ethics*, "The moral act is not that which satisfies some far-away principle, hedonistic or transcendental. It is that which meets the present, actual situation."[49]

Ideas, then, have value insofar as they are effective plans of action for solving problems and for modifying the conditions of life in more satisfying ways. But since experience is in constant flux, values themselves must continually be changed to meet new demands and expectations. Fixed systems of value render "men satisfied with the existing state of affairs and to take ideas and judgments they already possess as adequate and final."[50] An adequate theory of value must be concerned first of all with its own continued revaluation;

values must have the same doubling character as
experimental logic if they are to meet the requirements
of modern scientific thinking. Every idea men advance
as valuable must be prepared to give way to new values
and meaning as knowledge accumulates and new ideals
are forged; an adequate theory of values must primarily be concerned with its own improvement.

> This sense of wider values than those definitely
> apprehended or definitely attained is a constant
> warning to the individual not to be content with
> an accomplishment. Conscientiousness takes more
> and more the form of interest in improvement,
> in progress. . . . The good man not only measures
> his acts by a standard, but he is concerned to
> revise his standard. His sense of the ideal . . . for-
> bids his resting satisfied with any formulated
> standard; . . . the good can be maintained only
> in enlarging excellence. The highest form of con-
> scientiousness is interest in constant progress.[51]

Dewey was well aware that such a relativistic
approach to values was deeply disquieting to those who
longed for the security of some permanent standard
of meaning, some expression of "ultimate" or "intrinsic" value by which to measure their experiences.
Dewey's reply to his absolutistic critics was that since
values themselves came out of experience, it would
hardly be realistic to expect experience to reveal that
which it did not, and by its very nature could not,
encompass. Dewey did on occasion refer to a certain
order of values as intrinsic and ultimate, but his use
of such terms carried only a sequential significance.
"An instrumental value," he remarked in *Democracy and
Education*, ". . . has the intrinsic value of being a means
to an end."[52] Only if a given idea or value came at the

end of a series of inquiries into a series of problems might it be said to be ultimate. "There are things," Dewey wrote in reply to one critic,

> that come last in reflective valuation and, as terminal, they are ultimate. Now Dr. Geiger is quite right in saying that for me the method of intelligent action is precisely such an ultimate value. It is the last, the final or closing, thing we come upon in inquiry into inquiry. But the place it occupies in the temporal manifestation of inquiry is what makes it such a value, not some property it possesses in and of itself, in the isolation of non-relatedness. It is ultimate in use and function; it does not claim to be ultimate because of an absolute "inherent nature" making it sancrosanct, a transcendant object of worship.[53]

Values functioned essentially as agents for transforming inevitable change into conscious actions that made progress experientially possible. Yet wherever there was progress, wherever there was deliberate, planned change for the better, tension between custom and innovation was inevitably present. The exercise of value options always raised serious questions about how much of the present deserved conservation and how much change could be effected without mere anarchy "loosed upon the world." Demands on the one side for personal freedom, for variety and progress, were sure to be countered on the other side by demands for preservation of the established pattern of doing things. Dewey, like James, saw pragmatism as a middle way between the extremes of flux and stability: with experimentalism, "not order, but orderly progress, represents the social ideal."[54]

In the final analysis, Dewey's theory of value

assumed that progress resulted from people's desire to actualize in the future a moral order not currently extant, and it aimed at providing a standard that would itself progress as new experiences in this direction accrued. The role Dewey envisioned for logic and values—and for philosophy generally—was to provide individuals with a scientific, self-correcting method of reflection to help them accurately assess their present circumstances and realistically plan for their continual improvement.

*iv*

The social crisis John Dewey confronted arose principally from the lag of certain ideas and conditions behind intellectual—particularly scientific—advance. The world as he saw it was in profound dislocation; its progress was random and uneven, its values were reflexes from bygone days, its institutions were reactionary formalisms that too often had outlived the historical conditions that called them into being. As an intrinsic component of culture, philosophy reflected this dislocation and would continue to do so until it incorporated the tenets of experimental science. Once this was accomplished, experimentalism could be systematically applied to the pressing problems of society. So the experimental rendering of logic and values was only part of Dewey's reconstruction; the building of an experimental, progressive society remained.

Dewey's antidote for the crisis called for replacing all existing modes of authority with experimentalism. Only a society free and open enough to countenance scientific experimentalism might expect to order its problems and guide its future in a satisfactory, progressive way; and that kind of freedom and openness

could only obtain in a society whose institutions themselves emulated the ongoing, self-corrective processes
of science. So Dewey's prescription aimed at recon-
structing the forms of social authority along the lines
of the most humane and intelligent understanding of
experimentalism. Not unsurprisingly, this reconstruction resulted in a vigorous reassertion of the peculiar
virtues of democracy.

Dewey saw philosophy as not just a reflection of a
civilization—although it was indeed that—but as a vital
force contributing to its improvement. Experimentalism as a social philosophy was his attempt to put a scientific and moral foundation under progressive social
change. The "Good Society," the end-in-view of
Dewey's experimental philosophizing, could be reached
only by a philosophy that found the "ultimate measure
of intelligence in consideration of a desirable future
and in search for the means of bringing it progressively
into existence."[55] Intelligence, like morality, had traditionally been considered an individual rather than a
social quality, and this, in Dewey's view, was a major
tributary of the crisis in society.

The individual, for Dewey as for James, was the
basic, "irreducible" experiencer and social unit. But
Dewey recognized, as James did not, that individuality
was a social achievement, that society was prior to personality. The singular individual, while seemingly
unique and independent, was actually the product of
associations that nurtured him from birth and that provided his capacity for experiencing with its particular
sensibilities and limitations. While the biological
individual was unquestionably the locus of experience,
both the meanings he inferred and the subject matter
of his perceptions were largely supplied and conditioned by the society that produced him. Intelligence,
knowledge, and morality were in reality actions con-

sequent to those perceptions, and thus, for all practical purposes, they were social categories. There could be no demarcation between the individual and the social, between the private dimensions of experience and their public expression in action. If there was to be genuine social progress, there had first to be a redefinition of individualism according to the requirements of experimental science.

Historically, the classical Lockean idea of individualism was a key weapon in the revolt against the old and limiting absolutes of church and state. "A theory which endowed singular persons in isolation from any associations, except those which they deliberately formed for their own ends, with nature or natural rights,"[56] individualism reflected a receptive attitude toward change based on the assumption that human nature, once freed from restricting social institutions, would effect progress. "The so-called individualism of the eighteenth century enlightenment was found to involve the notion of society as broad as humanity of whose progress the individual was to be the organ."[57] Human nature, unfettered, would inevitably effect beneficial social change—an assumption justifying the doctrine of laissez-faire. But by separating the individual from society, the theory in Dewey's view lacked any agency for securing the development of its ideal, and this deficiency had become acute as social and economic conditions changed.

The industrial revolution made good use of its inheritance of laissez-faire and was itself in part a product of that philosophy. By the latter half of the nineteenth century, however, the effects of industrialization had largely destroyed the basis of this inheritance. By the turn of the century, the older individualism, with its central doctrine of a fixed and atomistic human nature, had become bankrupt, but many

people nevertheless clung to its obstructionist preach-
ments. "They ascribe all the material benefits of our
present civilization to this individualism—as if
machines were made by the desire for money profit,
not by impersonal science."[58]

In reality, Dewey believed, civilization had progressed because of man's manipulation of nature in an
increasingly scientific and cooperative fashion and not
because of any foreordained improvement deriving
from the " 'free' play of the natural equipment of
individuals."[59] The idea that social progress was produced by the actions of individuals seeking private gain
in isolation from the rest of society may have been valid
in the earliest stages of industrialization, but by the
twentieth century this view was no longer tenable. The
fragmentation of society accompanying the industrial
revolution had brought about the critical need for a
new individualism requiring, "if there is to be moral
progress, a *reconstructed individual*—a person who is
individual in choice and feeling, in responsibility, and
at the same time social in what he regards as good, in
his sympathies, and in his purposes. Otherwise
individualism means progress toward the immoral."[60]

In redefining individualism to take into account the
true dynamics of modern society and the advances of
experimental science, Dewey drew upon and extended
James's pioneering work in psychology. But since
James's theory of the stream of consciousness defined
experience as essentially subjective and private, Dewey
found it necessary to make a crucial modification of
James's view. Experience was indeed the unbroken,
selective ebb and flow of an intelligent and singular
consciousness, but what was experienced, Dewey
insisted, was as much a part of "experience" as were
the mental processes of the individual who engaged in
experiencing. The environment was just as much a

part of the individual's experience as his mental responses to it, and his interactions with that environment, especially the social environment, had to be included in any adequate definition of the individual.

Contrary to eighteenth- and nineteenth-century versions of individualism, with their stress on innate individual rights derived from an unchanging, autonomous human nature, only in a social context could individuality truly be meaningful: true individual and social fulfillment occurred simultaneously. Under the aegis of Lockean individualism, however, society had evolved to the point where concurrent fulfillment was no longer possible; industrial society was marked by aggregates of force that too often advanced at the expense of the opportunities of private citizens to develop their capacities to the fullest extent possible.[61] Yet society's ethical center was still the shopworn certitude that somehow the unchecked exercise of individual self-aggrandizement and self-interest would eventually be beneficial for all.

This was no longer the case, and Dewey accordingly called for a new individualism that recognized that individual acts had inseparable social consequences and that "complete morality is reached only when the individual recognizes the right or chooses the good freely, devotes himself heartily to its fulfillment, and seeks a progressive social development in which every member of society shall share."[62] Viewed experimentally, individualism was not the isolated exercise of once-given, unchanging human attributes but the interaction—the transactions—between a person's private consciousness, his experiences within society, his choices and actions, and their social consequences intelligently apprehended. The individual did not, could not, have meaning apart from his social context. And the same held true for his intelligence.

In the preexperimental world, intelligence was viewed as an individual affair, as the indwelling capacity for rightness of certain fortunate and independent thinkers. Experimentalism, however, required a more dynamic and social definition; intelligence in the modern world implied the power to modify and control the total conditions of life and inquiry. It meant an increment of freedom from chance and an emancipation from what would otherwise have happened had intelligence not been exercised. Intelligence was a quality of those acts which foretold their own consequences, thus extending further thought and action. Such a definition clearly implied that intelligence had intrinsic social dimensions and obligations that were not fully grasped in the preexperimental heyday of Lockean individualism.

Thus the crisis with which Dewey grappled was at least partly caused by the inadequate conception of intelligence that still prevailed in the power centers of society.[63] Science, the method of intelligence, had for too long been the servant of a conception of individualism unaware of or indifferent to the legitimate social claims upon its exercise. Just as individualism was created by the conditions of associated life, so intelligence denoted the power and the responsibility of modifying the environment in prefigured and calculated ways; hence society had an indisputable claim upon its uses. Thus, intelligence, like individualism, had to be socialized; it was in this connection that Dewey's writings on education became such an important part of his response to the crisis.

Much scholarly ink has been spilled—deservedly so—proclaiming the importance of Dewey's educational ideas for his philosophy. As Dewey himself believed, his writings on education put his more abstract opinions to work; the heart of his philosophy, he once admitted, was expounded in *Democracy and Education*.[64] The primary reason for this was that Dewey's philosophy of education embodied the paradigm of experimentalism in its most practical and concrete form. In education, experimental science, intelligent knowing, and progress became one. As Dewey summed it up, "The reconstruction of philosophy, of education, and of social ideals and methods . . . go hand in hand; . . . philosophy may even be defined as *the general theory of education*."[65]

Education until the twentieth century had largely been considered a preparatory process in which the student learned by rote what his elders decreed it necessary for him to know to "be educated." The orientation of schools was toward the past, and their authoritarian methods focused on the dissemination of predetermined, ready-made truths. The effect of these practices on the student was to produce "a lack of interest in the novel, an aversion to progress, and dread of the uncertain."[66] The products of such schools acquired habits that enslaved them to tradition and custom and taught them that intelligence was the innate ability to reproduce fixed, a priori certainties. The result was that learning became a spectator affair in which excellence was measured by reverence for the culture's achievements, not its promise. Students were discouraged, in effect, from learning in ways that reflected what modern science taught about the function of intelligence and the selective, experimental nature of knowing. The consequences, Dewey thought, were disastrous: "To educate on the basis of past surroundings is like adapting an organism to an environment which no longer exists. The individual is stultified, if not disintegrated: and the course of progress is blocked."[67]

In contrast with traditional views, Dewey's theory of

education was "progressive"; its object at every stage of the learning process was "added capacity for growth."[68] Dewey turned the process of experimental knowing into the ideal of education. If the emphasis in schools was on students' capacity to learn rather than on the digestion of prepackaged lumps of approved "knowledge," what would result was the start of an ongoing, self-corrective educational process in which the student provided the dynamics of his own expanding capacity for growth. "A possibility of continuing progress is opened up by the fact that in learning one act, methods are developed good for use in other situations. . . . The human being acquires the habit of learning. He learns to learn."[69]

In the past, students had acquired habits of learning that paralleled the older models of empirical science: learning was a unidirectional process of observation and emulation. The habits it inculcated were passive and conservative, and hence its products were ill prepared for life outside the confines of the school. Dewey's belief, on the other hand, was that students could learn habits that were progressive, not conservative, if the method of experimental science governed all the interactions in the schools. "In learning habits," Dewey argued, "it is possible for man to learn the habit of learning. Then betterment becomes a conscious principle of life."[70] For this reason, Dewey advocated nothing less than making the experimental method the primary lesson of the schools.

Thus reformed, the school would become the focal point for society's reconstruction because it was here that social values and mores were transmitted to the young. If children acquired early the habits of free inquiry and intelligent knowing, inevitably those habits would affect their society. If experimental knowing—the method of socialized intelligence—was society's educational model, then one could realistically expect that over time society itself might come to reflect the open, progressive habits of its members. The school, as Dewey put it, is "the essential distributing agency for whatever values and purposes any social group cherishes,"[71] and its methods and goals could be viewed as portents in microcosm of society's destiny.

This was why Dewey put such emphasis on the kind of knowing schools engaged in and made this, rather than any specific lesson, the goal of education. Such an education taught students how to know and how continually to grow in their capacity for knowing. Progressive schools would produce students who always quested for new knowledge and who would progressively seek newer and deeper meanings in that knowledge. Progressive education thus reflected the instrumental, doubling effect of experimentalism in a concrete way; its goal was the public teaching of intelligent knowing, and this by definition meant continual improvement in the process by which such knowing accrued. If society was in the midst of a protracted crisis arising from an inadequately socialized definition of intelligence, the place to attack the problem was where intelligent knowing was in fact defined and promulgated.

John Dewey had, then, a larger social purpose in mind when he advocated progressive education. If the schools taught first and foremost the method of experimental knowing, then the task of constructing an open, progressive society would be much easier. And a progressive society, for him, meant a democracy. It was for this reason that in choosing a title for his all-important book of 1916 Dewey yoked "democracy" and "education" together. As he stated, "The conception of education as a social process and function has no definite meaning until we define the kind of society we have in mind."[72] Democracy gave education its frame of reference just as progressive education furnished democracy with the socialized intelligence it so desperately needed.

The strong affinity between education and democracy rested, again, on the free, perpetually inquiring methodology of experimentalism. As Dewey expressed it, "the *problem* of education in its relation to [the] direction of social change is all one with the *problem* of finding out what democracy means in its total range of concrete applications; domestic, international, religious, cultural, *and* political."[73] Democracy, like progressive education, was open-ended in its goals and pluralistic and participatory in its methods. Both relied upon free communication and the uninhibited sharing of meanings in an ever-enlarging circle of experiences. Since knowing was an activity that purposefully modified the environment, it followed that the culture in which intelligent knowing functioned had to be receptive to change and ready to redirect its energies and priorities according to the new meanings discovered in new experiences. All of this, in Dewey's view, could best be realized in a democracy.

Why then was America, undisputably a democracy, gripped by a pervasive social and intellectual crisis? The answer was comparatively simple. Democracy in America had been shaped in the eighteenth and nineteenth centuries as a system wherein individuals, exempted from feudal or aristocratic restrictions, might freely exercise their natural rights and privileges. Such a society, guided by the invisible hand of a beneficent nature, would inexorably progress as individual wants and needs were gratified. But with the coming of industrialism, economic and technological consolidation, and conglomerate capitalism in the late nineteenth and early twentieth centuries, the social environment was radically transformed—often with tumultuous consequences for the individual. The "old" liberalism of John Locke, Adam Smith, and Jeremy Bentham, which advocated private self-interest, hopefully enlightened, as the vehicle for public progress —the philosophic credo of early American democracy—was an anachronism in this new environment. Just as the old individualism of Locke had to be redefined in the light of experimentalism's contributions to psychology, so the old liberalism that was its social extension had to be renovated according to the experimental method's criteria of effectiveness. The crisis of democracy was in large part a crisis of liberalism, and once again experimentalism promised a solution.

The ideological core of the old liberalism was its faith in automaticity. The free play of human nature, this liberalism assumed, would give rise to diverse interests which, in both the marketplace and the political arena, would somehow automatically find an equilibrium beneficial to everyone. This process allegedly reflected nature's laws and brooked no interference from such "artificial" agencies as government; governmental action had to be confined to a minimal, laissez-faire role that merely secured public order. Such order provided the optimal conditions for the natural give-and-take of competing individual interests out of which progress and community interest automatically arose and in which individual freedom and fulfillment were maximized.

But it had not worked out this way. Industrialism and laissez-faire capitalism combined to produce not progress and individual satisfaction but social stress, individual alienation, community fragmentation, and a haphazard kind of commercial growth that seemed to destroy with one hand as much of human value as it created with the other. "The local face-to-face community has been invaded by forces so vast, so remote in imitation, so far-reaching in scope and so completely indirect in operation, that they are, from the standpoint of the members of social units, unknown."[74] The old liberalism, in attempting to take account of human nature and provide latitude for its growth, ironically had helped create by the twentieth century conditions destructive of its individualistic ends. As Dewey summed it up:

> The present predicament may be stated as follows: Democracy does involve a belief that political institutions and law be such as to give fundamental account of human nature. They must give it freer play than any non-democratic institutions. At the same time, the [natural rights] theory, legalistic and moralistic, about human nature . . . has proved inadequate. . . . During the nineteenth century it was progressively overloaded with ideas and practices which have more to do with business carried on for profit than with democracy. . . . We cannot continue the idea that human nature when left to itself, when freed from external arbitrary restrictions, will tend to the production of democratic institutions that work successfully.[75]

Because of its faulty natural-law foundation, the old liberalism had to be replaced by a new liberalism if democracy was to survive. The foundation for this new liberalism was, of course, the experimental method and all that it implied about human nature, intelligence, and social change. The new liberalism's goals, generally, were the same as those of the older, laissez-faire liberalism: a progressive society permitting and encouraging maximum individual and community growth. But Dewey's new liberalism recognized that laissez-faire, natural-law doctrines that were "on the side of moral progress in the eighteenth and early nineteenth centuries" had by the twentieth century become "morally reactionary."[76] The new liberalism's ideal was democracy in the actual conditions of life experienced by individuals in the modern industrial and scientific world. Consequently, it "expresses the need for progress beyond anything yet attained; for nowhere in the world are those institutions which in fact operate equally to secure the full development of each individual and assure to all individuals a share in both the values they contribute and those they receive."[77]

Dewey was confident that since the method of experimental science and the processes of democracy were basically congenial, even parallel, democracy's most realistic hopes lay in science, which he believed was "by far the most potent social factor in the modern world." Yet science remained largely the property of a limited technology that had extended enormously "the scope and power of interests and values which antedated its rise."[78] Those interests, behind the bulwark of laissez-faire capitalism and a host of conservative social habits and values, steadfastly resisted science's application to large social and political questions. Science had to be democratized and democracy made scientific before true progress could be assured. Thus the real scientific revolution was yet to come; the old liberalism, an extension of the first scientific revolution, had produced a pervasive social crisis in the world's democracies, and it was up to the new, experimental liberalism to effect a cure. The scientific planning of public policy and the socialized intelligence created in the progressive schools were to provide the new liberalism with its method; democracy was to be its nexus.

Dewey believed that democracy, like experimental science, was open, provisional, and intrinsically public and communicative. Properly constituted, it stimulated original thinking by its citizens and evoked reactions to public policies so as to anticipate new problems and experiences.[79] There could be no single, compelling goal in a democracy beyond the continual refinement of the democratic process itself: a democracy aimed principally at maximizing the conditions for more intelligent and broader participation in public life and at the perpetual improvement of the means to this end. As with experimentalism, the policies it effected were ends-in-view rather than final, transcendent achievements.[80] For Dewey, the idea of a "progressive democracy" was a redundancy; a democracy was intrinsically progressive:

> To my mind the greatest mistake that we can make about democracy is to conceive of it as something fixed, fixed in idea and fixed in its outward manifestation. . . . No form of life does or can stand still; it either goes forward or it goes backward, and the end of the backward road is death. Democracy as a form of life cannot stand still. It, too, if it is to live, must go forward to meet the changes that are here and are coming.[81]

According to Dewey, democracy was both a humanistic and a scientific commitment. Its foundation was faith in the capacities of human nature, intelligence, and experience. It did not argue, however, that these things were complete in themselves, but that "if given a show they will grow and be able to generate progressively the knowledge and wisdom needed to guide collective action."[82] Such growth did not occur spontaneously, as the current crisis amply demonstrated. The new liberalism recognized that although democracy placed its reliance on the free capabilities of the citizenry, those capabilities could become systematically progressive only when linked with the experimental method. "The very foundation of the democratic procedure is dependence upon experimental production of social change; an experimentation directed by workable principles that are tested and developed in the very process of being tried in action."[83] The progress that resulted might mean different things to different ages, but its continuity was assured by its method.

Not only did democracy have to be explored and defined afresh by each generation, but its meaning could not be narrowly construed. A major part of Dewey's analysis of the crisis during the 1920s and 1930s arose from his recognition that political democracy was not, in and of itself, sufficient to realize the ends of the new liberalism. The challenge facing the new liberalism was nothing less than creating a progressive culture in which individuals and institutions were so imbued with the values and methods of intelligent, experimental knowing that no sector of social experience might be exempt from scientific inquiry. No single reform or public policy was sufficient to the needed transformation. Dewey's new liberalism was not so much a political program as a comprehensive social persuasion which included but went far beyond piecemeal political action. New liberalism was applied experimentalism, Dewey's act of faith in the compatibility and convergence of democracy, education, science, and progress.

*v*

Progress was the cornerstone of the entire range of John Dewey's thought. Every integrant of his philosophy—experience, intelligence, knowledge, logic, value, science, education—derived its essential meaning by how it improved man's relationship with his environment. The social categories of experimentalism —the individual, society, democracy—were all similarly defined and evaluated in the light of their progressive function and potential. And out of this casting, in turn, came a new definition of the idea of progress.

For Dewey, progress was open, processive, purposive, scientific, and democratic; it had no closed, fixed moral contours or teleology. Its constant reference was improving the means by which individual and social desires and experiences might be realized. Its standard was self-refining and self-redefining: the continued growth and development of "all the social capacities of every individual member of society."[84] Progress, in sum, was experimental.

This meant, among other things, that no single prescription or formula would guarantee progress. Progress, was, as Dewey liked to put it, a "retail," not a "wholesale," matter. The faith of previous generations in automatic, necessary progress was "childish and irresponsible." There were no cosmic forces outside human volition and action that impelled history's movement "whether or no." Change, to be sure, was a necessary, definitive ingredient of history, but change was merely the opportunity for progress; progress itself had meaning only in terms of the guidance and direction human beings gave to change. Science through experimentalism had given mankind the method for achieving progress on a broad social scale, but thus far its implementation had been piecemeal and fractional. Yet even if the scientific attitude did come to prevail, "progress in general" would still be an illusion.[85]

The notion of wholesale progress was the result of a rationalistic, holistic approach to social change without due regard for the actual processes by which change was effected. The idea that progress in general could take place tended to absolve the individual from responsibility for improving the conditions under which he lived. This was especially true if progress was seen as the result of some mechanical absolute such as divine providence, natural selection, economic determinism, or free competition. During the nineteenth century, such automatic conceptions of progress had become popular, and the results were disastrous. In Dewey's view, the notion of automatic progress resulted in thoughtless sentimentalism, itself partly to blame for such catastrophes as World War I. Confusing change with progress, Americans and Europeans had developed a fragile and irresponsible optimism that left them unnecessarily vulnerable to pessimism and resignation once the war came. Consequently, Dewey's experimentalism called for "the institution of a more manly and more responsible faith in progress than that in which we have indulged in the past."[86]

Progress, then, was particularistic. It occurred, in Dewey's Darwinian language, when obstacles to the free, continuous flowing of experiences provided "stimuli to variation" calling for new kinds of responses, and the mind of man consciously and intelligently planned for the obstacles' removal.[87] Progress was a case of "readjustment to certain environmental conditions by particular individuals."[88] Progress occurred when specific problems were met and mastered by intelligent planning.

Since progress was particularistic and subject to no overarching moral reference, there could be no absolute standard for its assessment. This immediately raised the question of whether, since progress was a relative term, it could have meaning as a social category. If progress was relative only to resolving the problems individuals experienced, would it not be legitimate to employ "progress" on behalf of private ends that were antisocial or even criminal? Could not one speak of progress as movement toward ends inimical to society's well-being and advance?

Such a problem might have been real in the preexperimental period when "the individual" and "society" were separate, even antithetical categories. The experimental redefinition of those terms, however, meant that individual conduct always had to be considered by its effects on society, and this criterion obviated the problem. Individual ends could not be considered in isolation from their social consequences; apart from society, there could be no moral standard for measuring the quality of action. As Dewey put it in *Experience and Education*,

> That a man may grow in efficience as a burglar, as a gangster, or as a corrupt politician, cannot be doubted. But from the standpoint of growth as education and education as growth the question is whether growth in this direction promotes or retards growth in general. Does this form of growth create conditions for further growth or does it set up conditions that shut off the person who has grown in this particular direction from the occasions, stimuli, and opportunities for continuing growth in new directions?[89]

Thus, while progress was indeed particularistic and

"retail," it was nonetheless inevitably a social phenomenon. Social growth provided the moral criterion
whereby individual actions might be termed progressive.

Just as social progress was the essential occasion for
Dewey's philosophy, so his experimentalism gave the
idea of progress its character and its reality. Qualitative
improvement in the lives of individuals in society had
always been the goal of progress, but experimentalism
now promised to provide this goal with a new measure
and a new method. While science had always been the
most efficient means for satisfying men's desires, it had
failed generally to modify the quality of human purpose. Real progress—what Dewey called sometimes
"significant" progress—had become possible only with
the advent of experimentalism, for the experimental
method provided a method of problem solving that
perpetually stretched men's imaginations with new possibilities and new meanings as their problems were
solved. Real progress, then, had the same doubling
character as the experimental method itself:

> Progress is sometimes thought of as consisting in
> getting nearer to ends already sought. But this is
> a minor form of progress, for it requires only
> improvement of the means of action or technical
> advance. More important modes of progress con-
> sist in enriching prior purposes and in forming
> new ones. Desires are not a fixed quality, nor does
> progress mean only an increased amount of satis-
> faction. With increased culture and new mastery
> of nature, new desires, demands for new qualities
> of satisfaction, show themselves, for intelligence
> perceives new possibilities of action. This projec-
> tion of new possibilities leads to search for new
> means of execution, and the progress takes place;

while the discovery of objects not already used leads to suggestion of new ends.[90]

Real progress, pragmatic progress, meant movement toward particular ends-in-view and the continuing modification and improvement of those ends as they became realized. The ends and means of progress were inseparable: progress was the deliberate movement toward constantly improving goals.

Dewey's faith in progress as a possibility challenging modern man continued to the end of his life. Two world wars and a depression only served to reinforce his conviction that most social problems were not so much the result of a Frankensteinian science as of the persistence of antiquated intellectual habits preventing men from using methods of experimentalism to achieve real progress. In 1916, he stated that "it depends upon man whether he wants [progress] or not."[91] After the war, in 1922, he wrote: "The doctrine of progress is not yet bankrupt. The bankruptcy of the notion of fixed goods to be attained and stably possessed may possibly be the means of turning the mind of man to a tenable theory of progress—to attention to present troubles and possibilities."[92] In 1940, with war in Europe threatening once again to engulf the United States, he reaffirmed his faith:

It is easy in the present state of the world to deny all validity whatever to the idea of progress, since so much of the human world seems bent on demonstrating the truth of the old theological doctrine of the fall of man. But the real conclusion is that, while progress is not inevitable, it is up to men as individuals to bring it about. Change is going to occur anyway, and the problem is the control of change in a given direction.[93]

And in 1948, only four years before his death, Dewey wrote that the events of the previous twenty-five years only clarified and underscored the need for philosophic reconstruction, for the creation of a new moral order based on "new ends, ideals and standards to which to attach our new means."[94]

Dewey's continuing faith in progress and science was not the unblinking naiveté of the sentimental liberal. He was keenly aware that the weight of tradition in the United States posed an intransigent barrier to the kind of forethought and planning his vision of progress required. Before experimental progress could become a systematic part of the American way of life, awareness of the interdependency of all components of culture had to dominate the public consciousness, and there was much in the American tradition of individualism that militated against this possibility. Dewey did believe, however, that a culture might be progressively reoriented through education, and his faith and work was directed to this end.

But Dewey's experimental definition of progress assumed an instrumental view of history he failed to expound fully. If it was possible for significant or real progress—realization of individual and social ends together with their progressive modification in light of evolving means—to take place, history had to reveal that such two-dimensional development was possible. Dewey on occasion asserted that it did and used such assertions to refute alternative historical interpretations, but his philosophy of history was insufficiently developed to serve as an adequate foundation for the pragmatic idea of progress.

From his very early years as a pragmatist, Dewey had viewed history instrumentally. His emphasis on thought and experience as processes of life adjustment inevitably pushed him in this direction. For Dewey, as for James, history was that part of the universe's development that derived from and had meaning in terms of human intelligence and purpose. History, as Dewey wrote in 1915, "is the record of how man learned to think, to think to some effect, to transform the conditions of life so that life itself became a different thing."[95] History's value was that it increased man's consciousness of how intelligence in the past had helped to create the present; only with that kind of awareness could the future be improved. "Intelligent understanding of past history is a lever for moving the present into a certain kind of future."[96]

Since history was essentially the record of human intelligence and purpose, no single principle could explain its development. Human interests were far too varied to be subsumed under any monolithic causal analysis. Dewey's view of historical change did tend to focus on the forces generated by interest and group conflict, and to this extent he was clearly in debt to Hegel's theory of the dialectic. But Dewey did not, like Marx, assume that any one type or mode of conflict was paramount and controlling throughout recorded time. For him, as for James, history was pluralistic and novel; it was not rigidly dialectical in any monistic fashion. As a Darwinist, Dewey felt the importance of natural and social conflict for historical change, but as an experimentalist, he also believed that man's mind could partly control the forces contained in his experience. "We do not merely have to repeat the past," he wrote in 1920, "or wait for accidents to force change upon us. We *use* our past experiences to construct new and better ones in the future. The very fact of experience thus includes the process by which it directs itself in its own betterment."[97]

This passage suggests the intimate linkage between Dewey's experimentalism and his view of history: experimentalism required that history be treated in precisely the same manner as any other mode of experience, as the raw material out of which current interests and desires shaped a more moral future. There were, of course, many kinds of human interests and desires. While Dewey saw conflict at the heart of historical change, he had far too vivid a sense of human complexity and cultural organicism to ascribe to any one kind of conflict the source of historical dynamism. Indeed, such a reductionist reading of history was in direct conflict with the openness and pluralism that experimentalism required.

It was for this reason that in dealing with Marxism, Dewey's historical assumptions became most explicit. Although by the 1930s Dewey had become an avowed socialist, he nonetheless felt Marxism to be false and "dated."[98] He firmly put the blame on laissez-faire capitalism for the imbalances and inequities of society in the 1920s and 1930s, but his new liberalism never embraced the extreme of national collectivism. Historical experimentalism, in Dewey's eyes, was a scientific middle ground between two paralyzing, unscientific historical views that actually prevented men from acting in morally responsible ways, for the rugged individualism of the old liberalism, like Marxist communism, called for "complete economic determinism."[99] Like Marxism, it posited a single, all-embracing historical law of social and economic change and progress:

> The person who holds the doctrine of "individualism" or "collectivism" has his program determined for him in advance. It is not with him a

matter of finding out the particular thing which needs to be done and the best way, under the circumstances, of doing it. It is an affair of applying a hard and fast doctrine which follows logically from his preconception of ultimate causes.[100]

The old liberalism had indeed produced a crisis, a "house divided against itself," in democratic countries.[101] And this crisis had been precipitated primarily because of the nonprogressive character of the philosophic basis of traditional individualism. But the substitution of one nonprogressive, monolithic theory of social action and historical causation for another would not ameliorate the situation. Dewey's criticism of Marxism paralleled directly his criticism of the old liberalism: "Marxism throws out psychological as well as moral considerations."[102] As an "illustration of the monistic block-universe theory of social causation,"[103] Marxist collectivism was inimical to significant social progress. "The collectivist fomula tends to set up a static social whole and to prevent the variations of individual initiative which are necessary to progress."[104] Just as James saw pragmatic meliorism as a philosophic middle ground between monism and empirical nihilism, so Dewey saw experimentalism as a middle ground between Marxism and laissez-faire individualism.

Fundamentally, Dewey rejected Marxism because its central doctrine of economic determinism was unscientific; as he charged in 1940, Marxism "violated most systematically every principle of scientific method."[105] By this, of course, Dewey meant that Marxism violated the principles of experimentalism, that its rigid adherence to a preconceived formula for understanding social change was diametrically opposed to free inquiry and that diversity of opinion on which modern science and true progress rested. Like the laissez-faire liberals of the nineteenth century, the Marxists could only read history as a flat, one-dimensional unraveling of an a priori causal scheme. Such a reading was intrinsically preexperimental and thus blind to the truly progressive character of historical change: "The radical who insists that the future method of change must be like that of the past has much in common with the hidebound reactionary who holds to the past as the ultimate fact. Both overlook the *fact that history in being a process of change generates change not only in details but also in the method of directing social change.*"[106]

Dewey's remarks about history represent the logical, inferential application of experimentalism to the problem of historical knowledge. Because of experimentalism's logic, Dewey believed that history had the same doubling quality as any other mode of inquiry: the historian, himself caught in the stream of current preoccupations, necessarily conveyed the present to the past and the past to the present. Each temporal sphere progressively propelled the other; history was a "double process. On the one hand, changes going on in the present . . . throw the significance of what happened in the past into a new perspective. . . . On the other, as judgment of the significance of past events is changed, we gain new instruments for estimating the force of present conditions as potentialities of the future."[107]

But such statements about history were really an experimentalist's act of faith, for they were unsupported by that meticulous, controlled research into the specifics of historical change that Dewey himself made the criterion of true knowledge. Experimentalism could logically expect that history would always be generating new change-making forces and that a crucial segment of those forces would be supplied by the ever-deepening pool of historical knowledge and meaning that was the precipitate of inquiry. Dewey was not a historian, and to a large degree he begged the all-important question of how inquiries into events long past afforded the inquirers that experience from whence came all knowledge. This crucial question, so central to the pragmatic approach to history and to the idea of historical progress, became the pivot of Charles Beard's most mature reflections.

# 6

# *Charles Beard:*

# *Civilization in America*

Two years before Henry Adams published his *Letter to American Teachers of History*, a young political scientist at Columbia University named Charles Beard presented a lecture on politics to his friends on the faculty. In that lecture Beard argued, as Adams had some years earlier in an essay "The Tendency of History," that only if the methods of science were applied to political studies and history could men ever achieve control over themselves and their future. But the "sciences" invoked by Adams and Beard belonged to different generations and to different intellectual expectations. Whereas Adams expected science to answer the riddles of cosmic destiny, Beard looked to science to reveal empirically the hidden realities beneath the surface of social and political experience; science for Beard was not entrée to infinity but an empirical "view of a certain aspect of human action."[1] While Beard would one day celebrate Adams for writing "at least one book that made Columbus's voyage worthwhile—the story of his education," in 1908 he had nothing but contempt for Adams's brand of grandiose, "scientific" imprecision.[2]

Beard was similarly contemptuous of the shirking of involvement that characterized Adams's response to the harsh, untidy realities of modern society. Whereas Adams had briefly thought of himself as a political reformer in the late 1860s, one glimpse of the sordid machinations of Grantism had shattered his resolve, and he had quickly withdrawn to contemplate in silence the serenity and order of medieval history. By contrast, Beard's response to the rough-and-tumble of politics was positive and strenuous: intimations of political wheeling and dealing only sharpened his appetite for deeper knowledge and personal involvement. When Beard turned to history for an explanation of politics, it was not out of fright or timidity but out of the tough-minded conviction that history was an instrument for righting political and social wrongs. History was not a refuge for the effeminate but a struggle in which only a strong assertion of moral principle might cause that principle to prevail; Beard's view of history combined Dewey's acute sense of process with James's "will to believe." While Adams cursed the formalistic darkness, Beard struck a progressive, antiformalistic flame.

Beard's attitude toward history was significant not only because of his spirited, persistent rejection of intellectual formalism but also because his rejection came to be witnessed and shared by an enormous and varied readership. Unlike Adams, whose most profound speculations about history were hurled at a tiny, neo-Brahmin elite, Beard wrote for the people—and he reached them. Writing on technical political subjects in traditional scholarly volumes, on public affairs and current events in popular essays and articles, on Euro-

pean and American history in widely circulating text-
books and monographs, Beard—often collaborating
with his wife Mary—was read by millions of his fellow
Americans. Not all of them liked or agreed with what
they read, for Beard could be as querulous and conten-
tious as he was eloquent and emphatic. But he could
not be ignored, and by the end of his life he had
become the most influential American historian of the
twentieth century. If the task and discipline of the historian had by then changed radically from what Henry
Adams believed them to be, Charles Beard as much
as anyone deserved the praise or blame.

Charles Austin Beard was born near rural Knights-
town, Indiana, in 1874. His father, a wealthy farmer,
banker, and real-estate speculator, was steeped in Radical Republicanism and in that familiar midwestern
Protestantism which confined itself to no denomination
but which gave to him a moral strength no mere synod
or congregation could impart. An admirer of Robert
Ingersoll and himself the son of an independent-
minded Quaker, Beard's father was also an impas-
sioned and optimistic defender of America's liberty
and destiny. Under his strong influence, Beard grew
up in an atmosphere marked by material comfort and
public-spirited individualism of the sort that produced
such ardent spirits as Jane Addams, Frederick C.
Howe, and Vernon L. Parrington.[3]

Most of Beard's precollege schooling was at the
Quaker Academy at nearby Spiceland, which he
attended in the 1880s. For several years thereafter, he
and his brother wrote, edited, and distributed a small
daily newspaper their father had bought for them. In
1895, Beard matriculated at DePauw University, a
Methodist college in Greencastle, Indiana. During his
student days, he spent several months in Chicago
where he listened to the speeches of William Jennings

Bryan and John P. Altgeld, visited and became lifelong friends with economist John R. Commons and Jane Addams at Hull House, and in general became aware of that world which had seemed so out of joint to Henry Adams only a few years before at the Chicago World's Fair. Beard's days in Chicago had a profound effect on him, and he soon became known at DePauw as a passionate advocate of social reform. A caricatured profile appearing in the university yearbook had Beard delivering an imaginary, but apparently characteristic, address to the student body:

> The time has come. . . . The old traditions and fossilized methods of the past must be smashed into smithereens and consigned to chaos. Let there now be ushered in an era of unlimited, unqualified and untrammeled freedom! Away with a moss-back faculty, moth-eaten orthodoxy, and give us true democracy! I move you that we declare war upon all things that at present exist.[4]

Upon graduating from DePauw in 1898, Beard embarked for England to study history and politics with Frederick York Powell at Oxford. England at that time, as Jane Addams observed, was the focal point for concerned social reformers.[5] The works of Kier Hardie, Beatrice and Sidney Webb, the Fabians, and the recently formed Labor party had opened new political vistas, and Beard found himself caught up in the swirl of reform. With another American, Walter Vrooman, he helped found Ruskin Hall, a labor college with semiofficial ties to Oxford, and for nearly two years he lectured at the college. His first book, *The Industrial Revolution* (1901), was an outgrowth of these early lectures.

Save for a half-year of graduate study at Cornell

University, Beard remained in England for nearly four years. Returning to the United States in 1902, he entered the graduate school at Columbia University, from which he received his Ph.D. in 1904. That year, he became lecturer in European and English history at Columbia, although by this time his interests were already shifting toward the emerging field of political science. In 1907, Beard became adjunct professor of politics, and in 1915 he became full professor. During this period, he organized and headed a new undergraduate major in politics and had close contact with such Columbia notables as Frank J. Goodnow, H. L. Osgood, John W. Burgess, E. R. A. Seligman, and, in particular, James Harvey Robinson and John Dewey.

In 1917, Beard abruptly resigned from Columbia to protest the firing of three faculty members whose pacifist views had incurred the wrath of Columbia's trustees and president, Nicholas Murray Butler. Although Beard happened not to agree with the views of the fired teachers, he felt that Butler and the trustees had infringed upon the sacred ground of academic freedom; in 1916, he himself had been hailed before the trustees, his views on the war had been sharply examined, and he had been ordered to warn his colleagues in political science not to teach anything that might inculcate students' disrespect for American institutions and values. Beard's letter of resignation in October 1917 charged, among other things, that Columbia was "really under the control of a small and active group of trustees, who have no standing in the world of education, who are reactionary and visionless in politics, narrow and medieval in religion."[6] His announcement to his class that he had resigned in protest of these conditions brought a standing ovation that lasted for fifteen minutes and left Beard mute, tears streaming down his cheeks. Ironically, one of the fired teachers later became an important New York City banker and a trustee of Columbia University, and Beard was awarded an honorary doctorate by Columbia in 1943. Yet his dramatic resignation, coming when it did, was widely hailed as an early, courageous blow for academic freedom in America.

After leaving Columbia, Beard bought and operated a four-hundred-acre dairy farm near New Milford, Connecticut; the farm was home for the rest of his life. Beard's return to the countryside, however, did not signal his withdrawal from academic and public affairs. In 1917, he became director of the Training School for Public Service, an offshoot of the Bureau of Municipal Research in New York City, and he remained in the post for five years. In 1917 and 1918, with James Harvey Robinson, Thorstein Veblen, and John Dewey, and others, he helped found the New School for Social Research, where he taught periodically for several years. In 1921, he took the lead in establishing the Workers' Education Bureau of America, and in 1922 he accepted an invitation from the mayor of Tokyo to study minicipal government in the Japanese capital. His success there led to his invitation to return the following year to assist in Tokyo's reconstruction after a devastating earthquake. Four years later, he was invited to Belgrade to help study efficiency in Yugoslavian government.

During the 1920s Beard lectured at various universities and continued to publish regularly on a variety of political, historical, and social topics. In 1926, he was elected president of the American Political Science Association, and, a year later, with his wife Mary, he published the first two volumes of the celebrated *Rise of American Civilization*, the work that secured his reputation as dean of American historians. From 1929 to 1934, Beard was active on the Commission on the

Social Sciences of the American Historical Association,
and in 1932 he authored *A Charter for the Social Sciences*,
the first of the sixteen volumes the commission produced. The following year, Beard was elected president of the American Historical Association and delivered to the membership his remarkable presidential
address, "Written History as an Act of Faith."

Throughout the 1930s, Beard was active on a
number of other fronts. In 1933, he helped organize
the stockholders of the Missouri Pacific Railroad (of
which he was one) to force the company, after a con-
gressional investigation, to pay interest due to owners
of its stock. Subsequently he helped to mediate a
threatening statewide strike of Connecticut dairy farm-
ers and to draft much of the dairy legislation enacted
following the settlement. In 1936, he was invited by his
old friend John Dewey to serve with Dewey on the
Commission of Inquiry into the infamous Moscow trial
of Leon Trotsky scheduled to meet in Mexico City, but
he, like his fellow historian, Carl Becker, decided to
decline.[7] Throughout the 1930s, Beard warned against
America's involvement in the quarrels of Europe, and
by the end of the decade he had become an active, vo-
ciferous isolationist; as war engulfed the world, Beard's
repeated message was that America should attend its
own concerns on its own continent, and he did his best
to get his message heard by as many as would listen.

Beard's apprehension over America's entry into
World War II evaporated after Pearl Harbor, but his
conviction that Franklin Roosevelt had cunningly ma-
neuvered the United States into war remained. This
conviction lay behind his last books, *American Foreign
Policy in the Making* (1946) and *President Roosevelt and
the Coming of the War, 1941* (1948), which contended
that Americans had been duped by a prowar president.
The two books triggered the outrage of the historical

profession, and Beard found himself vilified and criticized, often by former friends and supporters. The controversy made his last years unhappy ones, but he remained true to his beliefs and his instincts regardless of the personal or professional cost. When he died in September 1948, the tempest he had provoked was still raging.

Charles Beard was not an original, seminal thinker. His mind was quick, vigorous, ranging, and eclectic. He had, like James, a deep need to comprehend the "moral business," and throughout his life he searched for what Cushing Strout has called an "organizing vision of the historical process as a whole, moving toward some luminous goal."[8] In this, he was not unlike Henry Adams. But he also had an ingrained, equally deep skepticism about neat, formalistic historical systems that purported to explain the sweep of history. While Beard shared Dewey's sense of cultural organicism and historical continuity, he often expressed doubts about the extent to which the finite mind, limited by time and space and experience, could comprehend the totality of past and present. Beard had what James called the empirical temperament; while yearning for the repose enjoyed by the "tender-minded," he remained all the while a "Rocky Mountain tough." This combination led him, inevitably it would seem, toward pragmatism.

Yet Beard came to pragmatism late and not, as one might expect, primarily from exposure to the familiar American sources, James and Dewey. His pragmatism grew out of his native optimism, his persistent skepticism, and his reading in the late 1920s and early 1930s of such continental relativists as Benedetto Croce, Karl Heussi, Karl Mannheim, and Hans Vaihinger, all of whom were rebelling against the scientific positivism of the Ranke school. In the late 1920s, Beard also became aware that scientists themselves, as they assimilated the vast implications of Einstein's theory of relativity, were no longer certain of the ground on which they stood or of the tools with which they worked.[9] Uncertainty in mathematics and physics, coupled with new questions about historical relativity, forced him to reexamine the limitations and possibilities of historical knowledge. Out of that reexamination emerged a full-blown, if unsystematic, pragmatic theory of history. And central to that theory was a pragmatic conception of progress that Beard called the idea of "civilization."

Before Beard arrived at his pragmatic theory, however, he was subject to a number of important intellectual influences, all of which, sometimes incongruously, left their mark. In his student days, he had encountered and strongly rejected "the Johns Hopkins school of Teutonism"—the germ theory of Herbert Baxter Adams—which, Beard gibed, might almost be called "Totemism."[10] By contrast, Beard was strongly attracted to the environmentalism of Frederick Jackson Turner, to which he was introduced by his teacher at DePauw, Colonel James B. Weaver.[11] The result of his DePauw tutelage was a continuing sense of history as process, struggle, and change, out of which men slowly achieved a better life through their continuing efforts. From this historical sense grew Beard's predilection for the idea of progress, a concept that never lost its hold on his mind.

At Columbia, Beard's early assumptions about history did not substantially change, but his fifteen-year association with Dewey, Seligman, and Robinson made him increasingly cautious about large historical generalizations and increasingly preoccupied with empirically verified historical data, particularly economic data, and with their possibilities for explaining political events. The works of Seligman, Veblen, Robinson, and J. Allen Smith were particularly imporant, as his seminal *An Economic Interpretation of the Constitution of the United States (1913)* revealed. Beard's thinking at this time was very much in agreement with A. F. Bentley, whose *The Process of Government* (1908) stressed group conflict as the source of legal and political change. Beard's preoccupation with economic conflict persisted throughout the 1920s.

During that decade, Beard's thinking began gradually to change, and by 1930 he was becoming more philosophically self-conscious and more inclined to take seriously the speculative dimensions of history and social science. During the next decade, he kept in close contact with his friend and fellow relativist Carl Becker, and his writings made frequent allusions to Dewey, James, and Croce. Beard also reread the collected works of Marx and Engels (in the original German edition) and rediscovered Henry and Brooks Adams. While their influence is difficult to measure, these figures do reveal the length and breadth of his attempts to reach some concept of historical reality and understanding. But when Beard took up his pen to put all these diverse influences to work, the result was distinctly his own: a blend of pragmatic progressivism that combined John Ruskin's aestheticism, James Madison's realism, Croce's skepticism, James's intellectual courage and moral hardihood, Dewey's experimentalism, and Frederick Jackson Turner's sense of America's unique democratic heritage and destiny.

While it is difficult to measure the effect of particular influences on Beard, it is even more difficult to assess Beard's impact on others. Certainly he was a major contributor to that developing sense of historicity and confidence that marked the resurgence of reform sentiment in the Progressive era and helped keep Americans aware of the proud dissenting tradition that was theirs. His efforts to redefine history and

its relationship to the social sciences contributed
uniquely to the sociology of knowledge in America,
and his frequent criticisms of public policy, grounded
as they were in a thorough knowledge of American history, made a large reading public aware of the continuity of past and present. Beard's opinions on many
matters were heard far beyond the walls of the
academy. His forty-nine major books had, by 1954,
reached over eleven million readers, and since that
time many of his works have been reprinted in paper-
back.[12] For several generations of students, Beard's
interpretations of history and foreign policy were conventional wisdom; *A Basic History of the United States*
(1944) sold almost 650,000 copies, and *The History of
the American People* (1918) sold nearly two million! And
Beard's hundreds of articles, essays, and book reviews
reached an even wider audience. If his scholarship and
judgment were sometimes questioned and challenged,
there can be no gainsaying the extent to which he
defined the terms of the controversies that ensued.
Charles A. Beard was definitive in American historical
thought for several decades in the first half of the
twentieth century.

*ii*

Like many other scholar-reformers who came of age
around the turn of the century, Charles Beard was suspicious, even derisive, of holistic, a priori theories of
history and society. Historians and social scientists, he
insisted, should resist abstract systems, however allur-
ing their symmetry, and embrace instead thorough collections of empirically gathered data as they bore on
specific, carefully defined problems in human experience. From the beginning an ardent, instinctive anti-

formalist, Beard maintained that even such commonly used terms as "institution," "state," or "society" had to be employed cautiously, for such abstractions could easily become glib facades for the merely metaphysical. To approximate "reality," the investigator had to confine himself rigorously "to a description of concrete practices."[13] Law, he wrote in 1913, when "separated from the social and economic fabric, . . . has no reality."[14]

This stringent antiformalism expressed Beard's conviction that the scientific method was the only means to social and historical truth. To be scientific was to be objective, neutral, empirical; there was no margin for preconceived abstraction in the quest for the kind of knowledge true scholarship required. Fact and value were different modes of thought, and the scientific researcher was properly concerned only with the former. Scientific studies had to be divorced from ethical considerations, and only empirical methods could provide the data required for a science of society, a project toward which Beard saw his own research contributing. Thus, Beard could write that "the formation and expression of ethical judgments do not fall within the historian's province" and that the study of politics "for scientific purposes" should be disengaged from "ethics."[15] The methods of the physical and the social sciences were, ideally, the same. "Political science," he declared in 1917, "is to be the greatest of all the sciences. Physics and politics are to be united, but the former is to be the bondsman."[16]

Beard's early brand of empiricism assumed that historical reality was in essence political and economic and that the empirically revealed phenomena of society fell neatly into categories of cause and effect, which a discerning student could take apart and put together as "tiny bits of intricate machinery."[17] Society's problems

were to be met "out of the fullness of concrete experience which history records, not by reference to abstract
doctrines set up *en vacuo*."[18] Accordingly, Beard was
unwilling to give much weight to philosophy or
ideology as real causes of historical events, his antiformalism occasionally giving way to a rather shallow and
strident anti-intellectualism. Ideas in Beard's estimate
were somehow unscientific; they could not be
measured empirically and their influence could not be
traced with exactness. One of his frequent criticisms of
historical writing was that scholars emphasized too
strongly ideological conflict as the cause of historical
change.[19] Conflict was indeed at the center of history's
movement, but the significant conflicts were political
and economic, not conceptual. Underlying the
economic interpretation of history, which brought
Beard his early notoriety, was the assumption that historical change was the result of "contending [economic
and political] interests" in society.[20] The most generally
satisfying explanation for the "great transformations in
society," he long maintained, was James Madison's
theory of conflicting factions as outlined in the Tenth
Federalist.[21]

In taking such a posture, Beard was, of course,
merely extending into history the vision of social reality
that suffused the writings of the muckrakers and the
"insurgent scholars" of the Progressive era.[22] This conception of reality, as Richard Hofstadter noted, stood
Plato on his head: it assumed that the "real" after
which historians researched was rough, sordid, hidden,
and clandestine, a succession of external happenings
of which intellectual events were merely secondary,
pale reflections.[23] Reality was lumpy and material, full
of vested interests, class antagonisms, and corrupt bar-
gains over which fine-sounding ideas and tidy theories
were carefully draped to mask the clutter and the dirt.

Reality was what had sent Henry Adams scurrying back to Cambridge to commence the weaving of his own peculiar, formalistic drapery. Ideas, as the pragmatists themselves were testifying, were essentially instruments of human intention and purpose, and these intentions and purposes in history, Beard believed, were predominantly economic and materialistic.

Yet despite his aggressive insistence on the sufficiency of the empirical method, Beard's writings before the late 1920s often reflected views inconsistent with the objective fact gathering required by neutral science. At the same time he was rejecting nonempirically identifiable causes of historical change, together with James Harvey Robinson, Beard had become a leading spokesman of the school of historical writing known as the "new history." Holding that the past should be "consistently" subordinated to the interests of the present, Beard and Robinson advocated an instrumental historicism that purported to use historical knowledge in an attempt to illuminate current social problems.[24] A vital part of the revolt against established institutions and their formalistic glosses, the new history proposed that current needs and problems should transform the study of the past from a heroic celebration of the culture's sacred cows into an instrument for social reform and political reconstruction.

While the new history plainly affirmed that the ideas men held about the past could be useful to their interests in the present, Beard seemed strangely blind to the fact that men's ideas *in* the past had been useful also, that ideas had, in some respect, made history. His goals were essentially those of a reformer, yet his professed methodology required inducing limited conclusions from carefully processed data. Beard did not seem to recognize that the instrumental approach to history was in basic conflict with his commitment to written history as the product of strictly empirical, scientific methods of observation and reporting. Beard's too casual assumption that economic interests were sufficient to explain social change tended to obscure this fundamental inconsistency in his thinking. Not until around 1930 did he begin to turn instrumentalism on itself as a mode of historical understanding, and even then the problem was not wholly resolved.

Similarly, Beard from the beginning maintained that society was organic and evolutionary in nature, that its diverse elements were in constant, dynamic, and reciprocal interaction. This perception, partly a holdover from the early influence of Turner, took the form of the assumption that politics, economics, and the social process were subsumed under the larger dynamics of history. The boundaries between the old, formalistic divisions of knowledge could no longer be clearly defined in a world whose only certainty was change and interrelatedness. In particular, politics could not be divorced from the larger social context in which uniquely political activities occurred:

> We are coming to realize that a science dealing with man has no special field of data all to itself, but is rather merely a way of looking at the same thing—a view of a certain aspect of human action. The human being is not essentially different when he is depositing his ballot from what he is in the counting house or at the work bench. In place of a "natural" man, an "economic" man, a "religious" man, or a "political" man, we now observe the whole man participating in the work of government.[25]

One can scarcely find a more concise expression of what Morton White has called "cultural organicism" in the entire range of American social thought in the early part of the century.

Despite this organic view, however, Beard was also convinced that clashing economic interests were the fundamental causes of society's "transformations." In his view, the economic interpretation of history was a realistic, scientifically verifiable alternative to the formalistic explanations that prevailed in the nineteenth century. While Beard deliberately stopped short of overt economic determinism, he was confident that economic considerations bore the most weight of all the identifiable factors of social causation. *An Economic Interpretation of the Constitution* was an attempt to demonstrate the basic causality of economic interests in producing social change by showing that economic conflict could be detected in the shaping and ratification of the Constitution. As he put it, "The whole theory of the economic interpretation of history rests upon the concept that social progress in general is the result of contending interests in society—some favorable, others opposed, to change."[26] Beard's not unsurprising conclusion was that the Constitution was essentially an instrument forged to advance certain economic interests; that the moving spirits behind adoption held particular kinds of property and security was, he believed, sufficient evidence for this conclusion.

Beard seemed not to realize that economic determinism was at odds with his professed organicism, that if society were indeed analogous to an evolving organism, activity in one sector could not definitively be said to be the cause of change in another. Beard's book, and its companion piece of two years later, *Economic Origins of Jeffersonian Democracy*, showed clearly that no line of demarcation separated the political from the economic, yet the very freight of his interpretation was that the

"Constitution was a product of the struggle between capitalistic and agrarian interests."[27] The fact that Beard used the terms "economic interpretation" and "economic determinism" interchangeably when speaking of the Constitution may be evidence that he was aware of the problem and was hedging his bets.[28] Beard may have wished to imply determinism while only claiming—when pressed—to interpret. In any event, he did not appear to recognize that raising the economic interpretation to the level of determinism involved embracing a mode of the formalism he so quickly condemned in others.[29]

Thus by the early 1920s, Beard's thought contained a number of themes and assumptions which, if pushed to the extreme, were often contradictory. The Progressive perception of reality required both moral fervor for reform and reliance for its achievement on neutral, empirical science; Beard scarcely acknowledged the conflict. Society was organic and interrelated, yet economic activity was the principal cause of social change. The problem of how men translated their economic interests into conceptual schemes and ideologies received little attention. History was the slow, checkered story of man's gradual progress from barbarism to civilization, but no systematic formula could wholly account for the method by which this rise was accomplished; science and technology furnished the impetus for industrialization, but ideas remained epiphenomena to social change. The economic interpretation of history represented a realistic and scientific alternative to earlier, formalistic theories, but it, too, when applied to the sweep of civilization, became one more mode of formalism.

Over the next decade, however, Beard's thinking about history began to change. There was no single, illuminating break in his thought, but by the first years of the depression it is clear that he had subjected many of his early assumptions to critical analysis. The economic interpretation of history, the ambition to create a science of politics, the general suspicion of ideas, the faith in an austere empiricism, the instrumental approach to history—all the major themes since his Oxford days were changing. While generalization about the evolution of his thought is difficult, one thing seems certain: by 1930, Beard recognized that the study and writing of history was a vastly more complicated enterprise than he had hitherto suspected.

First, Beard's estimate of the role of ideas in history began to change. In 1922, he was still arguing that "the wordy creeds of mankind have little effect upon the main course of things, because . . . no philosophy can prepare and determine decisions in advance."[30] In 1923, he declared that those seeking to understand the shape of history needed "facts, facts, and still more facts verified and tested."[31] Two years later, he vigorously reasserted his faith in empiricism: "I have definitely cast off all my lingering suspicions about the value of science. . . . It offers the best hope to mankind struggling to conquer itself and the world."[32] By 1927 and 1928, however, he was expressing doubts about whether there could be a reliable, scientific explanation of the political life of society, and increasingly he seemed willing to recognize the intellectual dimensions of historical change. *The Rise of American Civilization* (1927), perhaps the important turning point in Beard's intellectual development, acknowledged that the conceptions men held in their minds had affected the course of history; the idea of progress, in particular, had become "the most dynamic social theory ever shaped in the history of thought."[33] Three years later in a new edition of *Rise*, when examining the relationship between ideas and external reality, he admitted that "in some mysterious way, thought and the materials of life evolve together."[34] And in 1932, he observed that "one might almost say that peoples are civilized in proportion as they mingle ideas with their labors and aspirations."[35]

Correspondingly, as ideas began to loom larger as the causes of change, the adequacy of the economic interpretation of history shrank. As early as 1922, Beard confessed that words such as "cause" and "effect" were "terrible" words which gave only the illusion of historical explanation:

> The truth is, as William James said, anyone who tries to think his way all through any subject runs into metaphysics. Metaphysically speaking, so-called economic interpretations are as bankrupt as the output of any other school of thought. . . . I do not think that economics determines or even explains politics in the philosophic sense. Neither does anything else that I have yet stumbled across in this vale of tears.[36]

At this juncture, it was not clear how important Beard held metaphysical explanations to be in any case. Nonetheless, he was well on the way to a deliberate repudiation of economic determinism. In 1927, he reported that modern democracy was advancing toward greater economic justice through "agitation, political action, economic pressure, and the spread of ideas. . . . A word, an article, a pamphlet, a speech or a book may set in motion forces of incalculable moment."[37] And in an essay on social thought published in 1930, he backed off still farther from the economic interpretation. Questioning whether the word or the deed came first in history, he again invoked the authority of James:

> The great debate has never been closed to the satisfaction of the contestants, but William James has given us a fair working formula in the declaration that the worlds of fact and idea have evolved together. Their relations are reciprocal and no sword of reason has yet been forged with an edge fine enough to separate them. Whoever would seek to penetrate to the heart of an age . . . must reckon with this instrument of thought.

Beard then turned to apply this conception to the rise of capitalism and concluded that the Marxist explanation of class conflict was inadequate precisely because it underestimated the role of ideas. "Movements in ideas," he declared, "either as a result of abstract speculation and dialectical processes or as the reflection of novel changes in material circumstances, must be taken into account in explaining the rise and development of capitalism."[38]

But the apprehension that "ideas" and "facts" evolved together also precluded the possibility of a strictly neutral, empirical science; if fact and idea were inseparable, then science and intellectuality were in some fashion united. Such a prospect was not as alarming to Beard in the late 1920s as it would have been some years earlier, for by this time he was becoming aware that scientists themselves could no longer pretend to a dispassionate neutrality. The physical sciences, which he always believed were to provide the mode and pattern for the social sciences, were increasingly shaken by doubt, uncertainty, and the spectre of relativity, reflecting the findings of Einstein, Werner Heisenberg, and Niels Bohr. By 1930, the possible implications of such relativity for the social sciences were being widely discussed, and Beard was well aware of the discourse.[39]

The new relativism, as expressed by such eminent
scholars as William B. Munro of Harvard (who succeeded Beard as president of the American Political
Science Association in 1927), James Harvey Robinson,
Beard's close friend and collaborator, and historian
Harry Elmer Barnes, was that history and politics
reflected the subjective predilections of the inquirer,
and thus no absolute laws governing historical and
political externals could obtain. Whenever a historical
event was examined, the examiner's own perspective
always produced distortion. As Barnes observed, "tests
of the significance of historical material are relative
and pragmatic. Is there no absolute and transcendental
test? Apparently not." Henry Osborn Taylor in his
address as president of the American Historical
Association in 1927 called attention to the concept of
relativity in physics and drew an extended parallel
between the apparent disintegration of solid matter
and the crumbling certainty of historical knowledge.
Taking a pragmatic tack, he concluded that the temper
of the times favored relativism and that written history
inevitably reflected the intellectual conditions that prevailed at its writing. Four years later, Carl Becker
amplified this view for the AHA by proclaiming every
man to be his own historian, and the following year
Edward M. Hulme told the association's Pacific Coast
branch that objectivity in historical writing was a discarded myth. Even physicists acknowledged the personal equation in their work, and historians, Hulme
argued, should do the same: "Historic truth is relative
and subjective, not absolute and objective."[40]

Americans were not alone in echoing these sentiments. In the years bracketing 1930, Beard was deeply
affected by his reading of Croce, Heussi, Vaihinger,
Kurt Riezler, and, a few years later, Mannheim and
Friedrich Meinecke. In one fashion or another, all

these writers were questioning scientific positivism as a mode of historical knowledge and were raising deep questions about the historian's relationship to his subject. Beard's son-in-law Alfred Vagts called his attention to Heussi's *Die Krises des Historismus* in 1932 and thereby helped to convert Beard to a more subjectivist position than he could have earlier considered.[41] Heussi and the other Europeans were frequently cited by Beard throughout the 1930s; their collective influence gave fresh evidence that his early obeisance to objective science had been uncritical, even misplaced. The instrumentalism implicit in the new history had never jibed with the determinism of scientific history, and Beard found himself increasingly questioning his customary servitude to science.

When he turned to the scientists themselves for light, his suspicions were only confirmed. His principal source was Ernest W. Hobson's graceful treatise of 1923, *The Domain of Natural Science*. This work, which Beard discovered in the late 1920s, was one of several books he mentioned as having a deep and abiding influence on his thought, and he unapologetically used Hobson as the "spokesman for natural science."[42] Writing in the tradition of Ernst Mach and Karl Pearson, Hobson had emphasized the essential discontinuity between the natural and the social sciences. Natural science, he argued, was a conceptual scheme designed by the intellect "for the purpose of representing particular classes of sequences and regularities in our percepts."[43] Natural science applied to those sequences and regularities that were repetitive and could be empirically perceived, but it could say little about causal phenomena lying behind singular, irregular events that occurred in no discernible sequence. Hobson concluded (and Beard was compelled to agree) that natural science concepts had only a limited and imperfect applicability to the data of history and the social sciences.

This conviction, which became fundamental to Beard's thought in the last two decades of his life, marked a major break with his earlier thinking. The change was occasioned primarily by Beard's consternation over Hobson's assertion that a science of society or history, if truly scientific, could be tested only by its warranted predictability; if such a science were created, Hobson maintained, the future would be charted and men could but helplessly await their fate. Such a prospect caused Beard to quickly jettison his ancient goal of a science of politics. In an essay "Political Science" (1929), he put much greater stress on the creative importance of political ideas than he ever had before, and he expressly rejected the notion that empirically based predictions could or should be made in politics. Such predictions, if true, would constitute a "trajectory" for the future that would be deterministic and "inexorable." "If we could get enough knowledge to make a science of politics, we should imprison ourselves in an iron web of our own making."[44]

In taking this tack, of course, Beard was mistakenly equating scientific prediction with absolute predestination. Even scientific knowledge, as John Dewey had stressed, was expressed in terms of probability and conditionality. The whole point of the scientific relativity sweeping the intellectual world at the time was to question the possibility of such absolute knowledge in the first place. Laws of history and society, even if generally and statistically verified, could hardly create an "iron web" of fate for every man. Scientific knowledge did not give to man that which, as James had put it, was vouchsafed only to God: knowledge of the beginning and the end and of the turbulent course of events in between. Yet Beard's instinct, like James's, was to flee from the determinism this knowledge seemed to imply. If this meant abandoning his lifelong faith in empirical science and turning to some other source of authority for knowledge of his world, Beard was prepared to do it.

The net result of these changes was the serious erosion of all of the major suppositions Beard had worked with over the preceding thirty years. Until about 1920, he had tried to keep his personal ethics subservient to the facts with which he worked in the hope that the data—and the obviousness of the acquisitive instincts of man—would supply the causal linkages and explanations between human motives, actions, and historical and political events. Beard the scientist tried hard to keep Beard the moralist under a tight rein. In the 1920s, however, the imperative of suppressing his personal values seemed to diminish, and by the end of that decade the picture had changed greatly. Science now seemed unpalatably deterministic, the economic interpretation seemed increasingly inadequate, and ideas, as William James had insisted, could not be separated from those objective "facts" in which Beard had placed such confident reliance. By 1930, Beard found himself, like Henry Adams three decades earlier, living between two intellectual worlds, one dead and the other not yet born.

*iii*

In the early 1930s, Charles Beard came to believe that the Western world was experiencing a dislocation so massive and significant as to compare with the Renaissance or the "dawn of the modern age."[45] On every side, social systems, institutions, and ideas long viable and useful were beginning to crumble. The stock-market crash in the United States in 1929 had been but the first sign of the pervasive weakening of capitalism that quickly swept Great Britain and the Continent, and this was only a small part of the picture. In Italy, Germany, and Japan, fascism was becoming more muscular and more militant each day, and these trends were being matched by mounting communist aggressiveness and by the defensive belligerency of the democracies. The faith in science that had been such a prominent feature of Beard's own outlook was beginning to buckle everywhere, and religion as an organizing principle of life was long since dead. Leaders in high places mouthed platitudes that scarcely concealed their confusion; politics seemed only to reveal that representative government "does not function efficiently in a closely meshed technological society."[46] Western civilization was reeling, and none of its marvelous technological accomplishments seemed equal to the task of saving it. And the historians, with all their horses and men, seemed helpless to explain the general disintegration, much less to suggest how society might be put back together again.

These problems were all comparatively easy to identify and to document, yet they were, it seemed to Beard, but symptoms of a more basic, fundamental malaise. How this could be proved defied the empirical method. Society, Beard had long believed, was an organic whole, and many of its components were clearly ailing. Isolated, particular social conditions could be described and measured, but whether in the aggregate they constituted sickness or health eluded empiricism's powers of revelation. At the outset, then, Beard had to consider the more basic question of how any large social situation came to be recognized as a problem. He concluded that problems become such

when conditions empirically observed failed to measure
up to the ideals men held in their minds. Recognition
of problems "grows out of the assumption that something better or more satisfactory than the present disarray of things is possible, as well as desirable, and that
a choice of new lines of action, positive or negative,
is possible and desirable."[47] On the strength of this
conclusion, Beard proceeded to locate the essence of
the crisis in the "tragic sense of the conflict between
the *ideal* and the *real*, between the noblest visions of
man and his performances."[48]

> The essence of the crisis itself is dissatisfaction
> with the present disarray of things. Were there no
> dissatisfaction there would be no crisis. Now dis-
> satisfaction springs from the belief that the pres-
> ent state of things is not wholly good, does not
> meet the requirement of some ideal existing in the
> mind. . . . The ideal, however dim, is at the bottom
> of the difficulty. No ideal, no intellectual discon-
> tent. No intellectual discontent, no crisis in
> economy or thought.[49]

Such a reading of the crisis implied that its exter-
nalities were but the tip of the iceberg; every overt historical event men perceived as problematic represented
some larger, "invisible" intellectual disjuncture. The
crisis involved both the known phenomena of public
life and the conceptualizations by which such
phenomena came to be known. As Beard reflected on
the nature of this all-engulfing "crisis in thought and
economy," the doubts he had come to entertain about
the scientific method seemed more and more endemic
to it. For years, Beard and others had deliberately
rejected traditional formalisms in favor of the empiri-

cal method. Was it possible that empiricism itself had
evolved into a kind of formalism, a procedure assuming, without consciously recognizing, a larger view? As
he analyzed the components of the crisis, Beard
realized this was precisely what had happened, for
associated with the sense of disjuncture between external reality and internal ideals

> likewise is the recognition of the fact that neither
> *theology* nor *science* can give to men and women the
> certitude which guarantees practice in human
> affairs to be correct, efficient and enduring. When
> the Victorian age discarded theology and took up
> science a certitude of empirical knowledge seemed
> to promise an infallible guide to life, action, prac-
> tice. Now even the hardest empiricists are divided
> forty ways on the issues of economics, politics, and
> culture.[50]

While there was no substitute for empirically gathered
information on existing conditions, such information
was merely raw material to be measured by human
ideals. "Empiricism does not and cannot reveal problems emerging from the facts. Problems do not come
out of facts."[51]

The limitations of the scientific method posed no
problems so long as social processes functioned
smoothly and the normal course of everyday life was
maintained. The ordinary, habitual responses of
individuals did not necessitate much reflection about
meaning and purpose in life: the need for thought was
diminished by routine. By the 1930s, however, the
stresses inherent in the social structures and
philosophies of the West were bursting the seams of
society, and the comfortable, mindless reliance on
objective empiricism as an infallible guide to life's prob-

lems no longer sufficed. In fact, this very reliance on objective science, with its contemptuous dismissal of ethics, was itself a major cause of the confusion:

> Herein, then, lies the substance of the crisis in thought. The contrast between the ideal that seems possible and the real that oppresses us is painfully evident to contemporary knowledge; and it is increasingly understood that science, which once supplanted theological assurance, can furnish no unequivocal prescriptions for national policy and action—prescriptions guaranteed to work as promised in human affairs—especially in bringing the ideal and the real into that degree of harmony which will relax the tension and resolve the crisis. Despite all the sayings, declarations, and prognostications, . . . unequivocal explanations and guidance are denied to us. Deprived of the certainty which it was once believed science would ultimately deliver, and of the very hope that it can in the nature of things disclose certainty, human beings must now concede their own fallibility and accept the world as a place of trial and error, where only those who dare to assume ethical and aesthetic responsibility, and to exercise intuitive judgment, while seeking possible command of realistic knowledge, can hope to divine the future and mould in some measure the shape of things to come.[52]

The empirical method, Beard now saw, had been substituted for "theological assurance"; at the heart of the crisis in thought lay the elemental recognition of science's limitations. The critical events of the 1930s pressed for analysis and redress, yet because of its basic neutrality, historical empiricism could neither identify problems nor indicate policies to ameliorate them. A major part of the crisis in thought arose because "no imperatives of choice and action arise out of the mere observation to which the empirical method is limited by its inherent nature."[53] Far from replacing "theological assurance" with a mode of thought by which human experience could be ordered and human aspiration realized, Western man, in espousing empiricism, had committed himself to a paralyzing and ethically impotent historical objectivity now proving itself to be a disastrously inadequate philosophy:

> To make a swift summation, the crisis in Western thought may be said to spring from the disconcerting recognition of the fact that science cannot of itself provide the certainty, understanding, and unequivocal direction to policy and practice profoundly expected after theological supremacy and assurance were disrupted in a conflict extending through several centuries.[54]

The trouble lay not in the empirical method itself, which had yielded an abundant harvest of facts about man's life in history and society, but in the assumption that empiricism could do what theology had failed to do, "namely, develop a complete social philosophy satisfactory to the human spirit."[55] Since the recognition of problems came only with awareness that "something better or more satisfactory than the present disarray of things is possible, as well as desirable," the center of the crisis in thought was at a level empiricism could not attain: "the tragic sense of conflict between the *ideal* and the *real*, between the noblest visions of man and his performances."[56] The crisis had been building, Beard wrote in 1931, "ever since the days of

Descartes when philosophers began to divide sharply into idealists, who soared off into transcendental heights, and materialists, who sank down at last with Darwinism into primeval slime, both equally cocksure and equally wrong."[57] Each had gone their separate way and, ultimately, had come to deny the validity of the other, science becoming neutral and contemptuous of ethics and idealism casting off the obligation to fact. The word and the deed became sundered by a deep, irreconcilable split between idealism on the one hand and realism or empiricism on the other.

According to Beard's analysis, solving the crisis at its most fundamental level meant unifying the real and the ideal, but this unification could come only after clear and widespread accord on what constituted the ideal had been reached. To this end, empiricism could offer no guidance, and hence the need for a "philosophy of ethical reconciliation" as the basis for policies specifically shaped to counter the crisis became every day more apparent. The compelling question, as Beard later put it, was no longer how to collect, collate, and verify data, but, "To what summation of values possessing the highest validity and utmost compulsion can minds turn for direction in framing policies calculated to overcome the crisis, for giving credence to such policies in the national consciousness and spirit? What unifying principle and faith can supply the optimism and ethical dynamics necessary to carry such policies into effect?"[58]

The knot of the crisis could not remain tied for much longer or the results would be disastrous for civilization. Everything was at stake, and nothing remained sacred—including old points of view. Indeed, Beard's call for a "unifying principle and faith" to help solve the crisis revealed how far he had

departed from his earlier quest for "facts, facts, and
still more facts" in order to know and to shape the
course of history. Solving the crisis required that the
empirical method, hitherto elevated above the personal
and the subjective, be subordinated to a dominant
"ethical and aesthetic purpose," an inversion that signified nothing less than an intellectual revolution. As
Beard declared ponderously in 1931, "a revolution in
thought is at hand, a revolution as significant as the
Renaissance: the subjection of science to ethical and
esthetic purpose."[59] Since science alone could not lead
the way out of the "Daedalian tangle,"

> We must retrace our steps and consider again first
> principles. . . . It is at this point that inquiry must
> start and thus a reversal of scientific procedure in
> the old style is required; the knot is cut by an act
> of will. . . . The condition precedent to attacking
> the problem of the crisis is then to determine:
> What is the ideal arrangement of economic and
> social life which we desire to bring into being. . . .
> Simple as this formula is, it constitutes a revolu-
> tion in the positive and scientific procedures to
> which contemporary minds have so widely
> enslaved themselves, to their own defeat.[60]

Beard's announcement of the crisis and the
"revolution" in thought required for its solution was
all the more sententious for its tardiness. Beard had
finally come to recognize the problem James had outlined in "The Present Dilemma in Philosophy" nearly
twenty-five years before, and which Dewey and other
antiformalists had been explicating for years.[61] The
"crisis in thought and economy" was none other than
Dewey's "crisis in liberalism" outfitted in Beard's own

distinctive garb. Beard's early instrumentalism had been subsumed by his firm faith in empiricism, and his belated recognition of empiricism's inadequacies as a social and historical philosophy came as a revelation. The crisis caused him to revert wholeheartedly to historical instrumentalism and, more importantly, to attempt consciously to construct a rationale on its behalf. Recognition of empiricism's limitations forced Beard to turn his attention toward the ethical framework in which the empirical method could be used to end the crisis. And when he did so, like James and Dewey before him, the result was an explicit form of pragmatism.

Thus James, Dewey, and Beard all perceived that the disjunction between idealism and empiricism lay at the heart of their common intellectual problems, and each agreed that the problem of reunification—with all that it implied for thought, culture, and history—was so momentous as to compare historically with the Renaissance or the Reformation. But each viewed the problem from a different vantage point and defined it with his own particular vocabulary. Whereas for James the schism between idealism (or "rationalism") and empiricism was largely a personal problem to be broached by a revised definition of experience, and for Dewey the problem was essentially a social and intellectual lag to be treated by applying experimentalism to social experience, for Beard the problem had different dimensions: for him it was both a crisis *in* history and, more vexingly, a crisis in thought *about* history. Only if historians came to a new understanding of what they were about could their own special reconciliation of fact and idea, of event and ethics, be accomplished, and this required a radical recasting of the historian's task.

Beard's emerging conviction was that the crisis in thought was largely a crisis in thought about history. This belief, which came to dominate his thinking in the 1930s, was given sharp focus by his reading of Heussi's *Die Krises des Historismus*. Heussi's book underscored the extent to which the changes in Beard's own thinking about history over the previous decade had been part of a worldwide defection from the thralldom of empiricism, and it provided a framework for his reading of Croce, Riezler, Vaihinger, Meinecke, and Mannheim. That framework, which in certain crucial ways distorted these European sources and used them in support of a distinctively American mode of pragmatism, in turn became a crucial part of Beard's response to the crisis.

Beard's analysis threw him on the horns of a dilemma. The crisis on one level was a split between the real and the ideal, and on another it was an event in history, and in the nature of things it had to be explained as such. As Beard put it, "efforts to deal with it in terms of the realities out of which it came involve knowledge of and interpretations of this history."[62] The crisis had revealed the ethical poverty of historical empiricism; not until an adequate account of the ethical as well as the historical dimensions of the crisis was rendered could it be resolved. Despite his longstanding aversion to philosophic overviews, Beard was forced to acknowledge that only fundamental agreement on some concept of the good could make possible the needed social and intellectual reconstruction. The way out of the dilemma lay in the discovery and assertion of an ethical center which, while transcending the limits of strict empiricism, avoided the artificiality and unrelatedness to fact of formalistic, a priori ethical systems.[63]

Yet no sooner had this dilemma become clear than

another, equally thorny, emerged. The task of explaining the crisis was to be undertaken, of course, by historians. But if the crisis was in large measure caused by a failure in thought about history, especially a failure of historical empiricism, what approach might historians take that was not tainted by the very failure that had produced the crisis in the first place? The primary assumption of scientific historians was that specific historical cause-and-effect relationships could be empirically identified and generalized upon. As Beard had become painfully aware, however, establishing a cause-and-effect relationship in history required more than mere data. To speak in terms of "cause" and "effect" required that the flow of time and the "seamless web" of the past be broken by the investigator; cause-and-effect, as William James had shown, did not leap unbidden out of "the big, buzzing, booming confusion of this universe" demanding to be recognized.[64]

> History . . . represents no known divisions —beginnings and endings. In its total context all human affairs are enclosed in a mesh so tight that the eye can discover no broken parts or gaps. To descend from the figurative, picking "events" and "causes" out of the totality is an act of the will, for some purpose arising in human conceptions of values and interests.[65]

If cause-and-effect had to be imputed by the mind and will of an investigator, himself presumably a victim of and contributor to the crisis, what could reliably be known about it that might then make its solution possible? Resolution of both these dilemmas thus had to wait upon a reconsideration of the nature of history and of the historian's relationship to it.

*iv*

Sparked by the crisis in thought and economy, Beard's growing dissatisfaction with historical empiricism after 1930 arose mainly from its restricted usefulness in comprehending social reality. The primary problem was that a strictly empirical approach to social conditions could not give an adequate explanation of growth and movement; empiricism could not detect causal relationships between events and their development in time. Society studied in one year might differ radically from society studied in another, but the mind of the investigator, not his method of verification, had to supply the reasons for the changes. In making this observation, Beard drew close to James's criticism of Hume and the British empiricists.

But there was a further element in Beard's criticism, and as it emerged, it suggested nothing so much as James's rejection of determinism and his faith in "the will to believe." Physical science had achieved its significance, Beard argued, primarily by its success in identifying the regularity, the lawfulness, of the phenomena with which it dealt. In this it had a distinct advantage over the so-called social sciences: physical science could duplicate its experiments so as to give its causal theories a high degree of probability. Moreover, the physical sciences worked with inanimate or subhuman materials and forces while the social sciences, because they gauged human actions, had to treat with "morals, purposes, aspirations, wills, esthetics," which made accurate measurement and predicted lawfulness impossible.[66] The physical sciences, to the extent they had validity, were deterministic, but no deterministic framework could be made wholly, or even largely, compatible with the irrepressible creativity of human volition. At bottom, the analogy between physical and social science, whether cast in the mold of physics or biology, was imperfect, and its imperfections became glaring when the analogy applied to the study of history. The day when empiricism might be expected to yield historical omniscience was past.

Yet if the goal of omniscience was denied, the crisis still had to be explained, and the historical approach was the only possible way this could be done; if one sought to "explain" the present or to "penetrate" the future, the only instrument available was "knowledge of the past, including the latest moment."[67] In attempting to approach the crisis without lapsing into the merely empirical on the one hand or striving for total omniscience on the other, Beard drew a fundamental distinction between what he called "history as actuality" and "history as thought." History as actuality he defined as "everything that has happened and is happening in this universe since time began."[68] It was that totality enclosing "all . . . phases of human affairs . . . in time unfolding. . . . It is the absolute totality of all personalities and occurrences, past, present, and becoming, to the end of time."[69] It was the only absolute, the only unconditioned occurrence in human affairs, the seamless web of time confronting and encompassing the historian as he worked. History as actuality embraced the whole of creation: nature, its processes and dynamics, and man, with all his thoughts and actions, bound up organically in an immense, evolving drama that left no personality or event, however insignificant or miniscule, standing alone. It was into this immense totality that the historian pushed when he sought an explanation for any specific part of the whole:

And whenever the human mind seeks to push any inquiry into any topic, theme, or phase of human affairs to the knowable limits, it pushes *endlessly* outward in the relationships of the total situation in time unfolding. . . . All single issues discussed under the head of human affairs when "fully" explored involve wide ranges of history and carry us toward the borders of its totality.[70]

Within the seamless web of history as actuality was history as thought, what people meant when they used "history" in an everyday sense. History as thought was simply thought about history as actuality. Such thought, however, was always selective, partial, and approximate; it could not begin to correspond in any exact sense to the infinite complexity of the seamless web. History as thought was what historians purposefully selected out of the actuality of past human experience; it was an abstract construct, checked and controlled to a certain extent by the verified record of the past. Even though historians might strive for completeness and objectivity in examining the most minute segment of the past, they still had to select and discriminate, and their selection was inevitably colored by their own purposes, prejudices, previous experience, and knowledge.[71] Historians could never know and write about the past as it actually was: "History as actuality," Beard declared flatly, "is not known and cannot be known."[72] The efforts of scientific historians to achieve complete, objective accounts of history were but a "noble dream," which indicated their failure to grasp the crucial difference between history as thought and history as actuality.[73]

History as thought, if responsibly and faithfully rendered, adhered closely, if always imperfectly, to the evidence, the residue, of history as actuality. This residue—documents, books, monuments, memoirs, records, buildings, institutions, social ideas and structures—was the material from which history as thought was constructed, but the events that had given rise to such residue had disappeared into the stream of time, and their measureless subtleties could only be approximated. The fact that historians could never experience wholly events they wrote about—even events in which they themselves had participated—was the basis for Beard's much touted and sharply criticized relativism in the last decades of his life.[74] To him, however, it seemed merely common sense to point out the obviously real experiental limits of the historians' relationship to their subject. And Beard, unlike his friend and fellow relativist, Carl Becker, carefully drew back from the abyss of complete historical relativity. If absolute historical determinism was an unacceptable possibility, Beard found similarly unpalatable the polar argument that nothing at all could be known about the past —what he referred to as "unlimited relativity."[75] Like James, Beard strove to find a middle way between the extremes of historical determinism and historical nihilism.

For this reason Beard qualified his relativism, and he qualified it in two ways. First, he insisted that while it was inevitable that historians could give only selected, partial accounts of the events they wrote about, they nonetheless were under the solemn obligation of the guild to be true to the evidence as revealed. The necessity for discriminating among relevant data and for arranging what was chosen in certain sequences always involved the human factor, but the empirical method could be used to its limits to assure a maximum amount of clarity and objectivity. While Beard criticized the old-style historians for their naive faith in the "noble dream," he nonetheless acknowledged their goal of completeness and fidelity to the record as his own: "The effort to grasp at the totality of history must and will be continued," he wrote after chastising the true believers, "even though the dream of bringing it to earth must be abandoned."[76]

The second qualification had to do with the particular ways historians chose to interpret events and sequences of events, and it was this qualification which allowed Beard entrée into the mysteries of the crisis. Events and their arrangements, like cause and effect, did not inexorably arise from the inner necessity of the data whenever the historian contemplated the record of history as actuality. Rather the historian, if sense was to be made of the past, entered into a kind of dialectical relationship with his data; whether tacitly or overtly, the historian supplied the necessary linkages and coherence that converted raw data into the stuff of story. At this juncture, the historian's view of the nature of reality always became operative; his philosophy of history, however dimly perceived, supplied the unity for his ordering of facts. Subsequent discoveries might force him to modify his account, for written history was always provisional and subject to qualification in the light of future disclosures. But when writing history, the historian imposed his own philosophy on the materials at hand, and the result was fundamentally an attempt at predicting the past.

Had he left matters here, Beard's relativism would scarcely have been qualified at all. But Beard went on to argue that selecting and arranging the data of history was a valuative or moral act undertaken as much in the spirit of philosophy or ethics as of science or social science. History as thought—written history—was by its very nature "a conception of what is taking place in the world—a philosophy of events."[77] Reality could not be described without "philosophic implications"; the historian, in fact, was actually "a philosopher work-

ing in time."[78] The choices exercised by the historian
sprang from his moral convictions about the thrust of
history. In turn, his interpretation (history as thought)
entered into the world of human activity (history as
actuality) to help provide the basis for other people's
understanding of history and for the assumptions
upon which they based their present actions. The historian's prediction of the past had greater or lesser
influence depending upon the scope of his writing and
upon how in the future his forecast was validated. As
Beard observed, quoting Croce, "History is philosophy
. . . and it is open at both ends."[79]

The relationship Beard thus established between the
historian and history was intrinsically moral and structurally dynamic. The historian, to use Dewey's phrase,
"interacted" with his historical environment in precisely
the same fashion that the individual interacted with
society. The historian studying the records of past actuality brought to his work both his presuppositions
about reality and his present purposes of inquiry, and
these interacted with the data of history as actuality to
form history as thought. His readers based their
actions and choices on this construction, and in this
way written history came to shape and condition present actuality. In the future, the process would continue, with other historians mediating between their
conceptions of the past and the needs and preoccupations of the times in which they lived. History as
thought thus maintained a reciprocal relationship with
history as actuality, with the historian serving in a
ministerial capacity; as Beard put it, the historian was
"a statesman, without portfolio, to be sure, but with a
kindred sense of responsibility."[80]

Beard's position reflected an observation Croce
made in a letter to him of June 1933, which he

appended to his presidential address to the American Historical Association in December of that year. Croce wrote:

> The nature of historical interpretation is closely linked with the nature of the moral life, and it is in a certain sense identical with these. That which appears defective and confused in the one is correspondingly defective and confused in the other; the restoration of health and the progress of one brings with it the restoration of health and the progress of the other.[81]

If the crisis, as Beard now believed, was largely the result of "ill health" among historians, its solution depended at least in part upon their recovery. That recovery, in turn, had to wait upon the construction of a more realistic basis for their collective moral acts in writing history.

In the recent past, historians' undue faith in science as an infallible guide to history had reduced man to a cipher in a causal sequence leading inexorably to a predetermined future. Their overestimation of the empirical method had prevented them from seeing how history as actuality involved the progressive development of "ideas and interests ever evolving together, reciprocally affecting each other, with interests now advancing far ahead of ideas and ideas now advancing far ahead of interests."[82] Distorted emphasis on the empirical method had produced a consensus in history as thought which, because it denied to man and his ideas a creative role in history, had helped to produce the crisis in thought and economy. Once the closed perfection of the scientific conception of history was denied, however, ideas and human creativity could be recognized and their role in history as actuality could be reaffirmed. If the notion of an ironclad chain of causes discoverable by empirical means was discarded,

> then there is room in the world for will, design, courage, and action, for the thinker who is also a doer. This does not mean that [the historian] is emancipated from all conditioning circumstances, that he can just make history out of his imagination; but it means that, by understanding the conditioning reality revealed by written history as thought and description, by anticipating the spirit of the coming age, he may cut new paths, through the present and cooperate with others in bringing achievement to pass.[83]

Although absolute knowledge of the past could not be attained, it did not follow that the historian had to remain mute. History as thought required some estimation of historical movement before history as actuality could be written. Even though he might be conditioned by present concerns and by his own experiences and predilections, the historian could still glean factual knowledge of particular bits of the past, verify them empirically, and then make an informed estimate of their relationship in time. Although the precise nature of the relationship of events could not be discerned by the finite mind of man, the historian could nevertheless legitimately assert "that something can be known about the movement of history," an assertion that was "a subjective decision, not a purely objective discovery."[84] Between the extremes of absolute knowledge of history as actuality and absolute denial of the possibility of knowing relationships between events in the past—"unlimited relativity"—lay a middle ground held by the historian willing to risk this assertion. Without such an assertion, such an "act of faith," useful knowledge about the past was impossible.

This act of faith was not a blind, intuitive commitment to the historian's own special brand of design but an informed, critical postulation achieved after a thorough examination of relevant data—after, as William James had put it, one thought "long and hard" about history.[85] The act of faith was made, to be sure, before all the facts which might one day be uncovered were known, but the needs of the present required that it be made: interpreting the past and understanding the present could not wait upon an infinite future. The act of faith was necessary if one were to find, albeit in a relative and circumscribed sense, unity and meaning in historical movement. For such meaning to be possible, history as actuality had to manifest elements of unity without becoming absolutely deterministic and elements of chance without devolving into chaos: the seemless web of past, present, and future had to be broachable at some point without, once broached, becoming fragmented into unknowable "isolated particularities."[86]

Beard believed, then, that simply because no transcendent law of history could be shown to exist, historians need not despair of the possibility of finding coherence and meaning in history's movement. While history was in some senses always to remain elusive and relative, historians could nonetheless trace with a high degree of accuracy the course of ideas and interests in the past without pretending to explain the world or to forecast the future. Confronted by the complexities and imponderables of history as actuality, the historian faced a series of choices; and—this was crucial to Beard's reasoning—those choices were not unlimited. The historian's act of faith—his historical affirmation of the will to believe—was always made in terms of some frame of reference, which took into account the various possibilities of history as actuality without attempting to reduce it to an absolute system of law. In fact, there were but three frames of reference within which the historian could make his act of faith, and in Beard's view they served as further limitations to relativism:

> Only three broad conceptions of all history as actuality are possible. History is chaos and every attempt to interpret it otherwise is an illusion. History moves around in a kind of circle. History moves in a line, straight or spiral, and in some direction. The historian may seek to escape these issues by silence or by a confession of avoidance or he may face them boldly, aware of the intellectual and moral perils inherent in any decision —in his act of faith.[87]

For support for this belief, Beard turned, surprisingly, to Machiavelli. In history, according to the author of *The Prince*, one found elements of *"virtù," "fortuna,"* and *"necessità,"* elements of the desirable, the possible, and the necessary.[88] *Necessità* was the complex of circumstances conditioning life which happened no matter what individuals desired: death, sex, language, geography, acts of nature. *Fortuna* was contingency in human affairs: chance, the appearance of choice, "oases of freedom, or fortune, in the great universe of necessity." *Virtù* was the force of human morality and preference "working in contingencies amid necessity, making life and history."[89]

Machiavelli's formula satisfied the requirements for Beard's own acts of faith by rendering a conception of history as actuality in which human choice and, consequently, moral considerations, might play a creative role. Although the boundaries between *virtù, fortuna*, and *necessità* could not be sharply defined, all three elements could be identified as parts of the events of the past. Systems of thought fixing on one element to the exclusion of the others, however, had caused historians much confusion. The primary fault with recent historical thought was its overemphasis of scientific *necessità* and its corresponding deemphasis of *virtù*, of the role human desires and choices had and could play in history. Using "history as philosophy," Beard set out to redress the balance in favor of human choice by seeking to establish a historically validated frame of reference to which historians and their readers could repair in treating the crisis in thought and economy. At this point the qualifications of Beard's relativism became explicitly pragmatic and positive.

So it was the historian, not the scientist or the philosopher, to whom society had to turn for light and understanding in explaining and escaping the crisis. Specifically, the historian had to discover a frame of reference that would both accurately explain the development of the crisis and help formulate some prescription for its cure. The success of the explanation—and, by extension, of the prescription—would depend "upon the degree of its realism, its continuing appropriateness for life and thought amid the remorseless changes of human affairs in time—which is the subject of historical inquiry."[90] With history defined as the dynamic evolution of ideas and interests amid the swirl of *necessità, fortuna*, and *virtù*, the historian had to discover an ethical center that would furnish a realistic frame of reference for explaining and resolving the crisis.

The historian's task was doubly difficult because the crisis, by definition, was testimony to the inadequacy of the frames of reference upon which existing historical and philosophical systems were based. In Beard's view, the traditional philosophical foundations for Western society were shattered almost beyond repair. "All the systems of social philosophy presented to us," he wrote, "are shaken and riven by theory and practice. . . . The business of rehabilitating any of the competing systems of social thought and restoring its former power and prestige is beyond our powers."[91] Theology and empirical science had failed as centers for historical understanding, and their failure was responsible for "our confused civilization."[92] Only a radically new philosophy, positing a new and historically realistic ethical center, would make possible the escape from the crisis.

> So the task before us is not that of devising new phrases for old operations. It is that of clarifying our conception of American society and our purposes in selecting, collecting, and organizing knowledge and thought bearing on the tensions, conflicts, and problems of American society in its world setting. This involves a searching of hearts as well as minds—construction for our guidance of a workable ideal for American society as it may be shaped by knowledge, thought, invention and effort.
>
> When we have done this, we can turn to the vast bodies of knowledge and thought covered by the term social studies and find rich materials to serve our purposes. Then we can make effective use of the various methods and devices developed by students of pedagogy, that is, use effective for our clarified purposes.[93]

Beard's reading of the crisis was strikingly autobiographical; his indictment of the enormities scholars had committed in the name of impartial science seemed nothing so much as a confession of his own culpability. Though Beard himself had been scarcely successful in repressing the moral fervor behind his research and writing, he had been unstinting in his requirement that true scholarship exhibit the neutrality of physical science. But the crisis was testimony to the fruitlessness of such pretensions, and its resolution required above all else that scholars frankly acknowledge and defend the ethical banners under which they worked. This new requirement became the occasion for Beard to enunciate the moral faith that had been his from the beginning and to attempt to justify that faith in the arenas of history and social necessity.

*v*

Thinking long and hard about the crisis drove Beard back to his own basic observation: the crisis represented a historically accrued disjunction between the real and the ideal. It pointed up, above all, the need for identifying a broad-based, normative moral center in history which might rally men's fragmented efforts in reshaping social reality. "The task of finding this center," he wrote in 1934, ". . . is categorical for all those concerned with the existence and progressive development of society."[94] Out of the morass of competing systems and ideologies whose collective failure *was* the crisis, a common "center of value" compelling all men's respect had to be located. If this were successfully accomplished, both dilemmas facing the historian would disappear, for the elusive center of value would serve as both a realistic frame of reference for explaining the crisis and as a historically validated ethic in terms of which policies for its resolution could be formulated.

Beard's search led him to conclude that underlying all the world's great philosophies and religions was a set of simple, basic affirmations leading to a common "telluric" goal: the good life.

> When all is said and done, the great systems of ethics, as distinguished from mere scholastic glosses and compilations, are assertions of values, and a conception of the good life lies at their core, the good life on this earth, to be attained and realized, more or less perfectly, by practice.[95]

Projections of the good life underlay the teachings of Jesus, Buddha, and Aristotle; Beard took the same idea as his ethical center "for the plain reason that there is no other immovable benchmark in the universal flux."[96] Man's continual striving after this goal, whatever its specific definition in any time and place, was the dynamic force behind human civilization; the quest for the good life and the process of civilization were the same. Hence, the task before those seeking to end the crisis was the selection of a specific set of modern values and criteria for living that would result in a nearer approximation of that for which men throughout history had striven. Efforts to realize the good life represented the lowest common denominator of human effort, and its extension over time as the idea of civilization—"The most desirable, the firmest foundation for a system of ethics"—provided Beard with the center and the frame of reference he was seeking.[97]

Notions of the good life varied widely, but "near some central points," Beard believed, there was a basic

consensus, "otherwise social life would disintegrate."[98]
Moreover, Beard found the specific terms of the consensus comparatively easy to define: the right to labor
and its rewards in a safe, healthful, and aesthetically
satisfying environment; preservation of the family's
structure and sanctity; encouragement of the
individual's sense of moral and social responsibility; a
cooperative, democratic government dedicated to
achieving humane objectives through national (rather
than international) planning and action; recognition of
the equal rights and status of women; education
spreading "knowledge of good and beautiful things
and conduct"; use of the science of public administration to raise the level of statecraft and politics; and,
above all, mobilization of the nation's scientific and
technological resources to implement these objectives
through empirically informed social engineering. In
constructing this definition, Beard drew freely from
such diverse sources as Thomas Jefferson, John Ruskin, Karl Marx, Beatrice and Sidney Webb, and
numerous writers in the tradition of twentieth-century
progressivism such as Stuart Chase, George Soule, Rex-
ford G. Tugwell, and, especially, John Dewey.[99]

By making the realization of the good life the goal
and measure of civilization, Beard expressly sought to
identify an ideal which was processive, which allowed
the "process of valuing and choosing [to go] on in
society."[100] The idea of civilization had to include provision for the good life's continual revision, else it
would become final and deterministic and eventually
result in the elimination of choice in history. Beard's
idea of civilization did not eliminate choice; it established it. Beard recognized that "a synthesis of ethics
must conform to the realities of the historical process,"
including the "changeful" nature of the world, the
"mutability" of human life and values, and the "falli-

bility" of the human intellect.[101] Visionaries in the past had projected conceptions of civilization that lacked the experimental openness a historically realistic ethic required. In contrast with these static, "utopian" ideals, Beard's idea of civilization explicitly recognized and took account of history

> as a continuous process involving ethics no less than necessity; and as a struggle within human personalities no less than within and between classes—a struggle pointed toward a higher objective for humanity, enlisting all the powers of men and women for progressive, civilizing purposes, yet with no final act in the drama of history, thus giving room for endless creativeness individual and social.[102]

Civilization represented something more than a set of materialistic goals and conditions. It meant also the process of achieving, through the deliberate assertion of ideals and choices, perpetually new levels of well being and freedom for the individual and society. By stressing the progressive, experimental nature of civilization, Beard was taking a new and more positive stance toward the role of ideas in history, as well as establishing an experiential relationship between various conceptions of the good life and their realization in time.[103] Specifically, the ethic of the good life was "geared into the idea of progress, of the future immense before us, of the continual adaptation of the material world and the instruments of knowledge to declarations of purpose in relation to the good life."[104]

Thus, Beard's idea of civilization had the same experimental, "doubling" quality as Dewey's pragmatic conception of progress. It was precisely this doubling quality that gave civilization, in Beard's view, its histori-

cal validity. The experimental definition of the good
life produced an ethic that conformed to the fluidity
and dynamism of history, an ethic that endured
throughout time but did not, in the process, become
fixed, deterministic, and fatalistic. The ebb and flow
of changing human needs and capacities did nothing
to qualify its validity or to diminish man's freedom and
creativity in acting on its behalf.

Moreover, the experimental definition of civilization
as a frame of reference conformed to the tripartite
schema for history as actuality outlined by Machiavelli:
it assumed that progress toward the good life was possible though not necessary, that human will and desire
(*virtù*) could work amid life's unchangeable imperatives
(*necessità*) because of the possibilities afforded by
chance (*fortuna*). But unlike the empirical approach to
history, which overemphasized *necessità*, civilization
stressed the creative role of human desires and ideas
in the historical process. By maximizing *virtù* and
reducing the scope and power of *fortuna* and *necessità*,
civilization encouraged men to increase their control
over their own destiny. The idea of civilization justified
the deliberate selection and positive assertion of that
which men deemed good or desirable in human
experience projected into the future and applied to
society. "Our problem" Beard wrote, echoing Dewey,
"is that of making the best of the best now in experience, of applying and realizing on a large scale that
which has been applied and realized sporadically."[105]

On what basis the "best" was to be determined Beard
was vague. He acknowledged that value was an assertion, an affirmation of purpose and choice. He denied
that science was capable of such an assertion—the
whole point of his "new" philosophy was to preserve
the ethical option for individuals on the basis of their

experience rather than having it determined by some artificial, mechanical method. History could provide no compelling moral laws, only singular instances of individuals acting to achieve particular goals. The sole authority for the good life, finally, was Beard's assumption that underlying all ethical systems was a common "telluric" unity. As expressions of this unity, Beard cited "the human spirit" revealing itself in the "first principles" of traditional Western thought, or in the "few common-sense aphorisms, fables, and maxims" distilled from the experience of "ordinary humanity."[106] Civilization rested on assertions of value deriving from these fundamentals.[107]

Satisfied that the ethic of civilization made the least strain on credulity and knowledge, Beard turned to examine the specific historical conditions that gave it sanction. Unless it was to be merely another utopian dream, he reasoned, civilization had to have a definite geographical and historical reference.[108] Therefore, as a prescription for dealing with the crisis as it affected America, those seeking to understand civilization had to start with

> an intensive study of American history as movement and conflict of ideas and interests, with a view to discovering what are the characteristics of American society that must condition every effort to realize any promise for American life. . . . Nothing can come out of nothing; wheat will not grow in sand. If there is promise of any kind for the future in America, that promise inheres in the past and present of American history. . . . The problem must be stated in language that corresponds to the inherited phraseologies of the American people, and it must find in the Ameri-

can consciousness a lodgment deep enough and wide enough to set in motion the forces of realization.[109]

The criteria for creating conditions of the good life in America had to be found in "the realities of [the American] experience, tried and tested in the fires of centuries" and in the potential that experience revealed.[110] To demonstrate that such an optimistic and pragmatic historical possibility existed, Beard turned to an examination of civilization—both as ideal and actuality—in America.

In the history of the United States, Beard found, the idea of civilization was not merely illustrated and documented; it was embodied and institutionalized, particularly in the Constitution and the government it created. "Nowhere," he wrote, "is the predominating ideal of a progressive society set forth more cogently or with greater authority than in the Constitution."[111] America's republican government had been designed to expedite the process of civilization, and as a result America's achievement was unique among nations. From the beginning, Americans had thought that the true end of government was to help men to realize the moral objectives of life, liberty, and the pursuit of happiness—in other words, the good life.[112] The founding fathers knew well that the definition of this ideal would change in time and, therefore, that a government which provided for the continuous alteration of social and economic arrangements within a broad framework of law was soundest.[113] Hence, Américan government, designed to combine "permanence with provisions for progress—something like our hills amid changing ways of life,"[114] conformed to the very "essence of history."[115] The builders of American institutions, through good sense and good fortune, had built a system allowing men to diminish *necessità*, control *fortuna*, and advance *virtù*. As a consequence, Beard concluded, the American people were identified by their continuing commitment to the idea of civilization, and their history could be seen as evidence of the idea's viability.[116]

This cluster of ideas crystallized in the fourth volume of "The Rise of American Civilization" series, which Beard and his wife entitled *The American Spirit: A Study of the Idea of Civilization in the United States* (1942). The earlier volumes in the series had dealt with the "outward" aspects of civilization in America; *The American Spirit* strove to identify those "interior or intellectual qualities which made American history unique in origins, substance, and development."[117] Commitment to the idea of civilization, Beard concluded—"a composite formulation [embracing] a conception of history as a struggle of human beings in the world for individual and social perfection—for the good, the true, the beautiful—against ignorance, disease, the harshness of physical nature, the forces of barbarism in individuals and society"—had made Americans the beneficiaries of a uniquely progressive, free, and democratic culture.[118] Because of their affirmation of "the ethical will to overcome suffering and other evils and make the good or better prevail in individual and social arrangements," Americans had found it possible to integrate the ideal and the real, to make their experiences in society and history correspond with increasing efficiency to their visions of what the good life in America should be.[119]

*The American Spirit* was a patchwork of brief, essentially laudatory explications of the ideas of several hundred Americans (most of them liberal reformers) who had contributed to what by the twentieth century had become an experimental, pragmatic conception of the idea of progress—what Beard called significantly "the new American philosophy." This philosophy, of course, was none other than the idea of civilization in its American context: a highly nationalistic world view and belief system representing the evolving American consensus on the good life. What made the book so significant was Beard's argument that fidelity to the idea of civilization had shaped America's values, institutions, and history and that now, in time of stress, it furnished Americans with a historically proven guide to social and ideological problems. The idea of civilization was the answer to both Beard's and America's search for a "usable past" in time of crisis; *The American Spirit* was Beard's own extended act of faith in writing American history.[120]

How, then, to account for the crisis? Taking a leaf from Dewey's text, Beard argued that while America's unique progress since the birth of the republic was due largely to the provision for change built into American institutions, understanding of the dynamics of civilization had lagged behind social development. While technology had produced the anticipated changes in American life, the laissez-faire philosophy of the Enlightenment still prevailed. "Technology," Beard complained, "has not made a single important contribution to the philosophy of government."[121] The discrepancy between the real and the ideal at the heart of the crisis was basically a reflection of the lag of political and social philosophy behind technological advance. Laissez-faire individualism may in the past have produced progress, but obviously such was no longer the case.

The cold truth is that the individualist creed of everybody for himself and the devil take the hindmost is principally responsible for the distress in

which Western civilization finds itself. . . .
Whatever merits the creed may have had in the
days of primitive agriculture and industry, it is not
applicable in an age of technology, science, and
rationalized economy. Once useful, it has become
a danger to society.[122]

Far from denying the validity of the ideals of civilization, Beard saw the crisis as pointing up the inadequacy
of the methods Americans had traditionally used to
achieve them. The need, in view of the crisis, was for
democratic government to utilize the techniques of scientific planning and experimentation long used in the
private sector to mobilize national intelligence against
the chaotic legacy of laissez-faire. Natural science and
technology had so altered American society as to
require the elevation of the government "to a new role
in the process of civilization."[123] Until science and
planning replaced chance and the acquisitive instinct,
true democracy in an industrial world was an empty
dream and the idea of civilization a diminishing prospect.

Beard's faith in a planned democracy as the best system of social organization for confronting the crisis
rested largely on the social and historical implications
of the idea of civilization. All social systems, he
believed, proceeded from specific interpretations of
history, from definite conceptions of the possible,
the necessary, and the desirable. In the twentieth century, three systems deriving from three possible
frames of reference competed for allegiance: Marxist
and fascist totalitarianism; Manchesterism, or laissez-
faire, capitalism; and progressive, cooperative democracy. The first assumed a materialistic, deterministic
philosophy of history; the second saw in history the
manifestations of natural law working automatically

through individual and national competition; the third saw history as the product of human will and intellect moving slowly but progressively toward a better life for mankind.

While looking for a philosophy that might help to explain the ethical dimensions of the crisis, Beard reread Marx and Engels in the 1930s, only to have his longtime reservations about Marxism strengthened by what he found.[124] Marxists saw history moving inexorably toward a final goal, after which, in the face of all historical precedent, the laws of history would supposedly cease to operate. Marx's ideal of a classless society would "freeze" history in the illusion of finality. Marxists were attempting to order the data of history in a rationalistic, deterministic sequence, rendering ethics and choice irrelevant and, revolution notwithstanding, *necessità* the only real element of history. A "true Marxian," according to Beard, could not allow for "moral choice" in history.[125] With violence and force as its method, Marxism, "one of the most deterministic of all systems," repudiated all the humane ideals of Western history that found expression in the idea of civilization.[126] The two versions of history, in fact, were mutually exclusive: "By its very origin and nature as an interpretation of history, the Marxian invention called dialectical materialism clashed with the idea of civilization."[127] Hence, for Beard Marxism rested on an unrealistic interpretation of history.[128]

More parochial and less systematic than Marxism, fascism was similarly based on determinism.[129] Alternatives to state policy and its implied historical interpretation were forbidden; the only ethic was conformity to the will of "irresponsible, dictatorial force."[130] "In essence . . . fascism is a combination of personal tyranny, state socialism, great capitalism, militarism and war."[131] Like communism, it repudiated the heri-

tage of liberal Western thought by declaring war on
the ideals of civilization. By denying the possibility of
the attainment of new historical truths, fascism too was
grounded on an unrealistic view of history.[132]

At the other extreme, Manchesterism offered a social
system based on a historical interpretation of Lockean
empiricism and natural law. The laissez-faire ideal of
"anarchy plus a constable" was the expression of a
primitive agricultural age and thus ill suited to a highly
integrated industrial order. Its assumption of natural
law perceived somehow through sensory experience
provided scant guidance to the meaning and uses of
history. As a social system, Beard concluded, Manchesterism was hopelessly obsolete: "Besides being repugnant to reason, the philosophy of laissez faire has been
tried and has failed to fulfill its promises."[133] To all
who had eyes to see, the crisis had proved Manchesterism's failure.

Curiously, the effects of Manchesterism and
totalitarianism were in certain respects the same.
"Though apparently opposed, in reality these two
schemes of ideas [have] much in common; perhaps
they [are] the obverse and reverse of the same
thing."[134] Both systems in effect denied that man's
intelligence could be organized cooperatively to affect
the course of history. While Marxism looked to an
inevitable future utopia, Manchesterism assumed the
present to be the best of all possible worlds. In either
case, human will as a creative, active historical force
was short-circuited. Both systems subscribed to a predetermined formula of history and society, and, consequently, neither could respond adequately to problems unforeseen by its particular theory. While one system assumed a dialectical historical absolutism and the
other a Lockean empiricism, the social effect of these
two extremes was the same: human will was rendered

impotent by a priori assumptions about historical *necessità*.

The third alternative—planned democracy based upon the idea of civilization—accepted neither current perfection nor an ultimate utopia. This alternative held that by making intelligent choices, positing realistic values, and using the scientific method, men could achieve their ideals in time. Civilization and democracy escaped the false and exclusive alternatives posed by Marxist absolutism and Lockean empiricism. As Beard wrote in *The American Spirit*:

> Caught in the clash between empiricism and absolutism, the idea of civilization yielded to neither. It countered the conservative and deadening influences of empirical servitude to habits, customs, and things experienced by three specific assertions: progress in human affairs is as much a fact as the perpetuation of customs and habits; human intelligence is creative as well as routine in nature; and a study of development in history—creative intelligence at work—yields truths indefeasible as those derived from a study of habitual experience.
>
> Without resort to an absolute reason above human experience, in connection with the idea of civilization was evolved the contention that the progressive realization of reason and good is in history, though not the sum of history. Carefully avoiding the efforts to "explain" the whole of the universe, exponents of the idea of civilization in the United States eschewed the mechanical limits of materialism and the mechanical logic of absolutism. For the idea of civilization it was sufficient that ideals and illustrations of the true, the

good, the beautiful, the social, the useful had
existed in human experience from the beginning
of recorded time—sufficient for inspiration and
guidance in conquering the forces of disorder and
opposition and bringing the real closer to the
ideal.

Civilization escaped the rigidity of both absolutistic and
empirical dogmatism; as a democratic, experimental
philosophy proclaiming the efficacy of "creative intelligence at work," it "offered to the reflective spirit such
a degree of unity and coherence that it became an
ultimate construct of values for countless Americans."[135]

Importantly, Beard saw civilization as an ideal
"universal in implication" but "national in application."[136] Though the crisis of politics, thought, and
economy had come to threaten the entire world, it
could be ameliorated most effectively by action on the
national level. Toward the end of the 1930s, as domestic conditions again worsened and the likelihood of
American involvement in another foreign war
increased, Beard became convinced that the idea of
civilization required American neutrality. Participation
in another war would be the result, he reasoned, of
the country's failure to solve the crisis; ironically,
American involvement in European quarrels would
create conditions at home that would destroy the very
ideal needed for its solution.[137] In reaching this conclusion, Beard seemed to assume that the nation-state was
part of the framework of historical *necessità* within
which men must work to achieve their ideals. This conviction underlay Beard's intransigent isolationism in
the late 1930s, and it conditioned his critical interpretation of America's foreign policy under Roosevelt's

leadership. War and democracy, he feared, were antithetical, and thus war posed a basic threat to the social conditions the idea of civilization required.

Civilization held up democracy as the social system most effectively fostering individual freedom, cooperation, discussion, creativity, planning, and experimentation—all weapons to be used in combating the crisis. Civilization affirmed that man's experience in history provided knowledge of the good and the useful but did not confine his choices accordingly. Civilization's universe was open-ended, continually giving man the option of improving his condition by whatever methods he deemed most effective and according to whatever criteria suited his estimate of the good life. The imperatives of war might result in a wider use of scientific planning and social organization, but they militated in crucial ways against the intellectual freedom of inquiry and expression that the idea of civilization required to endure and to perpetuate itself. Hence, war and social experimentalism were not compatible.

The idea of civilization was Beard's most profound and constructive answer to the crisis in thought, economy, and politics. It was the reasoned response of a traditional empiricist to a complex of problems that revealed the limitations of empiricism as a historical method and philosophy. Neither absolutism and its deterministic assumptions nor empiricism and its ethical limitations could solve the crisis; consequently, Beard arrived at a philosophic accommodation neither wholly systematic nor merely antiformalistic. Modeled on Machiavelli's threefold view of history, the idea of civilization was a pragmatic middle way, an approach to historical and current problems which affirmed human choice and intelligence as primary, though conditioned, agents of the civilizing process. Civilization found sanction in historical experience and, as a pragmatic ideal, affirmed the possibility of continued improvement presaged by that experience.

Both a historical interpretation and a call to action, civilization unified Beard's disparate, fragmentary thinking on ethics, social philosophy, and the philosophy of history over the last decade and a half of his life. While it failed to make of his thought a complete, fully reasoned philosophical system, it did furnish him with a consistent device for seeing, in realistic terms, human will as a major shaper of events past, present, and, especially, future. Once firmly in possession of the idea, Beard could look to American history and find his own pragmatic, democratic instincts verified and confirmed. Read rightly, he could assert, American history revealed and validated a concept of progress based on individual freedom, social experimentation, the humane use of science for democratic purposes, "for the good, the true, the beautiful—against ignorance, disease, the harshness of physical nature, the forces of barbarism in individuals and in society. . . .

> If there is anything which history demonstrates, it is this generalization. All legislation, all community action, all individual effort are founded on the assumption that evils can be corrected, blessings multiplied by rational methods, intelligently applied. Essentially by this faith is American civilization justified.[138]

Throughout his life, Beard provoked the wrath of historical orthodoxy, and much of the resulting criticism made him seem more radical—or more obtuse—than he actually was. Critics of his relativism in the 1930s made him seem nihilistic. Later, in the

1950s, it was easy for historians to dismiss him as a tedious and ill-tempered neo-Marxist whose writings reflected an annoying and even misguided concern with the conflicting polarities which made up good and evil for Progressive historians. Analyses of Beard's contributions to historical writing have dealt almost exclusively with his early economic interpretations or his later doubts about the validity of the scientific explanation of historical cause and effect. As a result, Beard's thinking has tended to be characterized as either naively mechanistic or skeptical and corrosive of the essential value of historical scholarship. Some, consequently, have charged him with anti-intellectualism.[139]

The tendency of critics to focus exclusively on Beard's economic preoccupations or his later relativism has caused them to miss the positive and constructive consequences of his revolt against empiricism and historical positivism. Specifically, the pragmatic way in which Beard qualified his relativism has scarcely been noted. When the idea of civilization in Beard's writings in the 1930s and 1940s is correctly viewed as an experimental frame of reference for the historian's act of faith, a more accurate appraisal of Beard's contribution as an intellectual historian—and as a pragmatist —becomes possible.

The way Beard employed the concept of civilization to criticize Marxism is particularly important. Beard, like Dewey, found Marxism not radical enough in its view of history as a creative process; Marxists failed to perceive that history involved ideas as well as interests and that it moved as men worked toward goals which themselves evolved as human needs and capacities changed. From the perspective of Beard's pragmatic definition of civilization, the Marxist approach to historical and social problems was simply another variety of that outdated formalism which had helped bring on the crisis in the first place.[140] Like Dewey, Beard found American history and culture inclined more toward democratic experimentalism than some alien, dialectical orthodoxy, and his criticism of Marxism displayed the instrumental edge of civilization honed to its finest. His criticism suggests, also, an important reason why many Americans in the 1930s who were disenchanted with laissez-faire capitalism still could not accept the teachings of Marx: to the extent that Americans subscribed to the pragmatic view of progress, Marxist determinism was unacceptable as a historical frame of reference.

Both as a pragmatist and an anxious observer of the crisis of the West, Beard felt keenly the need to resolve the conflict between social reality and men's conceptions of the good life. The idea of civilization became his frame of reference for doing so precisely because it represented his—and in his estimation, America's—most profound sense of history's nature, movement, and possibilities. In using civilization as the control for his act of faith in writing American history, Beard believed he was both speaking for and advancing the main drift and principal virtue of a unique culture. If American history meant anything, it meant that the idea of civilization was a living historical reality. And when his fellow Americans came to understand this luminous truth, civilization would know its finest hour. Then, truly, it would be the dawn and not the dusk of the gods.

# 7

# *Progress,*
# *Experience, and History*

William James, John Dewey, and Charles Beard shared a faith in the competency of thought to cope with the problems of ordering nature and society. In their view, human intelligence and its foremost achievement, the scientific method, had developed out of man's long struggle with nature and with himself for civilization. That man could know the process by which he and his civilization evolved and could conceive a pragmatic, experimental theory of progress was itself evidence of how successful that struggle had been. What remained was the consistent application of the pragmatic theory of progress to the larger problems of social life in the modern industrial world.

For the pragmatists, the comforting, formalistic certainties no longer availed, and James, Dewey, and Beard found it both necessary and sufficient to look to human experience for moral guidelines in the civilizing process. For them, the mind's primary function was the selective improvement of individual and social experience; the philosophy they constructed on this premise was from the outset a radical philosophy of progress. The key to their doctrine of progress, and to pragmatism generally, was their conception of experience as the dynamic, reciprocal interaction of the conscious self with its total natural, social, and historical environment.

Fundamentally, the pragmatists agreed that the universe known through experience was one of both continuity and change. Denial of rationalism's block universe, as James characterized it, was their common point of departure. But more than this, Dewey and Beard agreed—in their own vocabularies and with different emphases—with James's theory of radical empiricism. Their agreement resulted in the creation of an elaborate, if still not completely systematic, philosophy that encompassed the one and the many in experience and still left the way open for creative intelligence to function *in* as well as *on* historical development.

The stalemate between absolutism and empiricism which James called "the present dilemma in philosophy" arose essentially from philosophy's failure to keep pace with the changing world. James recognized that the stalemate, epitomized in the conflict between John Fiske and Chauncey Wright over the meaning of evolution, had to be forced, else philosophy would wither into mere unrelated speculation, a worse than useless encumbrance to the modern mind. Within two decades after his death, Dewey and Beard saw the dilemma James detected reach crisis proportions on a broad social and historical front. Philosophy's failure to progress had produced a major crisis in thought and society. James had been right; and his way out of the dilemma, amplified and extended, became their way out of the crisis.

"Meliorism," "experimentalism," "civilization"—each

had his own term for the pragmatic doctrine of progress. But at bottom they all meant the same thing: the
conviction that man, by using his intelligence to solve
specific problems, could with increasing effectiveness
create a future satisfying his developing moral requirements. Neither necessary nor impossible, progress was
a living option depending on man's will to believe in
a certain kind of future and on his willingness to act
in scientific, experimental ways to implement his
beliefs. In the context of twentieth-century America,
progress meant that Americans, by intellectual and
social cooperation and by democratic social planning,
might resolve the emergency in which they found
themselves.

As Beard insisted, however, a solution to the intellectual crisis had to precede a solution to the social
crisis. The main requirement was an act of faith in the
adequacy of knowledge derived from experience and
tested in the fires of experimental logic. Yet while the
scientific method could help insure accurate knowledge, it could provide no guarantees in the assault
upon the future. As a conscious goal and process,
progress was always to be limited by human knowledge
and understanding. The problem of progress was the
problem of knowledge, and the problem of knowledge,
especially moral knowledge, was the keystone to the
whole enterprise of pragmatism.

Hence, James, Dewey, and Beard strove consistently
to make morality knowable. The traditional philosophical extremes of rationalism and empiricism, by remov-
ing ideals from the realm of experience, in their
estimate denied that individuals could have reliable,
comprehensible experiences of the good. Rationalism
and empiricism were the polar philosophic expressions
of the ancient duality of real and ideal. All three saw
this artificial division as the heart of the crisis. Insisting

that individual, social, and historical experience was the source of all knowledge, they attempted to reunite and make usable these hitherto unyielding extremes. As Beard wrote, "the only tolerable goal of our labors must be an artistically perfect adjustment of our conduct and ideas to the noblest imagined potentialities of the constantly becoming situation, thus uniting the word and the deed which were not asunder in the beginning and will not be at the end."[1]

Since James's concern was primarily with the problem of knowledge for individuals, his focus was on individual morality, on fidelity to one's own experience. Rarely did he allude to the social implications of radical empiricism or the sentiment of rationality. Pragmatism for him was essentially a question of the individual coming to terms with and controlling himself and his unique destiny. Although meliorism clearly implied that society as a whole might progress through its own efforts and on its own terms, James did not explore the idea's social implications. He nevertheless saw the possibility of willed improvement in the quality of human experience as the source of morality. Dewey and Beard, on the other hand, focused on the social, cooperative implications of the will to believe, recognizing that significant progress (as Dewey used the term) required a social agency—whether school or government—dedicated to continued social and individual betterment through careful usage of the experimental method. All agreed, however, that the possibility of progress made morality real and that the experience of morality—of the choice between alternative futures—made progress possible.

Thus, the authority for the possibility of progress was human experience. In James's case, the authority was every man's experience of desire and purpose gratified by effort and guided, basically, by the senti-

ment of rationality. Because the individual's experience
revealed melioration, his relation to the future could
be at least partly creative; hence, James saw the
individual as morally involved in the world's salvation.
Dewey's broader experimentalist conception of experience provided a scientific basis for a socially defined
morality. But again it was the experienced possibility
of a deliberately improved social order that made morality and progress real. Beard's authority for civilization as an ethic and a historical frame of reference was
also experiential—the experience of necessity, chance,
and human desire and will on the course of history.
Since progress was in various ways given in human
experience, the pragmatists believed that still more
efficient and more conscious modes of progress could
be achieved in the future.

If the pragmatists saw progress implicit in experience, their conception of thought and intelligence rendered progress explicit. For James, thought was the
progressive reorganization of experience functioning
essentially to create a feeling of order, rationality, and
purpose for one's activities. Dewey similarly regarded
thought as the progressive reconstruction of experience, but he couched his views in evolutionary language: thought was an experimental instrument for
qualitative adaptation. And for Beard, thought—in
particular, thought about history or "history as
thought"—was the primary instrument for the process
of civilization.

For Dewey and Beard, pragmatism's conception of
thought and experience also implied a certain kind of
social order: a planned, cooperative, socialized democracy. Since experience was the source and authority for
all knowledge, only a social order permitting and
encouraging men to look freely to experience to discover the good and the true would suffice. Access to

experience and its possible meanings could not be the prerogative of vested social privilege or an arbitrary, absolutistic philosophical dogma. Holding the individual to be the fundamental consciousness in the universe, the pragmatists subscribed to an even more radical individualism than did advocates of traditional laissez-faire democracy.

Dewey and Beard argued—and James doubtless would have concurred—that the democratic process embodied best the experimental method by which old truths were tested and new ones created. Thought and its results were hypothetical, continually requiring testing by external action. Since democratic institutions were designed specifically to accommodate this kind of trial-and-error activity, they effected best the conditions required by the pragmatic quest for betterment. Only a democratic society provided the kind of open marketplace for the free competition of ideas and experience so crucial to the achievement of progress.

Yet American democracy by the twentieth century was no longer a free market, either for ideas or for individuals. Dewey's "crisis of liberalism" and Beard's "crisis in thought and economy" revealed the failure of American thought and institutions adequately to provide for, protect, and perpetuate individuality in an increasingly consolidated, impersonal society. Once considered a liberal doctrine in opposition to monarchy and autocracy, in their opinion laissez-faire individualism had irresponsibly generated social conditions in which truly liberal, responsible individuality could scarcely be achieved. Paradoxically, in the twentieth-century world, individuals had to cooperate to remain individual in any meaningful and fulfilling sense. While Dewey looked to the schools to achieve this goal, Beard looked to government and to public administration. Both denied the traditional equation of laissez-faire individualism with free democratic government.

The philosophic extremes James identified as determinism and nihilism Dewey and Beard saw underlying the alternatives to the crisis of Western society: Marxist and fascist totalitarianism on the one hand and laissez-faire capitalism or Manchesterism on the other. For the pragmatists, each of these systems at bottom repudiated thought and will as innovative forces in history, since the philosophic extremes on which they rested, by dogmatically insisting that the universe was either finished or fragmentary, denied the reality of the creative potential of human experience. Just as James saw pragmatism as a middle way between the horns of the dilemma in philosophy, so Dewey and Beard saw progressive, experimental democracy as the middle way between the deterministic and nihilistic alternatives to the crisis of liberalism.

Above all, the pragmatists insisted on scientific procedure. Truth happened to certain ideas publicly and in time; history, in this sense, was a leveling, democratic force. The pragmatists recognized that given the dynamic nature of thought, strict neutrality in gathering data and testing hypotheses was impossible. Nonetheless, they argued for reportorial fidelity and loyalty to the method of investigation; objectivity was to be achieved insofar as psychologically and methodologically possible.

Yet neither Dewey nor Beard, for all their insistence on the scientific method, delineated clearly its limitations for social or historical studies. Nor did they use the term consistently. Dewey distinguished carefully between science as a laboratory procedure, as a body of verified data, and as a general attitude toward problems of knowledge. In his writings on social problems, however, these important distinctions often became blurred. Gail Kennedy's observation that Dewey regarded a democratic society as a community of scientists was correct; Dewey's analogy, however, was wishful thinking. Moreover, science as a laboratory technique required a degree of control over the variables of the problem under investigation that precluded dissent. Should one be free to deny the scientific method, to act irrationally? In Dewey's scientific, experimental democracy, evidently not. At least Dewey did not address the problem, save to insist that the general public needed to be taught the principles of scientific procedure.

Beard's confusion was more profound. Accepting Hobson's view that the measure of science must be accuracy in predicting the future, Beard went on to assume that a science of history, if it could be constructed, would lock one in a predetermined future. As a pragmatist, he rejected this view. Yet with no apparent sense of inconsistency, Beard also rejected Marx's philosophy of history as "unscientific" because it attempted to establish the final, inexorable goal of historical movement. Beard seemed unaware that he, like Dewey, used "science" in at least two different senses.

Furthermore, the experiential approach to history raised basic problems, only some of which Beard recognized. He affirmed that the historian had to remain objective in his collection and assessment of data. Only true facts about the past were useful. Beard also knew that the historian was necessarily limited by his own previous experience, that he could see only what was already "behind his eyes." Aware of this discrepancy, Beard continued to demand an empirical approach to history and at the same time to deny its possibility. Because of his confusion over what a science of history meant precisely, he implied that the more accurate one's knowledge about the past, the lesser one's area of choice in the future. Yet the very purpose of acquiring knowledge validated by the empirical method was to inform human purpose with respect to achieving control over future events: to make possible progress in a certain direction. Beard frequently lost sight of the distinction between positive, verified knowledge of the past and prospective, conditional knowledge of the future. At one time, he conceived of knowledge as an instrumental, particularistic construct and at another time as a deterministic, general entity. He never resolved the resulting ambivalence.

Beard also failed to come to grips with the precise way in which experience of the past produced historical knowledge. His philosophy of history could not be systematic because his conception of knowledge was fragmentary and inconsistent. Beard the empiricist insisted that accurate knowledge of history was experiential; Beard the moralist assumed that underlying the events and writings of history was some kind of ethical consensus beyond experience revealing the eternal verities of the "humane spirit." The two roles remained separate even though civilization as a frame of reference strove to blend them.

Beard's conception of "history as actuality" raised additional problems. First, the conception was metaphysical speculation; it could not be validated empirically. Second, Beard did not treat the problem of how history *not* experienced—the largest part of history as actuality—was deterministic or even influential on the present. He further assumed that history as actuality was composed of elements of necessity, chance, and human will. The precise proportions of these ingredients in any given event, however, could not be known. The historian, society's professional knower of the past and guide for the future, could not himself experience total history. Rather, he experienced only part of the data or residue of historical events, and from them he drew his own picture of the past leading to the present. Was history as actuality influential, or only those leavings of the past which could be known experientially? If the latter, were only those parts of history's residue chosen by the historian to have an effect on the present? What, then, was the effect of data historians could know but chose to neglect? Beard's failure to explore adequately the implications of experience as method for the historian pointed up real limitations of the pragmatic approach to history.

Part of Beard's confusion derived from pragmatism's unproven assumption that science and logic were basically unified, intrinsically self-corrective processes united by a common method of inquiry. Hence, historical inquiry, like any other kind, was finally to be judged by the success, the usefulness, of the results. But only true knowledge of the past, Beard insisted, could produce such useful historical knowledge; to argue otherwise was to embrace—or at least sanction—historical error. Yet to state this was to admit at once the central fallacy of pragmatic historicism: acting on knowledge that was erroneous might also produce useful results. It was all well and good for Dewey to argue that any proposition that resolved an indeterminate situation successfully was logically adequate, but this was hardly sufficient for the seeker of historical truth, however relativistically that truth might be conceived. Knowledge was always provisional and action imperative; yet if the consequences of action predicated on historical error proved socially successful, by what criteria could one label such knowledge as erroneous?

History as actuality was nothing less than absolute truth ("everything that has happened and is happening in this universe since time began"), and how history as

thought could be accurately related to that grand
abstraction was something Beard could not finally envision. History as actuality could not be experienced, but
somehow it had to exert a control, a check, on that
which could. Always in the back of Beard's mind there
lurked the hope of knowing the whole truth of history,
even though on another level he recognized the hope
was vain. Yet to free history as thought from its solemn
obligation to history as actuality would be to render
knowledge of the past a creature of fancy, and such
a creature could give scant guidance for the future. In
the end, the precise relationship of history as thought
to history as actuality remained unclear, and Beard's
progressive historical philosophy remained nothing
more than he had claimed it to be: an individual act
of faith.

James and Dewey had less difficulty with history as
actuality than did Beard largely because they usually
ignored the questions it posed. Their concern was less
with understanding what had transpired in the past
than with the relationship of currently held ideas and
beliefs to prospective actions; and they were more concerned with criticizing the ideas than with depicting
and explaining consequent events. Theirs was, in one
sense, a much easier task, for the future was malleable
and ideas could easily be revised as events marched on.
But the past was past, and even though ideas about
it might change as new evidence came to light, the
events that gave rise to that evidence were irrecoverably lost. Only the evidence could be experienced, and
the knowledge that resulted would always be but a
pale, tantalizing reflection of the rich occurrences of
the past. Like a good historian, Beard never ceased
wanting to know, to possess, the wholeness of those
occurrences. As he once poignantly remarked to a
friend, "When I come to the end, my mind will still

be beating its wings against the bars of thought's prison."[2]

*ii*

While their preoccupations with diverse modes of
experience took James, Dewey, and Beard in different
directions, all three recognized that belief in the idea
of progress—whether on the personal, the social, or
the historical level—required an act of faith, and faith,
as James had insisted, was fundamentally a matter of
temperament. America had always produced an abundance of tough-minded thinkers who inclined toward
optimism and for whom obstacles to progress were perceived as merely occasions for more conscious, more
energetic exercise. The faith of the pragmatist, finally,
was that such a temperament might be shaped and
nurtured by intelligence, education, and science. And
such became the faith of the vast majority of America's
liberals in the early decades of the twentieth century.

Yet not all could subscribe to this progressive vision
with its enormous freight of hope and its pragmatic
assumption that thought and will might direct, if not
transcend, the "booming, buzzing" confusion of history. For a temperament like Henry Adams's this was
too much to ask. His inclinations led in the opposite
direction; for Adams, history was ultimately chaos, and
thought about history, despite all his efforts on its
behalf, created not order and progress but merely their
illusion. As he put it cryptically in *The Education*,
"Chaos [is] the law of nature; Order [is] the dream of
man."[3] Man was alienated from nature, and the source
of his alienation, ironically, was his dogged, persistent
belief that some sort of unity and meaning underlay
the chaos about him; and insofar as man pursued that

illusory unity, he strayed still further from the natural. Hence, man was left with the alternative of yielding mindlessly to nature's caprice, or—a vaster irony—of willfully striving after unity and meaning, thereby contributing one more source of random energy to the pervading chaos.[4] For much of his life, Adams found the strength to pursue the latter course, but toward the end, the effort began to seem as absurd and pretentious as the facile optimism of the liberals. And Adams then turned to bittersweet recollections of older, simpler, more heroic times.

Yet for all his aspect of an aging Miniver Cheevy, Adams shared the same sense of crisis that galvanized James, Dewey, and Beard. His criticisms of modern society were every bit as trenchant and insightful as theirs, and often they were expressed more elegantly. That the age-old moorings of cultural and intellectual coherence had been slipped they all agreed; but on the questions of where this left Americans and what their prospects were, Adams dissented. James, Dewey, and Beard put their faith in man's capacity for deliberately drawing, with the aid of science, more and better meanings from his accumulating experience; for them, intelligence, reason, logic, and experimentalism gave evidence that a progressive course could be steered in the future. Adams was less sure. "Every day Nature revolt[s]," he wrote in 1904, "causing so-called accidents with enormous destruction of property and life, while plainly laughing at man. . . . An immense volume of force [has] detached itself from the unknown universe of energy, while still vaster reservoirs, supposed to be infinite, steadily [reveal] themselves."[5] Whatever unity science uncovered in the curve of history, Adams concluded, promised still more acceleration, more dissipation, more chaos. Only the future would show who was right.

# *Notes*

## CHAPTER 1

1. Adams to Charles Milnes Gaskell, March 14, 1910, in Worthington Chauncey Ford, ed., *The Letters of Henry Adams, 1892-1918* (Boston and New York: Houghton Mifflin, 1938), II: 537; Adams to William James, June 20, 1910, Ford, ed., *Letters*, 543.

Adams wrote on August 2, 1910, to Gaskell: "When I flung my little volume in professional faces last winter, and—so to speak—kicked my American Universities in the stomach as violently and insultingly as I could, I calculated on getting one sharp reaction and protest for every hundred copies of the *Letter* I sent out. After all, I am the *doyen* of their School, and they have got to listen to what I tell them. As a matter of fact, every correspondence has taken the tone,—'Why, of course! We know, etc., etc. But, etc. etc.' My poor dear old friend and fellow William James alone has put up some sort of a fight. Society is ready for collectivism; it has no fight left in it; and our class is as defunct as the dodo." Ibid., 546.

At least one other person did respond critically to the *Letter*, although Adams had not received his reply at the time of his correspondence with James. Henry A. Bumstead, a Yale mathematical physicist, wrote to Adams on June 16, 1910, but his letter had apparently not arrived (or Adams failed to acknowledge it) before his letter of August 2 to Gaskell. See William H. Jordy, *Henry Adams: Scientific Historian* (New Haven: Yale University Press, 1952), 216*n*.

2. Adams to Margaret Chanler, September 9, 1909, in Newton Arvin, ed., *The Selected Letters of Henry Adams* (New York: Farrar, Straus, 1951), 263; James to Henry Adams, June 17, 1910, in Henry James, ed., *The Letters of William James* (Boston: The Atlantic Monthly Press, 1920), II: 344.

3. Max I. Baym, "William James and Henry Adams," *New England Quarterly* 10 (December 1937): 731.

335

4. Adams to Henry James, January 22, 1911, in Ford, ed., *Letters*, II: 558.

5. James, ed., *Letters*, II: 10. This club was not the so-called Metaphysical Club that Charles S. Peirce recalled convening in the late 1860s and early 1870s, although some of the figures were the same. James's letters refer occasionally to overlapping groups of dining companions, some of whom were among those recalled by Peirce as constituting the Metaphysical Club: James, Fiske, Chauncey Wright, Joseph B. Warner, Holmes, Nicholas St. John Green, and, of course, Peirce himself. Philip Wiener, in questioning the Metaphysical Club's existence save in Peirce's nostalgia-clouded memory, noted that no mention of the club appeared in the letters of the alleged principles. Particularly, he noted that James, whose writings were filled with "generous acknowledgements," omitted reference to it. Philip Wiener, *Evolution and the Founders of Pragmatism* (Cambridge: Harvard University Press, 1949), 25.

Four years after Fiske's death in 1901, however, James did recall a humorous incident that suggests Peirce's recollections may not have been entirely false. To T. S. Perry on August 24, 1905, James wrote: "If you want an extra anecdote, you might tell how, when Chauncey Wright, Chas. Peirce, St. John Green, Warner and I appointed an evening to discuss the 'Cosmic Philosophy,' just out, J. F. went to sleep under our noses!" This would have been sometime in 1874, and the phrase "appointed an evening" suggests this may have been a fairly routine procedure. James, ed., *Letters* II: 233.

6. James had sent Adams copies of the two essays, knowing that his voluntarism would bring a strong reaction. He was not wrong. Ernest Samuels wrote that the articles "instantly aroused in him [Adams] the demon of contradiction," and that Adams was "violently sceptical of James's attempt . . . to give scientific support to the great man theory of history." Ernest Samuels, *Henry Adams: The Middle Years* (Cambridge: Harvard University Press, 1958), 231.

7. The two essays were put together and published under the title of "The Sentiment of Rationality," in Alburey Castell, ed., *Essays in Pragmatism* (New York: Hafner Publishing Co., 1968), 11.

8. Ibid., 9.

9. Ibid., 27.

10. Ibid., 36.

11. Quoted in Jordy, *Henry Adams*, 74. Jordy's discussion of Adams's historical views remains definitive.

12. Adams to William James, July 27, 1882, Harold Dean Cater,

ed., *Henry Adams and His Friends* (Boston: Houghton Mifflin, 1947), 121-122.

13. Gay Wilson Allen, *William James: A Biography* (New York: The Viking Press, 1967), 476-477.

14. James had had to ask, too, for a copy of the *Education* in a letter to Adams dated December 7, 1907. The letter and Adams's reply, reveal much of the style of the two friends' correspondence:

"Don't you think that after this dark abyss of time and separation you owe me the approximation of letting me have a copy of your autobiography? Approximation, and reparation! for, seeing a copy last summer at Milly Warner's house, I hastily looked in the index for the word "James"—did *you* never perform a similar act of egotism?—and found myself accused (along with others) of having made Cambridge a conversational desert, or words to that effect. Properly only blood could wipe out such an insult, but you are an old man (70, by the living jingo, and I who have during all these years considered you as about 40!) so that in consideration of the volume I will compound the injury.

"I may add that autobiographies are my particular line of litera-ture, the only books I let myself buy outside of metaphysical trea-tises, and that I have the most extraordinary longing to read yours in particular.

"Pray indulge me in this appetite, and believe me, wishing I could see you sometimes, yours always faithfully."

To which Adams replied on December 9, 1907 (Ford, ed., *Letters*, II: 485-486):

"Of course you have a right to the volume you want. In fact it was printed only for communication to you and a few others who were to help me—I fondly hoped—to file it into shape.

"If I did not send it to you at once, as I did to Charles Eliot, it was because I feared your judgement more than his, but since, now, I must, let me explain.

"Weary of my own imbecility, I tried to clean off a bit of the surface of my mind, in 1904, by printing a volume on the twelfth century, where I could hide, in the last hundred pages, a sort of anchor in history. I knew that not a hundred people in America would understand what I meant, and these were all taught in Jesuit schools, where I was a hell-born scorpion. I need not publish when no one would read or understand.

"Then I undertook—always to clean my own mind—a compan-ion study of the twentieth century, where I could hide—in a stack of rubbish meant only to feed the foolish—a hundred more pages

meant to complete the first hundred of 1904. No one would take the smallest interest in these. I knew they were safe. So was I.

"Unless, indeed, you got hold of them! In that case, I was rather inclined to weep and wail in advance, for I knew your views better than my own.

"With this I send the volume, which, as personal to me, is all in the last chapter. I meant to bid good-bye with graceful and sympathetic courtesy. The devil take it! I feel that Sargent squirms in the portrait. I am not there.

"You, at least, and your brother Harry, have been our credit and pride. We can rest in that." *Letters*.

15. Allen, *William James*, 477. A facsimile of James's letter is reproduced on pp. 478-479.

16. Henry Adams, *The Degradation of the Democratic Dogma* (New York: The Macmillan Co., 1919), 129. Compiled by Henry's brother Brooks, *Degradation* contains Adams's "The Tendency of History," "A Letter to American Teachers of History," and "The Rule of Phase Applied to History," plus Brooks's long essay, "The Heritage of Henry Adams."

17. Henry Adams, *The Education of Henry Adams* (Boston: Houghton Mifflin Co., 1918), 301.

18. "Forty years ago our friends always explained things and had the cosmos down to a point, *teste* Darwin and Charles Lyell. Now they say that they don't believe there is any explanation, or that you can choose between half-a-dozen, all correct. The Germans are all balled up. Every generalisation that we settled forty years ago is abandoned. The one most completely thrown over is our gentle Darwin's Survival which no longer has a leg to stand on. I interpret even Kelvin as throwing it over." Adams to Charles Milnes Gaskell, June 14, 1903, Ford, ed., *Letters*, II: 407.

19. Jordy has shown how imperfectly Adams understood these two laws. See his *Henry Adams*, 158-219.

20. Adams, *Degradation*, 281.

21. Ibid., 308.

22. Ibid., 224-225.

23. Adams's first mention of the law of entropy appears in a letter of 1902 to Brooks Adams in Ford, ed., *Letters*, II: 392. *The Education*, written in 1904, contains only three fleeting references to Lord Kelvin and entropy, although there is much evidence to support the argument that Adams had been a fairly thoroughgoing degradationist before he had heard of Lord Kelvin. See Timothy Paul Donovan, *Henry Adams and Brooks Adams: The Education of Two American Historians* (Norman, Okla.: University of

Oklahoma Press, 1961), 102-125. Adams seemed to feel a strong affinity for Lord Kelvin that went beyond intellectual kinship. In the *Letter* he wrote: "Almost in his [Lord Kelvin's] last words he pathetically proclaimed that his life was a failure in its long effort to reduce his physical energies to a single term. Dying he left the unity, duality, or multiplicity of energies as much disputed as ever." Adams, *Degradation*, 238-239. Writing to Margaret Chanler two years earlier, Adams had said: "Did I tell you how deeply I was touched—in my own sense—by Lord Kelvin's dying confession,—that he had totally failed to understand anything? I, who refuse to face that admission, am delighted to have somebody do it for me by proxy." Adams to Chanler, September 4, 1908, Ford, ed., *Letters*, II, 506.

24. Adams, *Degradation*, 141.

25. Nearly all of the scientists Adams cited in support of his theory—Wilhelm Ostwalt, Johannes von Hartmann, Albert Dastre, Jean-Albert Gaudry, Heinz Hopf, Augustus de Morgan—were Europeans.

26. Adams, *Degradation*, 261.

27. "I've a notion of printing a Letter to Professors. Pure malice! but History will die if not irritated. The only service I can do to my profession is to serve as a flea." Adams to Margaret Chanler, September 9, 1909, Ford, ed., *Letters*, II: 524.

28. Adams, *Degradation*, 212-218. Adams wrote in 1909: "Kelvin was a great man and I am sorry I did not know enough mathematics to follow him instead of Darwin who was all wrong." Adams to Margaret Chanler, June 6, 1909, Ford, ed., *Letters*, II: 519.

29. Adams, *Degradation*, 157. Darwin's achievement was that of "bringing all vital processes under the law of development or evolution,—whether upward or downward being immaterial to the principle that all history must be studied as a science." Ibid., 153.

30. Ibid., 207-208.

31. Howard M. Munford, "Henry Adams and the Tendency of History," *New England Quarterly* 32 (March 1959): 88.

Adams wrote to Elizabeth Cameron on January 24, 1910, about a month before sending out the *Letter* to his friends and colleagues: "I'm amusing myself by printing a little volume to make fun of my fellow historians. The fun of it is that not one of them will understand the fun. The *pince-sans-rire* is not an American form of humor. I don't know that I would see the joke myself if I were not its author. I have to take so much trouble to keep it from being bitter that it has all its nails cut off and can't scratch. Luckily nothing matters, and no one cares. America is a vast mud-flat; you can pepper it with stones but they all disappear instantly without a splash." Ford, ed., *Letters*, II: 531.

Unwittingly, Adams revealed how seriously he took the *Letter* by confessing how difficult it was for him to keep his essay from being bitter. He seemed to know ahead of time that the *Letter*, despite its freight of doom, would fail as an attention-getting device; this made the whole enterprise all the more desperate.

32. See *n.* 19 above.

33. James to Henry Adams, June 17, 1910, James, ed., *Letters*, II: 345-347.

34. Ibid., June 19, 1910, James, ed., *Letters*, II: 346-347.

35. Adams to James, June 20, 1910, Ford, ed., *Letters*, II: 543-544.

36. James to Adams, June 26, 1910, James, ed., *Letters*, II: 347.

37. James to James Ward, June 27, 1909, Ralph Barton Perry, ed., *The Thought and Character of William James* (Boston: Little, Brown and Co., 1936), II: 656.

38. William James, *The Will to Believe, and Other Essays in Popular Philosophy* (New York: Longmans, Green and Co., 1897), 1, 26.

39. Frederick Cople Jaher, *Doubters and Dissenters: Cataclysmic Thought in America, 1885-1918* (New York: The Free Press of Glencoe, 1964), passim.

40. *Boston Herald*, February 17, 1899.

41. Quoted in Robert L. Beisner, *Twelve Against Empire: The Anti-Imperialists, 1898-1900* (New York: McGraw-Hill, 1968), 47.

42. Jaher, *Doubters and Dissenters*, 4-18.

43. Morton and Lucia White, *The Intellectual versus the City: From Thomas Jefferson to Frank Lloyd Wright* (New York: New American Library, 1964), 13-17.

44. John Fiske, "A Century's Progress in Science," *Atlantic Monthly* 78 (July 1896): 25.

45. Charles Saunders Peirce, "Pearson's Grammar of Science," *Popular Science Monthly* 58 (January 1901): 296-300. For a superb treatment of how science contributed to doubt and uncertainty at the end of the century, see Barbara Lynette McClung, "Science and Certainty at the Turn of the Century: A Study of Ideas Revealed in American Periodical Literature, 1899-1910" (Master's thesis, Tulane University, 1965).

46. David J. Brewer, *The Twentieth Century from Another Viewpoint* (New York: F. H. Reven Co., 1899), 30-33.

47. Washington Gladden, *The New Idolatry* (New York: McClure, Phillips and Co., 1906), 231.

48. H. W. Horwill, "Incongruities in American Life," *Current Opinion* 30 (March 1903): 351.

49. Jaher, *Doubters and Dissenters*, 4-18.

50. For an extended discussion of ambivalent American attitudes toward the idea of progress in the two decades following the turn of the century, see Henry F. May, *The End of American Innocence: A Study of the First Years of Our Own Time, 1912-1917* (Chicago: Quadrangle Books, 1959), 20-29ff.

51. Morton White, *Social Thought in America: The Revolt Against Formalism* (1949; rev. ed., Boston: The Beacon Press, 1957). First given currency by White, the term "formalism" has now entered into the general vocabulary of intellectual historians in describing certain features of nineteenth-century thought. Generally, formalism is the tradition of philosophic rationalism, a priori logic, legal absolutism, and the variant of scientific history which aimed at constructing overriding laws of historical growth and decay. See especially ibid., 11-31ff.

52. In addition to White, for other treatments of the intellectual transition of the turn of century see May, passim; Cushing Strout, *The Pragmatic Revolt in American History: Carl Becker and Charles Beard* (New Haven: Yale University Press, 1958), 15-29ff.; Henry Steele Commager, *The American Mind: An Interpretation of American Thought and Character Since the 1880's* (New Haven: Yale University Press, 1950), 41-54ff.; Richard Hofstadter, *The Progressive Historians: Turner, Beard, and Parrington* (New York: Vintage Books, 1968), 3-43ff.; Charles Forcey, *The Crossroads of Liberalism: Croly, Weyl, Lippmann and the Progressive Era, 1900-1925* (New York: Oxford University Press, 1961), passim; and David W. Noble, *The Paradox of Progressive Thought* (Minneapolis: University of Minnesota Press, 1958), passim. Noble's observations on the ambivalence of American thinkers toward the idea of progress at the turn of the century are particularly astute.

53. Oliver Wendell Holmes, *The Common Law* (Boston: Little Brown and Co., 1881), 1-2.

54. Oliver Wendell Holmes, "The Path of the Law," in Perry Miller, ed., *American Thought: Civil War to World War I* (New York: Holt, Rinehart and Winston, 1964), 204.

55. Herbert Croly, *Progressive Democracy* (New York: The Macmillan Co., 1914), 27-28.

56. Forcey, *Crossroads of Liberalism*, 16-17.

57. Herbert Croly, *The Promise of American Life* (Cambridge: Harvard University Press, 1956), 3. First published in 1909.

58. Ibid., 139.

59. Ibid., 452.

60. Thorstein Veblen, "Why Is Economics Not an Evolutionary Science," in his *The Place of Science in Modern Civilization and Other Essays* (New York: B. W. Huebsch, 1919). This essay was first published in 1898.

61. White, *Social Thought in America*, 22-23.

62. Thorstein Veblen, *The Theory of the Leisure Class* (New York: The Macmillan Co., 1899), 192-193.

63. James Harvey Robinson and Charles A. Beard, *The Development of Modern Europe* (New York: Ginn and Co., 1907-1908), I: iii.

64. Hofstadter, *The Progressive Historians*, 182-189ff.; White, *Social Thought in America*, passim.

65. Frederick Jackson Turner, "Social Forces in American History," in his *The Frontier in American History* (New York: Henry Holt, 1920), 323-324.

66. Walter Lippmann, *Preface to Politics* (New York: M. Kennerly and Co., 1913), 23.

67. Mark De Wolfe Howe, ed., *Holmes-Laski Letters: The Correspondence of Mr. Justice Holmes and Harold J. Laski, 1916-1935* (New York: Atheneum, 1963), I: 52-53; Forcey, *Crossroads of Liberalism*, 3-52.

68. David Noble has shown how certain traditional religious doctrines survived in the thinking of post-Darwinian reformers who in other respects fit the definition of antiformalism. See his *The Paradox of Progressive Thought*, passim, and "The Religion of Progress in America, 1890-1914," *Social Forces* 22 (Winter 1955): 417-440.


CHAPTER 2

1. Such a breakdown of the idea's history is to some extent arbitrary and is intended merely to suggest the changing frames of reference within which a multitude of opinions about progress were expressed at different times. The idea was debated vigorously, for at no other time in American history were assertions about progress unchallenged. The intellectual bases of both the assertions and the challenges, however, had their origin in the dominant assumptions about God, history, nature, and science prevailing in different periods, and there is common agreement among historians that rationalism, romanticism, and evolutionism represent reasonably distinct intellectual responses to these topics in the

American past. Each period or "phase" contained its own dialogue over the idea of progress, although there was perhaps more continuity to the idea than the phase approach seems to imply. Not all views of progress in any given phase fit the designation: there were progressive interpretations in the early nineteenth century that were not romantic, just as there were romantic views of history that were not progressive. Employment of the concept of phase always raises the danger of treating the history of ideas as a "bloodless dance of the categories," but it is nonetheless useful in relating variations in the idea of progress to the broader reaches of intellectual life in America, as well as in identifying the general types of progressive thinking that antedated pragmatism. The first two phases can be sketched only briefly. Since it established the milieu in which pragmatism was nurtured, evolutionism and its dialogue over progress must be examined in more detail.

2. J. B. Bury, *The Idea of Progress: An Inquiry into Its Growth and Origin* (1920; reprint ed., New York: Dover Publications, 1955) 64-77; Carl L. Becker, *The Heavenly City of the Eighteenth Century Philosophers* (New Haven: Yale University Press, 1932), 60-61. For analyses of the rationalist view of progress, see: Charles A. Beard, introduction to Bury, *The Idea of Progress* (1932 ed.); Charles A. and Mary R. Beard, *The American Spirit: A Study of the Idea of Civilization in the United States* (1942; reprint ed., New York: Collier Books, 1962), 94-152; Becker, *The Heavenly City*, passim; Daniel J. Boorstin, *The Lost World of Thomas Jefferson* (Boston: Beacon Press, 1948), passim; V. E. Gibbens, "Tom Paine and the Idea of Progress," *Pennsylvania Magazine of History and Biography* 66 (April 1942): 191-204; Merle Curti, *The Growth of American Thought* (1943; reprint ed., New York: Harper and Row, 1964), 165-169; Rutherford E. Delmage, "The American Idea of Progress, 1750-1800, *Proceedings of the American Philosophical Society* 91 (1947): 307-314; Arthur A. Ekirch, *The Idea of Progress in America, 1815-1860* (1944; reprint ed., New York: Peter Smith, 1951), 13-37, Zoltan Haraszti, *John Adams and the Prophets of Progress* (Cambridge: Harvard University Press, 1952), passim; Howard M. Jones, *O Strange New World* (New York: Viking Press, 1964), chaps. 1, 2, 3; E. T. Martin, "Thomas Jefferson and the Idea of Progress" (Ph.D. diss., University of Wisconsin, 1941), passim; Macklin Thomas, "The Idea of Progress in the Writings of Franklin, Freneau, Barlow, and Rush" (Ph.D. diss., University of Wisconsin, 1938), passim; Benjamin F. Wright, *American Interpretations of Natural Law* (Cambridge: Harvard University Press, 1931), passim.

3. J. A. Passmore, "The Malleability of Man in Eighteenth

Century Thought," in Earl J. Wasserman, ed., *Aspects of the Eighteenth Century* (Baltimore: The Johns Hopkins Press, 1965), 21-46; Merle Curti, *Human Nature in American Historical Thought* (Columbia, Mo.: University of Missouri Press, 1969), passim.

4. As R. G. Collingwood put it, "the eighteenth-century conception of progress was based on the . . . false analogy between knowledge of nature and knowledge of mind." R. G. Collingwood, *The Idea of History* (Oxford: Clarendon Press, 1964), 85.

5. Some Enlightenment thinkers—Diderot and Buffon, for example—did not wholly accept the idea of fixed species. Their assumption of an unchanging environment, however, helped prevent them from reaching a theory of evolution. See Norman Hampson, *A Cultural History of the Enlightenment* (New York: Pantheon Books, 1968), 225-230. Most scholars and students of nature, however, accepted gladly the orderly system of taxonomy set forth by Carolus Linneas in his *Systema Naturae* of 1735, in which all forms of life were arranged graphically in the seried structure of the great chain of being.

6. Hampson, *Cultural History*, 223-224; Boorstin, *The Lost World of Thomas Jefferson*, passim. One of the best illustrations of how eighteenth-century Americans viewed nature can be seen in the way Thomas Jefferson and the other founders of the American Philosophical Society, the new nation's closest approximation of an intellectual establishment, regarded the discovery of fossil remains of enormous animals in the western part of North America. Since the giant animals had obviously once existed and since the structure of nature did not vary, the Jeffersonian circle assumed that such exotic creatures still walked the earth. Accordingly, the society advised its permanent committee to collect remains of "unknown," not "extinct" animals, and Jefferson himself eagerly looked forward to receiving evidence of a live American mammoth. Boorstin, *The Lost World of Thomas Jefferson*, 30-40.

7. Jefferson to Richard Henry Lee, quoted in Carl L. Becker, *The Declaration of Independence: A Study in the History of Political Ideas* (New York: Alfred A. Knopf, 1956), 25-26.

8. After surveying the writings of Jefferson, Franklin, George Washington, Richard Henry Lee, John Witherspoon, James Wilson, Benjamin Rush, and a host of lesser luminaries, Rutherford Delmage concluded that "the dominant note in American thought between 1750 and 1800 was that of progress." Delmage, "The American Idea of Progress," 313.

9. For concise discussions of the rationalist meaning of "hap-

piness," see Adrienne Koch, *Power, Morals and the Founding Fathers: Essays in the Interpretation of the American Enlightenment* (Ithaca: Cornell University Press, 1961), 23-49, and Howard Mumford Jones, *The Pursuit of Happiness* (Cambridge: Harvard University Press, 1953), 1-28.

10. Boorstin, *The Lost World of Thomas Jefferson*, 99-108; Gilbert Chinard, "Eighteenth Century Theories on America as a Human Habitat," *Proceedings of the American Philosophical Society* 91 (1947): 27-57; Henry Ward Church, "Corneille de Pauw and the Controversy Over His *Recherches Philosophique sur des Americains*," *Publications of the Modern Language Association* 51 (1936): 178-206.

11. Thomas Jefferson, *Notes on the State of Virginia*, ed. William Peden (Chapel Hill: University of North Carolina Press, 1955), 59, 65, 83.

12. William Currie, *Historical Account of the Climate and Diseases of the United States of America* (Philadelphia, 1792), 405-409.

13. Ronald S. Crane, "Anglican Apologetics and the Idea of Progress," *Modern Philology* 31 (May 1934): 350; Harry Hayden Clark, "The Influence of Science on American Ideas, from 1775 to 1809," *Transactions of the Wisconsin Academy of Sciences, Arts and Letters* 35 (1943): 307-314.

14. Boorstin, *The Lost World of Thomas Jefferson*, 226-227.

15. Benjamin Rush, *Three Lectures upon Animal Life* (Philadelphia, 1799), 62, 67-68.

16. Jefferson to William Ludlow, September 6, 1824, *The Writings of Thomas Jefferson* (Washington, D.C.: The Library of Congress, 1869-1871), XVI: 75.

17. Bury, *Idea of Progress*, 98-176; Sidney Pollard, *The Idea of Progress: History and Society* (New York: Basic Books, 1968), 18-96.

18. Jones, *O Strange New World*, 61. See also Charles L. Sanford, *The Quest for Paradise: Europe and the American Moral Imagination* (Urbana, Ill.: University of Illinois Press, 1961); Arthur K. Moore, *The Frontier Mind: A Cultural Analysis of the Kentucky Frontiersmen* (Lexington: University of Kentucky Press, 1957), 13-43.

19. George Berkeley, *Works*, ed. A. C. Fraser (Oxford, 1871), III: 232.

20. Andrew Burnaby, *Travels Through the Middle Settlement in North America*, in John Pinkerton, ed., *Voyages and Travels in All Parts of the World* (London, 1812), XIII: 750.

21. Richard Price, *Observations on the Importance of the American Revolution* (London, 1784), 7.

22. Quoted in Henry Nash Smith, *Virgin Land: The American*

*West as Symbol and Myth* (New York: Vintage Books, 1957), 10; see also Daniel Boorstin, *The Americans: The Colonial Experience* (New York: Random House, 1958), 152-158.

23. From "The Rights of Man," quoted in Beard, *American Spirit*, 103.

24. Moncure Daniel Conway, ed., *The Writings of Thomas Paine* (New York, 1894), I: 114, 118-119.

25. A. H. Smyth, ed., *The Writings of Benjamin Franklin* (New York and London, 1905-1907), IX: 489.

26. Quoted in Ekirch, *Idea of Progress*, 32.

27. For discussions of the idea of progress in America during the middle period, see ibid., passim; Stow Persons, *American Minds: A History of Ideas* (New York: Holt, Rinehart and Winston, 1958), 153-157; Ralph Gabriel, *The Course of American Democratic Thought* (New York: The Ronald Press, 1954), chap. 2; Beard, *The American Spirit*, 153-244; Rush Welter, "The Idea of Progress in America," *Journal of the History of Ideas* 16 (June 1955): 401-415; Mildred Silverman, "Emerson and the Idea of Progress," *American Literature* 12 (March 1940): 1-19; Howard Mumford Jones, "The Influence of European Ideas in Nineteenth-century America," *American Literature* 7 (March 1935-January 1936): 241-273; John L. Thomas, "Romantic Reform in America, 1815-1865," *American Quarterly* 17 (Winter 1965): 656-681; R. W. B. Lewis, *The American Adam: Innocence, Tragedy and Tradition in the Nineteenth Century* (Chicago: University of Chicago Press, 1955), passim; Sanford, *Quest for Paradise*, 135-154; and A. N. Kaul, *The American Vision: Actual and Ideal Society in Nineteenth-century Fiction* (New Haven: Yale University Press, 1963), 1-44. Leo Marx, *The Machine in the Garden: Technology and the Pastoral Ideal in America* (New York: Oxford University Press, 1967), 194-209ff.; Yehoshua Arieli, *Individualism and Nationalism in American Ideology* (Cambridge: Harvard University Press, 1964), 246-276ff.

28. Ekirch, *Idea of Progress*, 267. Ekirch's encyclopedic study fails to treat adequately antiprogressive thought during this period. See Sanford, *Quest for Paradise*, passim; Marx, *Machine in the Garden*, passim; William R. Taylor, *Cavalier and Yankee: The Old South and American National Character* (New York: George Braziller, 1961), 95-141; and Lewis, *The American Adam*, passim.

29. Henry James, Sr., "Democracy and Its Issues," in his *Lectures and Miscellanies* (New York, 1852), 2, 44-45. For a discussion of America's rejection of tradition in the middle period, see Lewis, *The American Adam*, 13-27.

30. One common thread linking many reformers in the

antebellum period was impatience with—and sometimes hostility toward—social institutions whose habits and practices seemed to stifle needed reform. Numerous reformers became overtly anti-institutional, arguing for the primacy of individual conversion over against institutional reconstruction as the key to social progress. See Thomas, "Romantic Reform in America, 1815-1865," 656-685, and Stanley Elkins, *Slavery: A Problem in American Institutional and Intellectual Life* (New York: Grosset and Dunlap, 1963), 140-147.

31. For treatments of the interaction of European and American thought in the antebellum period, see Howard Mumford Jones, "Influence of European Ideas," 241-273, and his *America and French Culture, 1750-1848* (Chapel Hill: University of North Carolina Press, 1927), passim; F. O. Matthiessen, *American Renaissance: Art and Expression in the Age of Emerson and Whitman* (New York: Oxford University Press, 1954), passim; Paul R. Baker, *The Fortunate Pilgrims: Americans in Italy, 1800-1860* (Cambridge: Harvard University Press, 1964), passim; and, most importantly, René Wellek, *Confrontations: Studies in the Intellectual and Literary Relations Between Germany, England and the United States during the Nineteenth Century* (Princeton: Princeton University Press, 1965), passim.

32. Collingwood writes that "according to [the romantic conception of progress] past stages of history led necessarily to the present; a given form of civilization can exist only when the time is ripe for it, and has its value just because those are the conditions of its existing; if therefore we could bring back the Middle Ages we should only be going back to a stage in the process which has led to the present, and the process would go on as before. Thus the Romanticists conceived the value of a past stage of history like the Middle Ages in a double way: partly as something of permanent value in itself, as a unique achievement of the human mind, and partly as taking place in a course of development leading on to other things of still greater value." Collingwood, *The Idea of History*, 87-88.

33. George Bancroft, *Literary and Historical Miscellanies* (New York, 1855), 516. For useful accounts of the romantic view of the past in America see Lewis, *The American Adam*, 158-173; and David Levin, *History as Romantic Art: Bancroft, Prescott, Motley, and Parkman* (Stanford: Stanford University Press, 1959), passim.

34. George Bancroft, *History of the United States* (Boston, 1856), II: 267, 269. For a discussion of the complexities in Bancroft's conception of progress, see Merrill Lewis, "Organic Metaphor and Edenic Myth in George Bancroft's *History of the United States*," *Journal of the History of Ideas* 26 (October-December 1965): 587-592.

35. Boorstin, *The Lost World of Thomas Jefferson*, 54.

36. Jones, *America and French Culture, 1750-1848*, 472.

37. "The tendency of historic Romanticism was away from authority and toward liberty, away from the acceptance of caked wisdom and toward the exploratory development of the individual, away from the secure fixities and toward the drama of the unforeseeable, away from monarchy and toward the sovereignty of the people." Jacques Barzun, *Classic, Romantic and Modern* (New York: Doubleday and Co., 1961), xxi.

38. Jones, "The Influence of European Ideas," 257-261.

39. William Henry Channing, "Introduction," *The Present* 1 (September 1843): 5.

40. Jones, "Influence of European Ideas," 255.

41. James Dwight Dana, "Science and the Scientific Schools," *American Journal of Education* 2 (September 1856): 364.

42. Quoted in E. R. Corson, "Agassiz's Essay on Classification Fifty Years After," *Scientific Monthly* 11 (July 1920): 45.

43. E. C. Agassiz, *Louis Agassiz: His Life and Correspondence* (Boston: Houghton Mifflin Co., 1885), I: 92-93, 245.

44. John Weiss, *Life and Correspondence of Theodore Parker* (New York: D. Appleton and Co., 1864), II: 471.

45. Edward Hitchcock, *The Religion of Geology and Its Connected Sciences* (Boston, 1856), 439.

46. Loren Eiseley, *Darwin's Century: Evolution and the Men Who Discovered It* (New York: Doubleday and Co., 1961), 91-115.

47. Louis Agassiz, *Essay on Classification,* ed. Edward Lurie (Cambridge: Harvard University Press, 1962), 175, 177, 182, 137.

48. James, *Lectures and Miscellanies*, 261, 279-280, 285, 295, 298-299.

49. Mark Van Doren, ed., *The Portable Walt Whitman* (New York: Viking Press, 1945), 63.

50. Henry David Thoreau, *A Week on the Concord and Merrimack Rivers* (Boston: Ticknor and Fields, 1868), 29.

51. Henry David Thoreau, *Walden* (New York: Dodd, Mead and Co., 1946), 53.

52. Mildred Silver has explicated nicely Emerson's ambiguous attitude toward the idea of progress. Silver, "Emerson and the Idea of Progress," passim.

53. Charles Sanford traces how the concept of the sublime in Cole's paintings and William Cullen Bryant's poetry dissented from contemporary optimism. Sanford, *The Quest for Paradise*, 135-154.

54. Edward Waldo Emerson, ed., *The Journals of Ralph Waldo Emerson* (Boston: Houghton Mifflin, 1909-1914), III: 410.

55. Charles Sumner, *The Law of Human Progress* (Boston, 1849), 28.

56. There was, of course, a dark, pessimistic side of American romanticism that was also highly skeptical of the possibility of progress. Poe, Hawthorne, and Melville represent this perspective.

57. William Ellery Channing, *Works, II* (Boston: American Unitarian Association, 1855), 368.

58. David W. Marcell, "The Two Whitmans and *Democracy in America*," in Ray B. Browne et al., eds., *Challenges in American Culture* (Bowling Green, Ohio: Bowling Green University Popular Press, 1970), 182-183.

59. Steven Pearl Andrews, *Cost the Limit of Price* (New York, 1852), 20-21.

60. Michael Cowan has recently shown how Emerson employed the metaphor of the city to suggest that the individual and the community mutually supported each other. Michael Cowan, *City of the West: Emerson, America, and Urban Metaphor* (New Haven: Yale University Press, 1967), passim.

61. Bancroft, *Literary and Historical Miscellanies*, 418-419.

62. Thomas, "Romantic Reform in America, 1815-1865," 660.

63. Persons, *American Minds*, 154.

64. Rush Welter points out that Americans in the 1840s viewed the revolutionary turmoil in Europe with a good deal of alarm, despite the fact that these revolutions were widely rationalized in progressive, democratic terms. Progress thus seemed to have a much more radical connotation in Europe than it did in America. Americans of the middle period, Welter observed (citing Ralph Gabriel's *The Course of American Democratic Thought* and an article by Louis Hartz, "American Political Thought and the American Revolution," for corroboration), had had their revolution and were by and large satisfied with the results; what remained was "to find a way to extend the benefits of an existing perfection to as large a part of the population as possible." Welter, "The Idea of Progress in America," 404-408.

CHAPTER 3

1. John Dewey, *The Influence of Darwin on Philosophy* (New York: Henry Holt and Company, 1910), 8-9.

2. Darwin used this phrase in describing his conclusions to Harvard botanist Asa Gray in a letter dated July 20, 1856. George

Daniels, ed., *Darwinism Comes to America* (Waltham, Mass.: Blaisdell Publishing Company, 1968), 4.

3. Charles Darwin, *The Descent of Man, and Selection in Relation to Sex* (New York: D. Appleton and Company, 1871), 140, 240.

4. Ibid., 48, 605, 619.

5. Charles Darwin, *On the Origin of Species* (New York: D. Appleton and Company, 1860), 351.

6. Darwin noted in his copy of Robert Chambers's *Vestiges of Creation*, "never use the word[s] higher and lower." Gertrude Himmelfarb, *Darwin and the Darwinian Revolution* (New York: W. W. Norton and Company, 1968), 220.

7. Ibid., 202.

8. Perry Miller, ed., *American Thought: Civil War to World War I* (New York: Holt, Rinehart and Winston, 1964), xxiii.

9. Richard Hofstadter, *Social Darwinism in American Thought* (Boston: Beacon Press, 1955), 34.

10. Herbert Spencer, *First Principles of a New System of Philosophy* (New York: D. Appleton and Company, 1902), 367.

11. Herbert Spencer, *Social Statics* (New York: D. Appleton and Company, 1865), 74, 76, 79-80.

12. James McCosh, *The Religious Aspect of Evolution* (New York: Charles Scribner's Sons, 1888), 7.

13. Review of Darwin's *Origin of Species, American Journal of Science* (March 1860), quoted in Daniels, ed., *Darwinism Comes to America*, 18.

14. For useful accounts of the impact of Darwinian and Spencerian evolutionism on American thought, see: Hofstadter, *Social Darwinism*; Paul F. Boller, Jr., *American Thought in Transition: The Impact of Evolutionary Naturalism, 1865-1900* (Chicago: Rand McNally and Company, 1969); Philip P. Wiener, *Evolution and the Founders of Pragmatism* (Cambridge: Harvard University Press, 1949); and Stow Persons, ed., *Evolutionary Thought in America* (New Haven: Yale University Press, 1950). Two general works are helpful in treating Darwinism in its international and historical context: Loren Eiseley, *Darwin's Century* (New York: Doubleday and Company, 1961), and Himmelfarb, *Darwin and the Darwinian Revolution*. Two collections of documents are R. J. Wilson, ed., *Darwinism and the American Intellectual* (Homewood, Ill.: The Dorsey Press, 1967), and Daniels, ed., *Darwinism Comes to America*.

15. R. W. B. Lewis suggests an analogy between "the history of a culture . . . and the unfolding course of a dialogue: a dialogue more or less philosophic in nature and, like Plato's containing a number of voices." The vital aspect of a culture, Lewis argues, lies

not merely in the dominant ideas and images which preoccupy its artists and intellectuals, but in the clashes and debates which those ideas engender. These clashes, these "cultural conversations" over major ideas and issues, provide the culture's distinctive flavor and delineate the intellectual life of an age. R. W. B. Lewis, *The American Adam* (Chicago: University of Chicago Press, 1965), 1-5.

16. Henry Ward Beecher, *Evolution and Religion* (New York: Fords, Howard and Hulbert, 1885), 15, 16, 115; James McCosh, *Christianity and Positivism* (New York: Robert Carter and Bros., 1871), 51. See also Bert J. Lowenberg, "American Scientists and Darwinism," *American Historical Review* 38 (July 1933): 687-701; Sidney Ratner, "Evolution and the Rise of the Scientific Spirit in America," *Philosophy of Science* 3 (January 1936): 104-122; Herbert W. Schneider, "The Influence of Darwin and Spencer on American Philosophical Theology," *Journal of the History of Ideas* 6 (January 1945): 3-18.

Perhaps the most concise statement of how evolutionary postulates were used in the service of the traditional Christian optimism was McCosh's: "There is proof of Plan in the Organic Unity and Growth of the World. As there is evidence of purpose, not only in every organ of the plant, but in the whole plant; not only in every limb of the animal, but in the whole animal frame, and in the growth of both plant and animal from month to month and year to year: so there are proofs of design, not merely in the individual plant and individual animal, but in the whole structure of the Cosmos and in the manner in which it makes progress from age to age. Every reflecting mind, in tracing the development of the plant or animal, will see a design and a unity of design in it, in the unconscious elements being all made to conspire to a given end, in the frame of the animated being taking a predetermined form; so every one trained in the great truths of advanced science should see a contemplated purpose in the way in which the materials and forces and life of the universe are made to conspire, to secure a progress through indeterminate ages. The persistence of force may be one of the elements conspiring to this end; the law of Natural Selection may be another, or it may only be a modification of the same: all and each work in the midst of a struggle for existence, in which the strong prevail and the weak disappear. But in all this there is a starting point and a terminus, and rails along which the powers run, and an intelligence planning and guiding the whole, and bringing it to its destination freighted with blessings." McCosh, *Christianity and Positivism*, 90-91.

17. Wiener, *Evolution and the Founders of Pragmatism*, 137.

18. In Fiske's Cosmic Philosophy (Fiske always capitalized the term), the "religious attitude" prevailed, and the "antagonism between Science and Religion . . . is . . . utterly and for ever swept away." John Fiske, *Outlines of Cosmic Philosophy* (Boston: James R. Osgood and Company, 1875), I: 184.

19. Milton Berman, *John Fiske: The Evolution of a Popularizer* (Cambridge: Harvard University Press, 1961).

20. "To treat of the universe of phenomena with the noumenon of God is nonsense." John Fiske, *Darwinism and Other Essays* (New York: Macmillan and Company, 1879), 54.

21. Ibid., 19.

22. Fiske, *Outlines of Cosmic Philosophy*, II: 195.

23. John Fiske, *The Destiny of Man Viewed in the Light of His Origin* (Boston: Houghton Mifflin, 1884), 25.

24. Ibid., 113-114.

25. Fiske, *Outlines of Cosmic Philosophy*, II: 223-224.

26. Berman, *John Fiske*, 159.

27. John Fiske, *Studies in Religion* (Boston: Houghton Mifflin, 1902), 19-20.

28. In his later writings on American history, Fiske placed the United States—indeed, New England—at the pinnacle of civilization's historical and spiritual advance. Berman, *John Fiske*, 205-219.

29. John Fiske, *Through Nature to God* (Boston: Houghton Mifflin, 1899), 60-130.

30. Fiske, *Outlines of Cosmic Philosophy*, II: 187.

31. Ibid., 228.

32. John Fiske, *The Idea of God as Affected by Modern Knowledge* (Boston: Houghton Mifflin, 1885), xxv; see also his *The Destiny of Man*, passim.

33. Fiske, *Outlines of Cosmic Philosophy*, II: chaps. 16, 21, 22, *Darwinism and Other Essays*, 40-49, *A Century of Science* (Boston: Houghton Mifflin, 1899), 100-122.

34. Fiske, *A Century of Science*, 108-109.

35. In *Outlines of Cosmic Philosophy*, II: 164-190, Fiske attempted to resolve the question of free will by demonstrating that all volitional acts were deliberate and thus had causes. Such causes negated the notion of freedom and hence placed the question of will in the larger context of the total, evolving environment.

36. James's essay attacking Spencer, "Great Men, Great Thoughts, and the Environment," appeared in the October 1880 issue of *The Atlantic Monthly*. Fiske's reply, "Sociology and Hero Worship," appeared the following January in the same magazine;

it is reprinted in his *Excursions of an Evolutionist* (Boston: Houghton Mifflin, 1895), 175-202.

37. Fiske, *Outlines of Cosmic Philosophy*, II: 72-73, 83.

38. "Nevertheless, in spite of the fact that the career of progress has been neither universal nor unbroken, it remains entirely true that the law of progress, when discovered, will be found to be the law of history." Ibid., 195, 196, 209.

39. Fiske, *The Destiny of Man*, 118-119.

40. Thomas H. Huxley, "Evolution and Ethics," *The Popular Science Monthly* 44 (1893): 18-35, 178-191.

41. For example, see Robert Mathews, "Evolutionary Ethics," *The Popular Science Monthly*, 44 (1893): 192-195; Lesley L. Stephen, "Ethics and the Struggle for Existence," *The Popular Science Monthly* 44 (1893): 224-238; Lewis G. Janes, "Ethics in Natural Law," *The Popular Science Monthly* 46 (1894-95): 322-328.

42. Reprinted in the *Boston Index*, December 2, 1875, 56. The most detailed account of Wright's life is in Edward H. Madden, *Chauncey Wright and the Foundations of Pragmatism* (Seattle: University of Washington Press, 1963), 3-30.

43. Wiener, *Evolution and the Founders of Pragmatism*, 18-30.

44. William James, *Collected Essays and Reviews* (New York: Longmans, Green and Company, 1920), 21.

45. Charles Sanders Peirce, *Chance, Love and Logic* (New York: Harcourt, Brace, and Co., 1923), xviii.

46. James Bradley Thayer, ed., *Letters of Chauncey Wright* (Cambridge, Mass.: John Wilson and Son, 1878), 227.

47. Ibid., 370.

48. James, *Collected Essays and Reviews*, 21.

49. Ralph Barton Perry, *The Thought and Character of William James* (Boston: Little, Brown, 1935), II: 720.

50. Ibid., I: 525.

51. Charles Eliot Norton, ed., *Philosophical Discussions by Chauncey Wright* (New York: Henry Holt and Company, 1877), 400.

52. Ibid., 6.

53. Ibid., 397.

54. Ibid., 229.

55. Ibid., 407.

56. Thayer, ed., *Letters*, 193-194.

57. Ibid., 146.

58. Norton, ed., *Philosophical Discussions*, 7. Wright once referred to nature as "a never ending experiment in the possibilities of her laws." Thayer, ed., *Letters*, 169.

59. Madden, *Chauncey Wright*, 87-91.

60. Norton, ed., *Philosophical Discussions*, 69, 73.

61. Ibid., 63.

62. Thayer, ed., *Letters*, 111.

63. Norton, ed., *Philosophical Discussions*, 16.

64. Samuel Chugerman, *Lester Frank Ward: The American Aristotle* (Durham: Duke University Press, 1939). Richard Hofstadter devoted a chapter of his *Social Darwinism in American Thought* to Ward, as did Henry S. Commager in *The American Mind: An Interpretation of American Thought and Character Since the 1880's* (New Haven: Yale University Press, 1950). John C. Burnham, however, argues that Ward's significance and influence have largely been overestimated. See his *Lester Frank Ward in American Thought* (Washington, D.C.: Public Affairs Press, 1956).

65. Howard W. Odum, ed., *American Masters of Social Science* (Port Washington, N.Y.: Henry Holt and Company, 1927), 95.

66. In addition to these writings, Ward published approximately six hundred other articles, essays, and notes, many of which were collected in the six-volume *Glimpses of the Cosmos* (New York: G. P. Putnam's Sons, 1913-1917). *Glimpses* reveals Ward's incredible breadth of interest and capability: it contains writings on anthropology, geology, natural history, philosophy, religion, education, politics, economics, and sexology.

67. James Q. Dealey, "Lester Frank Ward," in Odum, ed., *American Masters of Social Science*, 61.

68. "True scientific progress tends constantly to increase the number of known facts and to reduce the number of fundamental concepts." Lester Ward, *Dynamic Sociology* (New York: D. Appleton and Company, 1883), 1: 220.

69. Lester Ward, *Pure Sociology* (New York: The Macmillan Company, 1903), 91.

70. Ward was among several critics who observed that, logically, the Spencerian idea of equilibrium involved an incongruous triumph of the law of entropy; rather than progressing to ultimate perfection and happiness, Spencer's evolutionary universe was moving inexorably to its death through the gradual dissipation of the solar system's heat and energy. Cynthia Eagle Russett, *The Concept of Equilibrium in American Social Thought* (New Haven: Yale University Press, 1966), 46.

71. In drawing the distinction between genesis and telesis, Ward was extending Darwin's observation that the laws of natural selection had only limited applicability in the case of man. See Darwin, *The Descent of Man*, chap. 5.

72. Ward, *Glimpses of the Cosmos*, III: 304.

73. Synergy is "the systematic and organic working together of the antithetical forces of nature." Ward, *Pure Sociology*, 171.

74. Ward, *Dynamic Sociology*, 1: 220-324. Ward's basic point in recounting the natural course of the development of life is "that life is a property of matter." Ibid., 320.

75. Ibid., 364-365.

76. Ibid., 1: 356.

77. Ibid., 11: 81-89.

78. Ibid., 1: 15-16.

79. "Civilization is the result of the activities of all men during all time, struggling against the environment and slowly conquering nature." Lester Ward, *Applied Sociology* (Boston: Ginn and Company, 1906), 132.

80. Ward, *Pure Sociology*, 544-545.

81. Ward, *Dynamic Sociology*, 11: 94, 111-157.

82. Ibid., 128-129.

83. Ibid., 155-156.

84. Ibid., 11: 632-633.

85. Ward, *Applied Sociology*, iii.

86. Ward, *Outlines of Sociology*, 292-293; Ward, *The Psychic Factors of Civilization* (Boston: Ginn and Company, 1893), 301-331; Ward, *Applied Sociology*, 331-339.

87. Ward, *Pure Sociology*, 175-176.

88. Ibid., 175.


CHAPTER 4


1. For accounts of William's youth, see F. O. Matthiessen, *The James Family* (New York: Alfred A. Knopf, 1947); Ralph Barton Perry, ed., *The Thought and Character of William James* (Boston: Little, Brown, 1935), I; and Gay Wilson Allen, *William James: A Biography* (New York: The Viking Press, 1967).

2. Perry, ed., *Thought and Character*, I: 332.

3. William James, *The Varieties of Religious Experience: A Study in Human Nature* (1902; reprint ed., New York: Collier Books, 1961), 138.

4. Quoted in Perry, ed., *Thought and Character*, I: 322-323.

5. James, *The Varieties of Religious Experience*, 138-139. James called attention in a footnote to his father's similar experience.

6. Ibid., 139.

7. Henry James, ed., *The Letters of William James* (Boston: The Atlantic Monthly Press, 1920), I: 147-148.

8. Perry, ed., *Thought and Character,* II: 11.

9. Paul Conkin, *Puritans and Pragmatists: Eight Eminent American Thinkers* (New York: Dodd, Mead Company, 1968), 278.

10. Quoted in Perry, ed., *Thought and Character*, II: 457. In a letter to his brother Henry, James forecast that *Pragmatism* was potentially an " 'epoch-making' book . . . something like the protestant reformation." Ibid., 453.

11. Philip Wiener, *Evolution and the Founders of Pragmatism* (Cambridge: Harvard University Press, 1949).

12. William James, *The Principles of Psychology* (New York: Henry Holt, 1890), I: 183.

13. Ibid., 8.

14. Ibid., 78.

15. Ibid., 138-139.

16. Ibid., 288-289.

17. William James, "What the Will Effects," *Scribner's* 3 (1888): 240.

18. James, *Principles*, I: 141.

19. Ibid., 246.

20. Ibid., 235.

21. Ibid., 243. There are, James insisted, no discrete sense impressions of the kind used by Locke and Hume and the British empiricists as the basic unit of experience. Even though the structure of language, with its separation of substantive and transitive domains, tended to support the notion that each sensation is a separate entity, the physiological continuity of consciousness denied sensational separation. There may be a separation of external objects, James allowed, but the perception of their separateness is itself a part of "one protracted consciousness, one unbroken stream." The old psychology, based on the associationist tradition that ideas and perceptions are compounded amalgams of atomistic, unchanging wholes impressed upon a passive tabula rasa, was conceptually inadequate to approach the mind's true dynamism and essential interestedness in all it apprehends. Ibid., 243-248.

22. Ibid., 465.

23. In summing up his chapter on conception, James put it this way: "*This whole function of conceiving, of fixing, and holding fast to meanings has no significance apart from the fact that the conceiver is a creature with partial purposes and private ends*." Ibid., 482.

24. Ibid., II: 634. Here James is quoting from his 1881 essay, "Reflex Action and Theism."

25. Ibid., 559-567.

26. Ibid., 572.

27. Ibid.

28. Ibid., 573.

29. Ibid. But it was clear that the *Principles* left the door open for healthy-minded individuals to will the kind of future they desired without any absolute psychic impairments.

30. Like all of James's other books, *The Will to Believe* was a collection of previously published essays.

31. James, ed., *Letters*, II: 259.

32. William James, *Pragmatism: A New Name for Some Old Ways of Thinking* (New York: Meridian Books, 1955), 26. First published in 1907. *Pragmatism, A Pluralistic Universe*, and *Some Problems of Philosophy* all began with essays that outlined the dilemma.

33. As James put it, "In short, the notion that real contingency and ambiguity may be features of the real world is a perfectly unimpeachable hypothesis. Only in such a world can moral judgments have a claim to be." William James, *The Will to Believe and Other Essays in Popular Philosophy* (New York: Longmans, Green and Co., 1897), 292.

34. James, *Pragmatism*, 18.

35. James, *The Will to Believe*, 150.

36. Ibid., 158.

37. William James, *Selected Papers on Philosophy* (New York: E. P. Dutton, 1917), 253.

38. James, *The Will to Believe*, 168.

39. James's attacks against extreme empiricism are contained in many essays in *Pragmatism* and *Essays in Radical Empiricism*; for his criticism of Wright, see "Against Nihilism," an unpublished paper possibly read before the Metaphysical Club in the early 1870s, reprinted in Perry, ed., *Thought and Character*, I: 525-528.

40. Perry, *Thought and Character*, I: 497-499.

41. James, *The Will to Believe*, 109.

42. Ibid., 54-55.

43. "It is almost incredible that men who are themselves working philosophers should pretend that any philosophy can be, or ever has been, constructed without the help of personal preference, belief, or divination." Ibid., 93.

44. Ibid., 130.

45. James, *Pragmatism*, 133.

46. Ibid., 58.

47. James, *The Will to Believe*, 151.

48. James, *Pragmatism*, 184.

49. James, *The Will to Believe*, 178.

50. Ibid., 226.

51. William James, *Memories and Studies* (New York: Longmans, Green and Co., 1924), 227.

52. William James, *Some Problems of Philosophy* (New York: Longmans, Green and Co., 1911), 3.

53. James, *Pragmatism*, 255-257.

54. Ibid., 286-287.

55. James, *Some Problems of Philosophy*, 223.

56. Ibid., 230.

57. Ibid.

58. James, *Pragmatism*, 297-298.

59. William James, *Essays on Faith and Morals* (New York: Longmans, Green and Co., 1943), 305.

60. Quoted in Lloyd Morris, *William James: The Message of a Modern Mind* (New York: Charles Scribner's Sons, 1950), 86.

61. For accounts of James's social views see Perry, ed., *Thought and Character*, II: 280-322; Morris, *William James*, 68-83; and Robert Beisner, *Twelve Against Empire: The Anti-Imperialists, 1898-1900* (New York: McGraw-Hill, 1968), 35-58.

62. James, *Memories and Studies*, 286.

63. James, ed., *Letters*, II: 90.

64. James, *Memories and Studies*, 313, 318.

CHAPTER 5

1. John Dewey, *Characters and Events*, ed. Joseph Ratner (New York: Henry Holt and Co., 1929), II: 11.

2. John Dewey, *Studies in Logical Theory* (Chicago: University of Chicago Press, 1903); Dewey letter quoted in Ralph Barton Perry, ed., *The Thought and Character of William James* (Boston: Little, Brown and Co., 1936), II: 521.

3. Quoted in Perry, ed., *Thought and Character*, II: 519.

4. William James, *Collected Essays and Reviews* (New York: Longmans, Green and Co., 1920), 446.

5. John Dewey, "From Absolutism to Experimentalism," in George P. Adams and William P. Montague, eds., *Contemporary American Philosophy* (New York: The Macmillan Co., 1930), II: 21.

6. Ibid., 13.

7. Ibid., 19.

8. For a recent account of the group around Dewey at Chicago, see Darnell Rucker, *The Chicago Pragmatists* (Minneapolis: University of Minnesota Press, 1969).

9. Quoted in Jane Dewey, "Biography of John Dewey," in Paul

G. Schilpp, ed., *The Philosophy of John Dewey* (New York: The Tudor Publishing Co., 1951), 45.

10. Morton White notes that the *Outlines* was Dewey's last idealist work. Morton White, *The Origins of Dewey's Instrumentalism* (New York: Columbia University Press, 1943), xiv.

11. Sidney Hook, ed., *John Dewey: Philosopher of Science and Freedom* (New York: The Dial Press, 1950), 29.

12. White, *Origins of Dewey's Instrumentalism*, 18-19.

13. Schilpp, *Philosophy of John Dewey*, 23. But Dewey did feel that *The Principles* carried a great deal more freight than James allowed. When James criticized the Chicago School for neglecting the psychological dimensions of pragmatism, Dewey responded by pointing out how adequately *The Principles* had already covered this ground. "I have a good mind," he wrote to James in 1903, "sometime to make an inventory of all the points in which your psychology 'already' furnishes the instrumentalities for a pragmatic logic, ethics and metaphysics." Quoted in Perry, ed., *Thought and Character*, II: 525.

14. James, *Memories and Studies* (New York: Longmans, Green and Co., 1924), 102-103.

15. William James, *The Will to Believe, and Other Essays in Popular Philosophy* (New York: Longmans, Green and Co., 1897), 24.

16. John Dewey, *Reconstruction in Philosophy* (1920; reprint ed., Boston: Beacon Press, 1948), 18.

17. John Dewey, *The Quest for Certainty: A Study of the Relation of Knowledge and Action* (New York: Minton, Balch and Co., 1929), 7-8, 13.

18. John Dewey, *The Influence of Darwin on Philosophy* (New York: Henry Holt and Co., 1910), 54.

19. John Dewey, *Human Nature and Conduct* (1922; reprint ed., New York: The Modern Library, 1929), 261.

20. John Dewey, *Intelligence in The Modern World*, ed. Joseph Ratner (New York: The Modern Library, 1939), 353.

21. Dewey, *Reconstruction in Philosophy*, 32-33.

22. Ibid., 93.

23. Ibid., 40-41.

24. Dewey, *The Influence of Darwin*, 287.

25. John Dewey, "Time and Individuality," in Daniel Webster Hering, et al., *Time and Its Mysteries* (New York: New York University Press, 1940), 88.

26. Dewey, *Reconstruction in Philosophy*, 82.

27. Dewey, *The Influence of Darwin*, 221.

28. John Dewey, *Essays in Experimental Logic* (Chicago: Univer-

sity of Chicago Press, 1916), 312-312. Dewey did not always make a careful distinction between the empirical or "first" and the experimental or "second" revolutions. But a careful reading of *The Influence of Darwin* and *Reconstruction in Philosophy* reveals the delineation he had in mind. It was on the basis of such a delineation that he claimed, "Intellectually speaking, the centuries since the fourteenth are the middle ages"; Darwinism marked their end. Dewey, *The Influence of Darwin*, 60.

29. Dewey, *Reconstruction in Philosophy*, ix.

30. John Dewey, *Philosophy and Civilization* (New York: Minton, Balch and Co., 1931), 324. This failure to apply science to all realms of experience was the core of the crisis: "Here, then, lies the reconstruction work to be done by philosophy. It must do for the development of inquiry into human affairs and hence into morals what the philosophers of the last few centuries did for the promotion of scientific inquiry in physical and physiological conditions and aspects of human life. . . . From the position here taken, reconstruction can be nothing less than the work of developing, of forming, of producing (in the literal sense of that word) the intellectual instrumentalities which will progressively direct inquiry into the deeply and inclusively human—that is to say moral—facts of the present situation." Dewey, *Reconstruction in Philosophy*, xxiii-xxvii.

31. John Dewey, *Democracy and Education* (1916; reprint ed., New York: The Macmillan Co., 1961), 329.

32. An excellent example of Dewey's strategy is his reply to his critics, "Experience, Knowledge and Value," in Schilpp, ed., *Philosophy of John Dewey*, esp. 520-529.

33. Ibid., 524.

34. Dewey, *Reconstruction in Philosophy*, 87.

35. Dewey, *Democracy and Education*, 343.

36. John Dewey, *The Problems of Men* (New York: The Philosophical Library, 1946), 195.

37. Dewey, *The Quest for Certainty*, 245. Although he made no mention of Lester Ward, Dewey's account of the history and function of intelligence is strikingly parallel to Ward's depiction of how telesis had emerged from genesis.

38. I am here paraphrasing Dewey's language in a letter to James of March 27, 1903, in which he described his early articles as all going "back to certain ideas of life activity, of growth, and adjustment, which involve teleological and dynamic conceptions rather than ontological and static ones." Quoted in Perry, ed., *Thought and Character*, II: 522.

39. John Dewey, "The Need for a Recovery of Philosophy," in

John Dewey et al., *Creative Intelligence: Essays in the Pragmatic Attitude* (New York: Henry Holt and Son, 1917), 65.

40. John Dewey, *How We Think* (Boston: D. C. Heath and Co., 1910), 154-155.

41. John Dewey, *Logic: The Theory of Inquiry* (New York: Henry Holt and Co., 1938), 14.

42. Dewey, *Essays in Experimental Logic*, 22.

43. Dewey, *The Influence of Darwin*, 223.

44. Dewey, *Logic*, 108.

45. Edwin A. Burtt, "The Core of Dewey's Way of Thinking," *Journal of Philosophy* 57 (June 1960): 403.

46. Dewey, *Philosophy and Civilization*, 108.

47. Dewey, *Essays in Experimental Logic*, 133.

48. John Dewey, *A Common Faith* (New Haven: Yale University Press, 1934), 48.

49. John Dewey, *Outlines of a Critical Theory of Ethics* (Ann Arbor: Register Publishing Co., 1891), 134.

50. John Dewey and James H. Tufts, *Ethics*, rev. ed. (New York: Henry Holt and Co., 1932), 311-312.

51. John Dewey, *Ethics* (New York: Henry Holt and Co., 1908), 421-422.

52. Dewey, *Democracy and Education*, 243.

53. Schilpp, ed., *Philosophy of John Dewey*, 594.

54. Dewey, *Ethics*, 485.

55. John Dewey, *Education Today*, ed. Joseph Ratner (New York: G. P. Putnam's Sons, 1940), 355.

56. John Dewey, *The Public and Its Problems* (New York: Henry Holt and Co., 1927), 86, 87.

57. Dewey, *Democracy and Education*, 99.

58. John Dewey, *Individualism, Old and New* (1929; reprint ed., New York: Capricorn Books, 1962), 77.

59. Dewey, *Philosophy and Civilization*, 281.

60. Dewey, *Ethics*, 75-76.

61. Dewey, *The Public and Its Problems*, 69. Even before he read James's *Principles* and arrived at his own synthesis of experience, Dewey had been drawn to the problem of traditional individualism and its social effects. As he wrote in 1930, when he was an undergraduate at the University of Vermont in the 1870s he was impressed by Comte's "idea of the disorganized character of Western modern culture, due to a disintegrative 'individualism,' and his idea of a synthesis of science that should be a

regulative method of organized social life." Dewey, "From Absolutism to Experimentalism," 20. For Dewey's amplification of the Jamesian notion of experience, see his *Experience and Nature* (1929; reprint ed., LaSalle, Ill.: Open Court, 1968).

62. Dewey, *Ethics*, 73.

63. John Dewey, *Liberalism and Social Action* (1935; reprint ed., New York: Capricorn Books, 1963), 44.

64. Adams and Montague, *Contemporary American Philosophy*, 23.

65. Dewey, *Democracy and Education*, 331, 383.

66. Ibid., 51.

67. Dewey, *Education Today*, 18-19.

68. Dewey, *Democracy and Education*, 54.

69. Ibid., 45.

70. Dewey, *Human Nature and Conduct*, 105.

71. Dewey, *Education Today*, 362.

72. Dewey, *Democracy and Education*, 97.

73. Dewey, *Education Today*, 97.

74. Dewey, *Public and Its Problems*, 131.

75. Dewey, *Freedom and Culture*, 123-124.

76. Dewey and Tufts, *Ethics*, 373.

77. Ibid., 387-388.

78. Dewey, *Philosophy and Civilization*, 318, 324.

79. Dewey, *Human Nature and Conduct*, 65-66.

80. Progress, Dewey wrote, "is never judged . . . by reference to a transcendental eternal value, but in reference to the success of the end-in-view in meeting the needs and conditions of the specific situation." Dewey, *Essays in Experimental Logic*, 387.

81. Dewey, *Problems of Men*, 47.

82. Dewey, *Education Today*, 339.

83. Dewey, *Problems of Men*, 157.

84. Dewey, *Ethics*, 474.

85. Dewey's most succinct statement on the idea of progress was an essay called: "Progress" which first appeared in *The International Journal of Ethics* in 1916 and was later reprinted in his *Characters and Events*, II: 820-830.

86. Ibid., 820.

87. Dewey, "The Need for a Recovery of Philosophy," 12.

88. Dewey, *Democracy and Education*, 87.

89. John Dewey, *Experience and Education* (New York: The Macmillan Co., 1938), 26.

90. Dewey, *Democracy and Education*, 223-224.

91. "Progress," in Ratner, *Characters and Events*, II: 823.

92. Dewey, *Human Nature and Conduct*, 287.

93. Dewey, "Time and Individuality," 107.

94. Dewey, *Reconstruction in Philosophy*, xxxviii.

95. John Dewey, *The School and Society*, rev. ed. (Chicago: The University of Chicago Press, 1915), 157.

96. *Logic*, 239. See pp. 230-239 for Dewey's most cogent remarks on history as an instrumental enterprise.

97. Dewey, *Reconstruction in Philosophy*, 94-95.

98. Dewey, *Problems of Men*, 60.

99. Dewey, *Freedom and Culture*, 84.

100. Dewey, *The Public and Its Problems*, 202.

101. Dewey, *Individualism, Old and New*, 17.

102. Dewey, *Freedom and Culture*, 98.

103. Ibid., 88. Dewey uses James's terms.

104. Dewey, *Ethics*, 484.

105. Dewey, *Freedom and Culture*, 101.

106. Dewey, *Liberalism and Social Action*, 83.

107. Dewey, *Logic*, 237-239.

## CHAPTER 6

1. Charles Beard, *Politics* (New York: The Columbia University Press, 1908), 6.

2. Charles Beard, "Henry Adams," *New Republic* 22 (March 31, 1920): 162.

3. The most detailed account of Beard's youth is Paul Schmunk, "Charles Austin Beard: A Free Spirit, 1870-1919," (Ph.D. diss., University of New Mexico, 1957); there are also useful accounts of Beard's life in Mary R. Beard, *The Making of Charles A. Beard* (New York: Exposition Press, 1955); Bernard C. Borning, *The Political and Social Thought of Charles A. Beard* (Seattle: University of Washington Press, 1962); Howard K. Beale, ed., *Charles A. Beard: An Appraisal* (Lexington: University of Kentucky Press, 1954); and Richard Hofstadter, *The Progressive Historians: Turner, Beard, Parrington* (New York: Vintage Books, 1970. First published in 1968).

4. Clifton J. Phillips, "The Indiana Education of Charles A. Beard," *Indiana Magazine of History* 55 (June 1959): 6.

5. In her autobiography, Miss Addams noted that in the 1890s "it seemed . . . as if the hopes of democracy were more likely to come to pass on English soil than upon our own." Jane Addams, *Twenty Years at Hull House* (New York: New American Library, 1960), 189.

6. Charles Beard, "Letter of Resignation from Columbia University," *School and Society* 6 (October 13, 1917): 446-447.

7. See Harold Kirker and Burleigh Taylor Wilkins, "Beard,

Becker and the Trotsky Inquiry," *American Quarterly* 13 (Winter 1961): 516-525, for the most complete account of this episode.

8. Cushing Strout, *The Pragmatic Revolt in American History: Carl Becker and Charles Beard* (New Haven: Yale University Press, 1958), 50.

9. For an account of this influence on Beard, see Hugh I. Rogers, "Charles A. Beard, the 'New Physics,' and Historical Relativity," *Historian* 30 (August 1968): 545-560.

10. Beard, "Henry Adams," 163.

11. Merle Curti, "A Great Teacher's Teacher," *Social Education* 13 (October 1949): 263-267.

12. Beale, ed., *Charles A. Beard*, 312.

13. Beard, *Politics*, 12; Charles Beard, review of *The Political History of England* by George B. Adams, *Political Science Quarterly* 21 (September 1906): 533. Beard at this time made no methodological distinction between history and politics.

14. Charles Beard, *An Economic Interpretation of the Constitution of the United States* (New York: The Macmillan Co., 1913), 12.

15. Charles Beard, review of *Histoire Socialist: Du 9 thermidore au 18 brumaire* by Gabriel Deville, *Political Science Quarterly* 21 (March 1906): 112, and *Politics*, 14.

16. Charles Beard, "Political Science in the Crucible," *New Republic* 13 (November 17, 1917): 4.

17. Charles Beard, "Self-Education," *Young Oxford* 1 (October 1899): 17.

18. Charles Beard, "A Plea for Greater Stress Upon the Modern Period," *Proceedings of the Association of History Teachers of the Middle States and Maryland* 6 (1908): 13.

19. Charles Beard, review of *Die Lehre vom Pouvoir Constituant* by Egon Zweig, *Political Science Quarterly* 24 (September 1909): 522-523, review of *The Courts, the Constitution, and Parties* by A. C. McLaughlin, *American Historical Review* 18 (January 1913): 378-379, review of *A History of the United States*, IV, by Edward Channing, *New Republic* 11 (July 7, 1917): 282-283.

20. Beard, *An Economic Interpretation*, 19.

21. Charles Beard, "The Economic Basis of Politics," *New Republic* 32 (September 27, 1922): 128.

22. Hofstadter, *The Progressive Historians*, 182; see pp. 181-189 for a discussion of this background.

23. Richard Hofstadter, "Beard and the Constitution," *American Quarterly* 2 (Fall 1950): 208.

24. Charles Beard and James Harvey Robinson, *The Development of Modern Europe* (Boston: Ginn and Co., 1907, 1908): I: iii; see

also James Harvey Robinson, *The New History: Essays Illustrating the Modern Historical Outlook* (New York: The Macmillan Co., 1912).

25. Beard, *Politics*, 6.

26. Beard, *An Economic Interpretation*, 19.

27. Charles Beard, *Economic Origins of Jeffersonian Democracy* (New York: The Macmillan Co., 1915), 3.

28. Lee Benson, *Turner and Beard: Historical Writing Reconsidered* (Glencoe, Ill.: Free Press, 1960), 99ff.

29. Cushing Strout has written: "If he had rejected the vision of history as a plot controlled by the moving finger of Providence, whether in pietistic or scientific terms, his economic interpretation appears to be only a secularized version of it." Strout, *The Pragmatic Revolt*, 103.

30. Charles Beard, "Potency of Labor Education," *American Federationist* 29 (July 1922): 501.

31. Charles Beard, "Rebuilding in Japan," *Review of Reviews* 68 (October 1923): 382.

32. Charles Beard, "Municipal Research Abroad and at Home," *Journal of Social Forces* 3 (March 1925): 495.

33. Charles and Mary Beard, *The Rise of American Civilization* (New York: The Macmillan Co., 1927), I: 443. One can see the change in Beard's thinking by comparing the superficial treatment of ideas in *An Economic Interpretation* with the genuine, if still tangential, acknowledgment of the role of thought in *Rise*. In the later book, for example, Beard spoke of the American Revolution as "an economic, social, and intellectual transformation of prime significance—the first of those modern modern world-shaking reconstructions in which mankind has sought to cut and fashion the tough and stubborn web of fact to fit the pattern of its dreams." Ibid., I: 296. And toward the end of the book, he observed that the writing of history itself was changing: "The monopoly of the political chronicle was coming to a close. . . . The narrow confines of Clio's kingdom were widening to include the history of the intellectual classes and the role of the intelligence in the drama of mankind." Ibid., II: 764.

34. Ibid., xi.

35. Charles Beard, Introduction to J. B. Bury, *The Idea of Progress* (1932; reprint ed., New York: Dover Publications, 1955), x.

36. Beard, "The Economic Basis of Politics," 128-129.

37. Charles Beard, "Recent Gains in Government," *World Tomorrow* 10 (November 1927): 439.

38. Charles Beard, "The Development of Social Thought and Institutions: Individualism and Capitalism," in E. R. A. Seligman

and Alvin Johnson, eds., *Encyclopedia of the Social Sciences* (New York: Macmillan Co., 1930), I: 145, 147.

39. Rogers's "Charles A. Beard" provides a helpful treatment of this development, and rebuts Cushing Strout's assertion that Beard was generally unaware of trends in modern physical science in the 1920s. See Strout, *The Pragmatic Revolt*, 160.

40. Quoted in Rogers, "Charles A. Beard," 547-551; this paragraph encapsulated Rogers's observations.

41. Higham, *History*, 126. For these various influences on Beard —and of his often questionable understanding of them—see Lloyd R. Sorenson, "Charles A. Beard and German Historical Thought," *Mississippi Valley Historical Review* 42 (September 1955): 274-287, and Gerald D. Nash, "Self-education in Historiography: The Case of Charles A. Beard," *Pacific Northwest Quarterly* 52 (July 1961): 108-115.

42. Charles Beard, "Neglected Aspects of Political Science," *American Political Science Review* 42 (April 1948): 213. The other books Beard cited were Brooks Adams's *Law of Civilization and Decay*, Mannheim's *Ideology and Utopia*, Croce's *History: Its Theory and Practice*, and Vaihinger's *The Philosophy of "As If."*

43. Earnest W. Hobson, *The Domain of Natural Science* (Cambridge, England: Cambridge University Press, 1923), 90.

44. Charles Beard, "Political Science," in Wilson Gee, ed., *Research in the Social Sciences* (New York: The Macmillan Co., 1929), 273-275.

45. Charles Beard, "Ruskin and the Babble of Tongues," *New Republic* 87 (August 5, 1936): 371.

46. Charles Beard, "Congress Under Fire," *Yale Review* 22 (September 1932): 42.

47. Charles Beard and G. H. E. Smith, *The Open Door at Home* (New York: The Macmillan Co., 1934), 15.

48. Beard, "Ruskin and the Babble of Tongues," 370. Also see his "The Task Before Us," *The Social Studies* 25 (May 1934): 215, and "Rushlights in Darkness," *Scribner's Magazine* 90 (December 1931): 577-578.

49. Beard and Smith, *The Open Door*, 135-136.

50. Beard, "Ruskin and the Babble of Tongues," 370.

51. Charles Beard, "Limitations to the Application of Social Science Implied in Recent Social Trends," *Social Forces* 2 (May 1933): 510.

52. Beard and Smith, *The Open Door*, 19-20.

53. Charles Beard, *The Nature of the Social Sciences* (New York: Charles Scribner's Sons, 1934), 154.

54. Beard, "Limitations to the Application of Social Science," 506.

55. Ibid.

56. Beard and Smith, *The Open Door*, 15.

57. Beard, "Rushlights in Darkness," 577.

58. Charles and Mary Beard, *The American Spirit: A Study of the Idea of Civilization in the United States* (New York: Collier Books, 1962), 523. *The American Spirit* was first published in 1942 as volume 4 of *The Rise of American Civilization*.

59. Beard, "Limitations to the Application of Social Science," 510.

60. Beard and Smith, *The Open Door at Home*, 135-136. The same phrasing appears in Charles Beard, *Public Policy and the General Welfare* (New York: Farrar and Rinehart, 1941), 14-15.

61. For example, editorials in *New Republic* during the 1920s had stressed the point that "reform must be more than a matter of empirical method. If liberalism were to have any deeper personal meaning, Herbert Croly insisted in 1922, it must transcend technology and achieve a spiritual reconstruction of society." John P. Diggins, "Flirtation with Fascism: American Pragmatic Liberals and Mussolini's Italy," *American Historical Review* 71 (January 1966): 497.

62. Charles Beard, "Grounds for a Reconsideration of Historiography," *Theory and Practice in Historical Study: A Report of the Committee on Historiography* (New York: Social Science Research Council, 1946), 6.

63. Harry Elmer Barnes noted the effects of Beard's dilemma in a review of *The Nature of the Social Sciences* (1934): "The book as a whole conforms to the somewhat discrepant and paradoxical trend observable in Dr. Beard's recent writings. On the one hand he is eminently practical and shows a wide acquaintance with the literature of contemporary social descriptions and analysis. On the other hand, in his theoretical observations he espouses that extreme abstraction of which he was himself at one time perhaps the foremost American critic. . . . Even Hegel, who was once veritably Dr. Beard's personal devil, is mentioned with affection." Harry Elmer Barnes, review of *The Nature of the Social Sciences* by Charles Beard, *American Historical Review* 40 (October 1934): 99.

64. Quoted by Beard in "Time, Technology, and the Creative Spirit in Political Science," *American Political Science Review* 21 (February 1927): 6.

65. Charles Beard, *The Discussion of Human Affairs* (New York: The Macmillan Co., 1936), 79.

66. Beard, "Limitations to the Application of Social Science," 506.

67. Charles Beard, "National Politics and War," *Scribner's Magazine* 97 (February 1935): 70.

68. Charles Beard, "A Historian's Quest for Light," *Proceedings of the Association of History Teachers of the Middle States and Maryland* 29 (1931): 16.

69. Beard, *The Discussion of Human Affairs*, 75-76.

70. Ibid., 117.

71. Charles Beard, "Written History as an Act of Faith," *American Historical Review* 39 (January 1934): 219, and *The Nature of the Social Sciences*, 52.

72. Beard, *The Discussion of Human Affairs*, 87.

73. Charles Beard, "That Noble Dream," *American Historical Review* 41 (October 1935): 75.

74. Harry J. Marks, "Ground Under Our Feet: Beard's Relativism," *Journal of the History of Ideas* 14 (October 1953): 628-633. As Whitaker Deininger observed, "While he was not always clear, nor perhaps even consistent, Beard never seriously doubted that historians can know the past sufficiently well to form tentative predictions and anticipations of the future." Whitaker Deininger, "The Skepticism and Historical Faith of Charles Beard," *Journal of the History of Ideas* 15 (October 1954): 588.

75. Charles Beard and Alfred Vagts, "Currents of Thought in Historiography," *American Historical Review* 42 (April 1937): 481.

76. Beard, "That Noble Dream," 86-87.

77. Beard, *The Nature of the Social Sciences*, 64.

78. Beard, "Political Science," 272-273, and his review of *Making Fascists* by Herbert W. Schneider and Shepard B. Clough, *American Political Science Review* 24 (February 1930): 181.

79. Ibid.

80. Beard and Smith, *The Open Door*, 228. In summing up this relationship, Beard adopted James's phraseology: "In seeking to determine what has been and is, we can only select facts which seem relevant to the problem at hand, that is, significant for the formulation of conclusions. When we come to drafting conclusions we inevitably mingle thought with the operation. We posit criteria and ends which we deem desirable, make an assertion of will to believe and act. The force of that determination, its effectiveness in making history, depends upon the degree of accurate prediction contained within it and its influence on the course of affairs." Ibid., 201-202.

81. "Written History as an Act of Faith," *American Historical Review* 39 (January 1934): 229.

82. Beard used Kurt Riezler's definition of history as "ideas and interests, ever evolving and involving in time" repeatedly throughout the 1930s, but there is strong evidence that he read Riezler through native American lenses. See Sorenson, "Beard and German Historical Thought," 283-285. Beard used Riezler's phrase "idea and interest" in precisely the same way James had spoken of the "word" and the "deed," and this was not what Riezler, a neoromantic, had had in mind at all. See, for example, Beard and Smith, *The Open Door*, 157-158.

83. Beard, *The Nature of the Social Sciences*, 61.

84. Beard, "Written History as an Act of Faith," 226.

85. Beard, *The Nature of the Social Sciences*, 71.

86. Beard, *The Discussion of Human Affairs*, 114.

87. Beard, "Written History as an Act of Faith," 228-229. The concept of the "frame of reference," which Beard used repeatedly in the 1930s and 1940s came from Croce. See Nash, "Self-education in Historiography," 112-114.

88. Beard, *The Nature of the Social Sciences*, 191. Beard discovered this Machiavellian formula in Friedrich Meinecke's *Die Idee der Staatsräson* (Munich: R. Oldenbourg, 1924).

89. Charles Beard, "American in Midpassage," in *John Dewey and the Promise of America* (Columbus, Ohio: Progressive Education Association, 1939), 19.

90. Charles Beard, "History and Social Science," *Saturday Review of Literature* 12 (August 17, 1935): 22-23.

91. Beard, *Public Policy and the General Welfare*, 8.

92. Charles Beard, "Search for the Centre," *Scribner's Magazine* 91 (January 1932): 2.

93. Charles Beard, "The Task Before Us," *Social Studies* 25 (May 1934): 217.

94. Beard, *The Nature of the Social Sciences*, 45.

95. Beard, *Public Policy and the General Welfare*, 27-28.

96. Beard, "Rushlights in Darkness," 578.

97. Beard, "A Search for the Centre," 3-4.

98. Beard, *The Nature of the Social Sciences*, 45.

99. Beard and Smith, *The Open Door*, 32-33. Various facets of Beard's definition of the good life can be found in his: *Public Policy and the General Welfare*, 57-71ff.; "Rushlights in Darkness"; "Ruskin and the Babble of Tongues"; "A Search for the Centre"; "A Five-year Plan for America," *Forum and Century* 81 (July 1931): 1-11; "The Task Before Us"; "A Historian's Quest for Light"; "A Memorandum on Social Philosophy," *Journal of Social Philosophy* 5 (October 1939): 7-15; "The World as I Want It," *Forum and Century*

91 (June 1934): 332-334; "Creating the Good Life for America," *Journal of the American Association of University Women* 28 (June 1935): 195-198; "That Promise of American Life," *New Republic* 81 (February 6, 1935): 350-352.

100. Beard, "A Search for the Centre," 7.

101. Ibid.

102. Beard, *The American Spirit*, 462.

103. By the end of the 1930s, Beard not only accepted the notion that ideas were truly causal in history, but he was approaching the position that ideas had a certain historical autonomy unrelated to identifiable "interests." Charles Beard, review of *The Course of American Democratic Thought: An Intellectual History Since 1815* by Ralph H. Gabriel, *American Historical Review* 46 (October 1940): 165.

104. Beard, "A Search for the Centre," 7.

105. Beard, "The World as I Want It," 334.

106. Beard, "Rushlights in Darkness," 578, "The Historian and Society," 2, review of *Abraham Lincoln: The War Years* by Carl Sandburg, *Virginia Quarterly Review* 16 (January 1940): 112-116, "Essentials of Democracy," *School and Society* 50 (August 19, 1939): 234.

107. Beard and Smith, *The Open Door*, 152.

108. Beard, "A Search for the Centre," 5.

109. Beard, "That Promise of American Life," 351-352.

110. Beard, *Public Policy and the General Welfare*, 24-25, 70, "America's Quest for Security," *Journal of the American Association of University Women* 28 (1935): 141-144.

111. Charles Beard, *A Charter for the Social Sciences* (New York: Charles Scribners Sons, 1932), 57-58.

112. Charles Beard, *The Republic: Conversations on Fundamentals* (1943; reprint ed., New York: Viking Press, 1962), 18.

113. Charles Beard, "The Rise of the Democratic Idea in the United States," *Survey Graphic* 26 (April 1937): 205.

114. Beard, *The Republic*, 15.

115. Beard, "The Rise of the Democratic Idea," 203.

116. Beard, *The American Spirit*, 7ff., especially chap. 11.

117. Ibid., 7, 581.

118. Ibid., 580-581.

119. Ibid., 13.

120. Robert Skotheim has observed that *The American Spirit* was Beard's response to the challenges of totalitarianism. While this is undeniably true, the crisis Beard was struggling with was much larger than the issue of totalitarianism, and the concept of civilization should accordingly be given greater significance as part of

Beard's later thought. See Robert Skotheim, *American Intellectual Histories and Historians* (Princeton: Princeton University Press, 1966), 105-106.

121. Charles Beard and William Beard, *The American Leviathan* (New York: Macmillan Co., 1930), 9.

122. Charles Beard, *The Myth of Rugged American Individualism* (New York: The John Day Co., 1932), 26-27.

123. Beard and Beard, *The American Leviathan*, 3.

124. Beale, *Charles A. Beard*, 70, 121, 236.

125. Charles Beard, "An Economic Interpretation of Navies," *New Republic* 69 (November 25, 1931): 47.

126. Beard, "A Memorandum on Social Philosophy," 13, *The American Spirit*, 68, 461; Beard and Smith, *The Open Door*, 109-111.

127. Beard, *The American Spirit*, 461.

128. Beard and Smith, *The Open Door*, 141-142, 305-307, 310-311. Beard by the 1930s had little use for "those Marxians who think that ideas automatically arise from given economic conditions." Charles Beard, "Making a Bigger and Better Navy," *New Republic* 67 (October 14, 1931): 223.

129. Charles Beard, "The Twilight of the Social Systems," *Living Age* 357 (January 1940): 412.

130. Beard and Smith, *The Open Door*, 305.

131. Beard, "A Memorandum on Social Philosophy," 10.

132. Beard and Smith, *The Open Door*, 306.

133. Beard, "A Five-year Plan for America," 3.

134. Beard, *Public Policy and the General Welfare*, 43-44.

135. Beard, *The American Spirit*, 580.

136. Beard, "A Search for the Centre," 5.

137. Charles Beard, "Collective Security," *New Republic* 93 (February 2, 1938): 359, "Our Choice in Foreign Policy," *Events* 1 (March 1937): 164ff. Beard's reaction to the gathering war clouds in Europe and Asia was to advocate a national policy of "American civilization" or "continentalism" which took as its credo "let us keep out of the next world war; mind our own business; till our own garden." Charles and Mary Beard, *America in Midpassage* (New York: The Macmillan Co., 1939), 452. In 1940, he argued that Americans should focus "on the continental domain and on building here a civilization in many respects peculiar to American life and the potentialities of the American heritage." Charles Beard, *A Foreign Policy for America* (New York: Alfred A. Knopf, 1940), 12.

138. Beard, *The American Spirit*, 580-581, 565. It should be noted that Beard's interpretation of Marx in the 1930s focused primarily

on the deterministic nature of Marx's dialectic. More sympathetic readers of Marx may argue that Beard was interpreting his determinism too severely and that his criticism in *The Open Door*, for example, did not take adequate account of the fact that Marxists too held that men made history.

139. Cushing Strout, one of Beard's most perceptive critics, maintained that Beard "failed to make clear just what new responsibilities the historian assumes when he no longer pretends to be a scientist." Having destroyed historical positivism, Beard made "the verdict of future events" the sole standard for evaluating the historian's work, and this was little more, in Strout's view, than "a demand for blind faith." (Strout, *The Pragmatic Revolt*, 29, 56.) Similarly, Lloyd Sorenson acknowledged Beard's awareness of many problems in the writing of history in the 1930s, but he then went on to argue that Beard "failed . . . to make any systematic analysis of just what this historiographical crisis was supposed to be." (Sorenson, "Beard and German Historiographical Thought," 277.) Neither Strout nor Sorenson gives adequate weight to the role of the idea of civilization as a positive, pragmatic ethical conception in Beard's thinking. And John W. Ward, in maintaining that "the major thrust of Beard's thought was to make ideas epiphenomena in history," seems simply not to have read Beard's later writings. (John W. Ward, "Direction in American Intellectual History," *American Quarterly* 18 (Winter 1966): 703).

140. Beard and Smith, *The Open Door*, 102-111; Beard, *The American Spirit*, 461-462.

## CHAPTER 7

1. Beard, "Political Science," in Wilson Gee, ed., *Research in the Social Sciences* (New York: The Macmillan Co., 1929), 287.

2. Quoted in Howard K. Beale, ed., *Charles A. Beard: An Appraisal* (Lexington: University of Kentucky Press, 1954), 7.

3. Henry Adams, *The Education of Henry Adams* (Boston: Houghton Mifflin, 1918), 451.

4. Melvin Lyon, *Symbol and Idea in Henry Adams* (Lincoln: University of Nebraska Press, 1970), 227-228.

5. Adams, *Education*, 495.

# Selected Bibliography

In preparing the following bibliography, I have included works of special significance for the preparation of this book. Not all works cited in the preceding pages are included; and for some works, no previous citations appear. For comprehensive bibliographies of the writings of William James, John Dewey, and Charles A. Beard see: John M. McDermott, ed., *The Writings of William James* (New York: The Modern Library, 1967), 811-853; Thomas M. Halsey, ed., *John Dewey: A Centennial Bibliography* (Chicago: University of Chicago Press, 1962); Bernard C. Borning, *The Political and Social Thought of Charles A. Beard* (Seattle: University of Washington Press, 1962), 257-295.

*General Bibliography*

## BOOKS

Adams, George P., and Montague, William P. *Contemporary American Philosophy*. New York: The Macmillan Company, 1930. 2 vols.

Adams, Henry. *The Degradation of the Democratic Dogma*. New York: The Macmillan Company, 1919.

————. *The Education of Henry Adams*. Boston: Houghton Mifflin Company, 1918.

Addams, Jane. *Twenty Years at Hull House*. New York: New American Library, 1960.

Allen, Gay Wilson. *William James: A Biography*. New York: The Viking Press, 1967.

American Studies Association, Texas Chapter. *Impact of Darwinian Thought on American Life and Culture*. Austin: University of Texas Press, 1959.

Arieli, Yehoshua. *Individualism and Nationalism in American Ideology*. Cambridge: Harvard University Press, 1964.

Aron, Raymond. *Progress and Disillusion: The Dialectics of Modern Society*. New York: New American Library, 1968.

Arvin, Newton, ed. *The Selected Letters of Henry Adams*. New York: Farrar, Straus, 1951.

Barzun, Jacques. *Classic, Romantic and Modern*. New York: Doubleday and Co., 1961.

Beale, Howard K., ed. *Charles A. Beard: An Appraisal*. Lexington: University of Kentucky Press, 1954.

Beard, Mary R. *The Making of Charles A. Beard*. New York: Exposition Press, 1955.

Becker, Carl L. *The Declaration of Independence: A Study in the History of Political Ideas*. New York: Alfred A. Knopf, 1965.

————. *The Heavenly City of the Eighteenth Century Philosophers*. New York: Yale University Press, 1932.

Beisner, Robert L. *Twelve Against Empire: The Anti-Imperialists, 1898-1900*. New York: McGraw-Hill, 1968.

Benson, Lee. *Turner and Beard: Historical Writing Reconsidered*. Glencoe, Ill.: Free Press, 1960.

Berman, Milton. *John Fiske: The Evolution of a Popularizer*. Cambridge: Harvard University Press, 1961.

Boller, Paul F., Jr. *American Thought in Transition: The Impact of Evolutionary Naturalism, 1865-1900.* Chicago: Rand McNally and Company, 1969.

Boorstin, Daniel J. *The Americans: The Colonial Experience.* New York: Random House, 1958.

————. *The Lost World of Thomas Jefferson.* Boston: Beacon Press, 1948.

Borning, Bernard C. *The Political and Social Thought of Charles A. Beard.* Seattle: University of Washington Press, 1962.

Burnham, John C. *Lester Frank Ward in American Thought.* Washington, D.C.: Public Affairs Press, 1956.

Bury, J. B. *The Idea of Progress: An Inquiry into Its Growth and Origin.* New York: Dover Publications, 1955.

Cater, Harold Dean, ed. *Henry Adams and His Friends.* Boston: Houghton Mifflin Company, 1947.

Chugerman, Samuel. *Lester Frank Ward: The American Aristotle.* Durham: Duke University Press, 1939.

Collingwood, R. G. *The Idea of History.* Oxford: Clarendon Press, 1964.

Commager, Henry Steele. *The American Mind: An Interpretation of American Thought and Character Since the 1880's.* New Haven: Yale University Press, 1950.

Conkin, Paul. *Puritans and Pragmatists: Eight Eminent American Thinkers.* New York: Dodd, Mead Company, 1968.

Cowan, Michael. *City of the West: Emerson, America, and Urban Metaphor.* New Haven: Yale University Press, 1967.

Croly, Herbert. *Progressive Democracy.* New York: The Macmillan Company, 1914.

————. *The Promise of American Life.* New York: The Macmillan Company, 1909.

Curti, Merle. *The Growth of American Thought.* New York: Harper and Row, 1964.

————. *Human Nature in American Historical Thought.* Columbia, Mo.: University of Missouri Press, 1969.

Daniels, George, ed. *Darwinism Comes to America.* Waltham, Mass.: Blaisdell Publishing Company, 1968.

Darwin, Charles. *The Descent of Man, and Selection in Relation to Sex.* New York: D. Appleton and Company, 1871.

————. *On the Origin of the Species.* New York: D. Appleton and Company, 1859.

Donovan, Timothy Paul. *Henry Adams and Brooks Adams: The Education of Two American Historians.* Norman, Okla.: University of Oklahoma Press, 1961.

Eiseley, Loren. *Darwin's Century: Evolution and the Men Who Discovered It.* New York: Doubleday and Company, 1961.

Ekirch, Arthur A. *The Idea of Progress in America, 1815-1860.* New York: Peter Smith, 1951.

Ferkiss, Victor C. *Technological Man: The Myth and the Reality.* New York: New American Library, 1969.

Fiske, John. *A Century of Science.* Boston: Houghton Mifflin Company, 1899.

————. *Darwinism and Other Essays.* New York: Macmillan and Company, 1879.

————. *The Destiny of Man Viewed in the Light of His Origin.* Boston: Houghton Mifflin Company, 1884.

————. *Excursions of an Evolutionist.* Boston: Houghton Mifflin Company, 1895.

————. *The Idea of God as Affected by Modern Knowledge.* Boston: Houghton Mifflin Company, 1885.

————. *Outlines of Cosmic Philosophy.* Boston: James R. Osgood and Company, 1875. 2 vols.

————. *Studies in Religion.* Boston: Houghton Mifflin Company, 1902.

————. *Through Nature to God.* Boston: Houghton Mifflin Company, 1899.

Forcey, Charles. *The Crossroads of Liberalism: Croly, Weyl, Lippmann and the Progressive Era, 1900-1925.* New York: Oxford University Press, 1961.

Ford, Worthington Chauncey, ed. *The Letters of Henry Adams, 1892-1918.* Boston and New York: Houghton Mifflin Company, 1938. 2 vols.

Gabriel, Ralph. *The Course of American Democratic Thought.* New York: The Ronald Press, 1954.

Gee, Wilson, ed. *Research in the Social Sciences.* New York: The Macmillan Company, 1929.

Hampson, Norman. *A Cultural History of the Enlightenment.* New York: Pantheon Books, 1968.

Haraszti, Zoltan. *John Adams and the Prophets of Progress.* Cambridge: Harvard University Press, 1952.

Himmelfarb, Gertrude. *Darwin and the Darwinian Revolution.* New York: W. W. Norton and Company, 1968.

Hobson, Ernest W. *The Domain of Natural Science.* Cambridge, England: Cambridge University Press, 1923.

Hofstadter, Richard. *The Progressive Historians: Turner, Beard, and Parrington.* New York: Vintage Books, 1968.

―――. *Social Darwinism in American Thought.* Boston: Beacon Press, 1955.

Holmes, Oliver Wendell, Jr. *The Common Law.* Boston: Little, Brown and Company, 1881.

Hook, Sidney, ed. *John Dewey: Philosopher of Science and Freedom.* New York: The Dial Press, 1950.

Jaher, Frederick Cople. *Doubters and Dissenters: Cataclysmic Thought in America, 1885-1918.* New York: The Free Press of Glencoe, 1964.

Jefferson, Thomas. *Notes on the State of Virginia.* Edited by William Peden. Chapel Hill: University of North Carolina Press, 1955.

Jones, Howard Mumford. *America and French Culture,*

*1750-1848*. Chapel Hill: University of North Carolina Press, 1927.

―――. *O Strange New World*. New York: Viking Press, 1964.

―――. *The Pursuit of Happiness*. Cambridge: Harvard University Press, 1953.

Jordy, William H. *Henry Adams: Scientific Historian*. New Haven: Yale University Press, 1952.

Kaul, A. N. *The American Vision: Actual and Ideal Society in Nineteenth-century Fiction*. New Haven: Yale University Press, 1963.

Kennedy, Gail, ed. *Pragmatism and American Culture*. Boston: D. C. Heath and Co., 1950.

Koch, Adrienne. *Power, Morals and the Founding Fathers: Essays in the Interpretation of the American Enlightenment*. Ithaca: Cornell University Press, 1961.

Lasch, Christopher. *The New Radicalism in America: 1889-1963*. New York: Vintage Books, 1967.

Levin, David. *History as Romantic Art: Bancroft, Prescott, Motley, and Parkman*. Stanford: Stanford University Press, 1959.

Lewis, R. W. B. *The American Adam: Innocence, Tragedy and Tradition in the Nineteenth Century*. Chicago: University of Chicago Press, 1965.

Lippmann, Walter. *Preface to Politics*. New York: M. Kennerly and Company, 1913.

Lyon, Melvin. *Symbol and Idea in Henry Adams*. Lincoln: University of Nebraska Press, 1970.

Madden, Edward H. *Chauncey Wright and the Foundations of Pragmatism*. Seattle: University of Washington Press, 1963.

Martland, Thomas R., Jr. *The Metaphysics of William James and John Dewey: Process and Structure in Philosophy and Religion*. New York: Philosophical Library, 1963.

Marx, Leo. *The Machine in the Garden: Technology and*

*the Pastoral Ideal in America*. New York: Oxford University Press, 1967.

Matthiessen, F. O. *American Renaissance: Art and Expression in the Age of Emerson and Whitman*. New York: Oxford University Press, 1954.

————. *The James Family*. New York: Alfred A. Knopf, 1947.

May, Henry F. *The End of American Innocence: A Study of the First Years of Our Own Time, 1912-1917*. Chicago: Quadrangle Books, 1959.

Miller, Perry, ed. *American Thought: Civil War to World War I*. New York: Holt, Rinehart and Winston, 1964.

Moore, Addison W. *Pragmatism and Its Critics*. Chicago: University of Chicago Press, 1910.

Morris, Charles. *The Pragmatic Movement in American Philosophy*. New York: George Braziller, 1970.

Morris, Lloyd. *William James: The Message of a Modern Mind*. New York: Charles Scribner's Sons, 1950.

Noble, David W. *The Paradox of Progressive Thought*. Minneapolis: University of Minnesota Press, 1958.

Odum, Howard W., ed. *American Masters of Social Science*. Port Washington, N.Y.: Henry Holt and Company, 1927.

Perry, Ralph Barton, ed. *The Thought and Character of William James*. Boston: Little, Brown and Company, 1935, 1936. 2 vols.

Persons, Stow. *American Minds: A History of Ideas*. New York: Holt, Rinehart and Winston, 1958.

Pollard, Sidney. *The Idea of Progress: History and Society*. New York: Basic Books, 1968.

Robinson, James Harvey. *The New History: Essays Illustrating the Modern Historical Outlook*. New York: The Macmillan Company, 1912.

Rucker, Darnell. *The Chicago Pragmatists*. Minneapolis: University of Minnesota Press, 1969.

Russett, Cynthia Eagle. *The Concept of Equilibrium in*

*American Social Thought.* New Haven: Yale University Press, 1966.

Sanford, Charles L. *The Quest for Paradise: Europe and the American Moral Imagination.* Urbana, Ill.: University of Illinois Press, 1961.

Schilpp, Paul G., ed. *The Philosophy of John Dewey.* New York: The Tudor Publishing Company, 1951.

Skotheim, Robert A. *American Intellectual Histories and Historians.* Princeton: Princeton University Press, 1966.

Smith, John E. *The Spirit of American Philosophy.* New York: Oxford University Press, 1966.

———. *Themes in American Philosophy: Purpose, Experience and Community.* New York: Harper and Row, 1970.

Smojee, A. H. *The Political Theory of John Dewey.* New York: Teachers College Press, 1968.

Strout, Cushing. *The Pragmatic Revolt in American History: Carl Becker and Charles Beard.* New Haven: Yale University Press, 1958.

Veblen, Thorstein. *The Place of Science in Modern Civilization and Other Essays.* New York: B. W. Huesbsch, 1919.

———. *The Theory of the Leisure Class.* New York: The Macmillan Company, 1899.

Ward, Lester Frank. *Applied Sociology.* Boston: Ginn and Company, 1906.

———. *Dynamic Sociology.* New York: D. Appleton and Company, 1883. 2 vols.

———. *Glimpses of the Cosmos.* New York: G. P. Putnam's Sons, 1918. 6 vols.

———. *The Psychic Factors of Civilization.* Boston: Ginn and Company, 1893.

Wasserman, Earl J., ed. *Aspects of the Eighteenth Century.* Baltimore: The Johns Hopkins Press, 1965.

Wellek, René. *Confrontations: Studies in the Intellectual*

and Literary Relations Between Germany, England and the United States during the Nineteenth Century. Princeton: Princeton University Press, 1965.

White, Morton. *The Origins of Dewey's Instrumentalism*. New York: Columbia University Press, 1943.

———. *Science and Sentiment in America: Philosophical Thought from Jonathan Edwards to John Dewey*. New York: Oxford University Press, 1972.

———. *Social Thought in America: The Revolt Against Formalism*. Boston: Beacon Press, 1957.

White, Morton and Lucia. *The Intellectual versus the City: From Thomas Jefferson to Frank Lloyd Wright*. New York: New American Library, 1964.

Wiener, Philip. *Evolution and the Founders of Pragmatism*. Cambridge: Harvard University Press, 1949.

Wilson, R. J., ed. *Darwinism and the American Intellectual*. Homewood, Ill.: The Dorsey Press, 1967.

Wright, Benjamin F. *American Interpretations of Natural Law*. Cambridge: Harvard University Press, 1931.

Wright, Chauncey. *Letters of Chauncey Wright*. Edited by James Bradley Thayer. Cambridge, Mass.: John Wilson and Son, 1878.

———. *Philosophical Discussions*. Edited by Charles Eliot Norton. New York: Henry Holt and Co., 1877.

## ARTICLES

Aiken, Henry D. "The Revolt against Ideology." *Commentary* 37 (April 1964): 29-39.

Bates, Earnest. "John Dewey, America's Philosophic Engineer." *Modern Monthly* 7 (August 1933): 387-404.

Baym, Max I. "William James and Henry Adams." *New England Quarterly* 10 (December 1937): 417-442.

Bernard, L. L. "Scientific Method and Social Progress." *American Journal of Sociology* 31 (July 1925): 1-18.

Blau, Joseph L. "Chauncey Wright: Radical Empiricist." *New England Quarterly* 19 (December 1946): 495-517.

———. "John Dewey's Theory of History." *Journal of Philosophy* 57 (February 1960): 89-100.

Blum, Harold J. "Perspectives in Evolution." *American Scientist* 43 (October 1955): 595-609.

Boller, Paul. "Charles A. Beard." *Forum* 6 (Fall-Winter 1968): 4-12.

———. "Freedom in the Thought of William James." *American Quarterly* 16 (Summer 1964): 131-152.

Bourne, Randolphe. "Twilight of Idols." *Seven Arts* 2 (October 1917): 688-703.

Burtt, Edwin. "The Core of Dewey's Way of Thinking." *Journal of the History of Philosophy* 57 (June 1960): 401-419.

Chamberliss, J. J. "Chauncey Wright's Enduring Naturalism." *American Quarterly* 16 (Winter 1964): 628-634.

Chambers, Clark A. "The Belief in Progress in Twentieth-century America." *Journal of the History of Ideas* 19 (April 1958): 197-224.

Chinard, Gilbert. "Eighteenth Century Theories on America as a Human Habitat." *Proceedings of the American Philosophical Society* 91 (1947): 27-57.

Church, Henry Ward. "Corneille de Pauw and the Controversy Over His *Recherches Philosophique sur des Americains.*" *Publications of the Modern Language Association* 51 (1936): 178-206.

Clark, Harry Hayden. "The Influence of Science on American Ideas, from 1775 to 1809." *Transactions of the Wisconsin Academy of Sciences, Arts and Letters* 35 (1943): 307-314.

Crane, Ronald S. "Anglican Apologetics and the Idea of Progress." *Modern Philology* 31 (May 1934): 350.

Cunliffe, Marcus. "American Watersheds." *American Quarterly* 13 (Winter 1961): 480-494.

Curti, Merle. "A Great Teacher's Teacher." *Social Education* 13 (October 1949): 263-267.

Deininger, Whitaker. "The Skepticism and Historical Faith of Charles Beard." *Journal of the History of Ideas* 15 (October 1954): 573-588.

Delmage, Rutherford E. "The American Idea of Progress, 1750-1800." *Proceedings of the American Philosophical Society* 91 (1947): 307-314.

Diggins, John P. "Flirtation with Fascism: American Pragmatic Liberals and Mussolini's Italy." *American Historical Review* 71 (January 1966): 487-506.

East, John P. "Pragmatism and Behavioralism." *Western Political Quarterly* 21 (December 1968): 597-605.

Fay, Sidney B. "The Idea of Progress." *American Historical Review* 52 (January 1947): 231-246.

Fisch, Max H. "Evolution in American Philosophy." *Philosophy Review* 86 (July 1947): 357-373.

Gibbens, V. E. "Tom Paine and the Idea of Progress." *Pennsylvania Magazine of History and Biography* 66 (April 1942): 121-204.

Goldman, Eric F. "The Origin of Beard's Economic Interpretation of the Constitution." *Journal of the History of Ideas* 12 (April 1952): 234-249.

Greenlee, Douglas. "On Pragmatism." *Journal of the History of Ideas* 30 (October 1969): 603-608.

Higham, John. "Beyond Consensus: The Historian as Moral Critic." *American Historical Review* 67 (April 1962): 609-625.

Hirschfield, Charles. "Brooks Adams and American Nationalism." *American Historical Review* 71 (January 1964): 371-392.

Hofstadter, Richard. "Beard and the Constitution." *American Quarterly* 2 (Fall 1950): 195-213.

Holmes, Robert. "John Dewey's Moral Philosophy in Contemporary Prospective." *Review of Metaphysics* 20 (September 1966): 42-70.

Hook, Sidney. "John Dewey and the Crisis of American Liberalism." *Antioch Review* 29 (Summer 1969): 218-232.

————. "John Dewey—Philosopher of Growth." *Journal of Philosophy* 56 (December 1959): 1010-1018.

Hoover, Dwight D. "Some Comments on Recent U.S. Historiography." *American Quarterly* 17 (Summer 1965): 299-318.

Hutchinson, William. "Liberal Protestantism and the End of Innocence." *American Quarterly* 15 (Summer 1960): 126-139.

Iggers, George G. "The Idea of Progress: A Critical Reassessment." *American Historical Review* 71 (October 1965): 1-18.

Jones, Howard Mumford. "The Influence of European Ideas in Nineteenth-century America." *American Literature* 7 (March 1935-January 1936): 241-273.

Kallen, Horace M. "The Modern World, the Intellectual, and William James." *Western Political Quarterly* 13 (December 1960): 863-870.

Kaufman, Marjorie R. "William James's Letters to a Young Pragmatist." *Journal of the History of Ideas* 24 (July 1963): 413-421.

Kennedy, Gail. "Evaluation in a Democratic Society." *Journal of Philosophy* 16 (March 12, 1959): 253-263.

————. "The Hidden Link in Dewey's Theory of Evolution." *Teachers College Record* 56 (May 1955): 421-435.

Kennedy, T. C. "Charles A. Beard on Mid-Passage." *Historian* 30 (February 1968): 179-198.

Kirker, Harold, and Wilkins, B. T. "Beard, Becker and the Trotsky Inquiry." *American Quarterly* 13 (Winter 1961): 516-524.

Lamont, Corliss. "Materialism and John Dewey." *New Masses* 62 (February 25, 1947): 17-23.

———. "New Light on Dewey's Common Faith." *Journal of Philosophy* 58 (January 1961): 21-28.

Lewis, Merrill. "Organic Metaphor and Edenic Myth in George Bancroft's *History of the United States.*" *Journal of the History of Ideas* 26 (October-December 1965): 587-592.

Lowenberg, Bert J. "American Scientists and Darwinism." *American Historical Review* 38 (July 1933): 687-701.

———. "Darwinism comes to America." *Mississippi Valley Historical Review* 28 (December 1941): 338-368.

———. "The Reaction of American Scientists to Darwinism." *American Historical Review* 38 (July 1933): 687-701.

McGill, V. J. "John Dewey in Theory and Practice." *Science and Society* 5 (Spring 1941): 61-71.

———. "Pragmatism Reconsidered." *Science and Society* 3 (Summer 1939): 289-322.

Marks, Harry J. "Ground Under Our Feet: Beard's Relativism." *Journal of the History of Ideas* 14 (October 1953): 628-633.

Mead, George Herbert. "The Philosophy of Royce, James and Dewey in Their American Setting." *International Journal of Ethics* 40 (June 1930): 211-231.

Metz, Joseph G. "Democracy and the Scientific Method in the Philosophy of John Dewey." *Review of Politics* 31 (April 1969): 242-262.

Munford, Howard M. "Henry Adams and the Tendency of History." *New England Quarterly* 32 (March 1959): 88.

Murphy, Arthur E. "John Dewey and American Liberalism." *Journal of Philosophy* 57 (June 1960): 420-436.

Nash, Gerald D. "Self-education in Historiography:

The Case of Charles A. Beard." *Pacific Northwest Quarterly* 52 (July 1961): 108-115.

Nash, Roderick. "The American Cult of the Primitive." *American Quarterly* 18 (Fall 1966): 517-537.

Nichols, Roy H. "The Dynamic Interpretation of History." *New England Quarterly* 8 (June 1935): 163-178.

Noble, David. "The New Republic and the Idea of Progress." *Mississippi Valley Historical Review* 38 (December 1951): 387-402.

————. "The Religion of Progress in America." *Social Research* 22 (Winter 1955): 417-440.

Phillips, Clifton J. "The Indiana Education of Charles A. Beard." *Indiana Magazine of History* 55 (June 1959): 1-15.

Phillips, Harlan B. "Charles Beard: The English Lectures, 1899-1901." *Journal of the History of Ideas* 14 (June 1953): 451-456.

Purcell, Edward A., Jr. "American Jurisprudence Between the Wars: Legal Realism and the Crisis of Democratic Theory." *American Historical Review* 75 (December 1969): 424-445.

Ratner, Sidney. "Evolution and the Rise of the Scientific Spirit in America." *Philosophy of Science* 3 (January 1936): 104-122.

————. "Facts and Values in History." *Teachers College Record* 56 (May 1955): 429-434.

————. "History as Experiment." *Antioch Review* 19 (Fall 1959): 315-327.

Rogat, Yosal. "The Judge as Spectator." *University of Chicago Law Review* 31 (Winter 1964): 213-256.

Rogers, Hugh I. "Charles A. Beard, the 'New Physics' and Historical Relativity." *Historian* 30 (August 1968): 545-560.

Roth, R. J. "The Religious Philosophy of William James." *Thought* 41 (Summer 1966): 249-281.

Salomon, Albert. "The Religion of Progress." *Social Research* 13 (December 1946): 441-462.

Schirmer, Daniel B. "William James and the New Age," *Science and Society* 33 (Fall 1969): 434-445.

Schneider, Herbert W. "The Influence of Darwin and Spencer on American Philosophical Theology." *Journal of the History of Ideas* 6 (January 1945): 3-18.

Schuyler, Robert L. "Forrest McDonald's Critique of the Beard Thesis." *Journal of Southern History* 27 (February 1961): 73-80.

Shafer, Boyd C. "The American Heritage of Hope, 1865-1940." *Mississippi Valley Historical Review* 37 (December 1950): 427-450.

Silverman, Mildred. "Emerson and the Idea of Progress." *American Literature* 12 (March 1940): 1-19.

Sorenson, Lloyd R. "Charles A. Beard and German Historical Thought." *Mississippi Valley Historical Review* 42 (September 1955): 274-287.

Stone, James. "Henry Adams's Philosophy of History." *New England Quarterly* 14 (September 1941): 538-548.

Stourch, Gerald. "Charles A. Beard's Interpretations of American Foreign Policy." *World Affairs Quarterly* 28 (Spring 1957): 111-148.

Strout, Cushing. "Pragmatism in Retrospect: Legacy of James and Dewey." *Virginia Quarterly Review* 43 (Winter 1967): 123-134.

———. "The Twentieth Century Enlightenment." *American Political Science Review* 49 (June 1955): 321-339.

———. "The Unfinished Arch: William James and the Idea of History." *American Quarterly* 13 (Winter 1961): 505-515.

———. "William James and the Twice-Born Sick Soul." *Daedalus* (Summer 1968): 1062-1082.

Susman, Warren. "History and the American Intellec-
   tual: Uses of a Usable Past." *American Quarterly* 16
   (Summer 1964): 243-263.
Thomas, John L. "Romantic Reform in America, 1815-
   1865." *American Quarterly* 17 (Winter 1965): 656-681.
Welter, Rush. "The Idea of Progress in America."
   *Journal of the History of Ideas* 16 (June 1955): 401-415.
White, H. B. "The Political Faith of John Dewey."
   *Journal of Politics* 20 (May 1958): 353-367.
Wilkins, Burleigh T. "James, Dewey and Hegelian
   Idealism." *Journal of the History of Ideas* 17 (June
   1956): 332-346.
———. "Pragmatism as a Theory of Historical Knowl-
   edge: John Dewey on the Nature of Historical
   Inquiry." *American Historical Review* 64 (July 1959):
   878-890.
Williams, Lloyd P. "A Note on John Dewey's View of
   History." *Southwest Social Science Quarterly* 38
   (December 1957): 228-235.
Williams, William Appleman. "A Note on Beard's
   Search for a General Theory of Causation." *American
   Historical Review* 62 (January 1956): 59-80.
Zilsel, Edgar. "The Genesis of the Concept of Scientific
   Progress." *Journal of the History of Ideas* 6 (June 1945):
   325-349.


*Writings by William James*


*Collected Essays and Reviews*. New York: Longmans,
   Green and Company, 1920.
*Essays in Pragmatism*. Edited by Alburey Castell. New
   York: Hafner Publishing Co., 1968.
*Essays on Faith and Morals*. New York: Longmans,
   Green and Company, 1943.

*The Letters of William James.* Edited by Henry James. Boston: The Atlantic Monthly Press, 1920. 2 vols.

*Memories and Studies.* New York: Longmans, Green and Company, 1924.

*Pragmatism: A New Name for Some Old Ways of Thinking* New York: Meridian Books, 1955. Originally published in 1907.

*The Principles of Psychology.* New York: Henry Holt Company, 1890. 2 vols.

*Selected Papers on Philosophy.* New York: E. P. Dutton, 1917.

*Some Problems of Philosophy.* New York: Longmans, Green and Company, 1911.

*The Varieties of Religious Experience: A Study in Human Nature.* 1902. Reprint ed., New York: Collier Books, 1961.

*The Will to Believe, and Other Essays in Popular Philosophy.* New York: Longmans, Green and Company, 1897.

*The Writings of William James.* Edited by John J. McDermott. New York: The Modern Library, 1967.

## Writings by John Dewey

*A Common Faith.* New Haven: Yale University Press, 1934.

*Creative Intelligence: Essays in the Pragmatic Attitude.* New York: Henry Holt and Son, 1917.

*Democracy and Education.* 1916. Reprint. New York: The Macmillan Company, 1961.

*Education Today.* Edited by Joseph Ratner. New York: G. P. Putnam's Sons, 1940.

*Essays in Experimental Logic.* Chicago: University of Chicago Press, 1916.

*Ethics.* New York: Henry Holt and Company, 1932.

*Experience and Education.* New York: The Macmillan Company, 1938.

*Experience and Nature.* 1929. Reprint. Lasalle, Ill.: Open Court, 1968.

*How We Think.* Boston: D. C. Heath and Company, 1910.

*Human Nature and Conduct.* 1922. Reprint. New York: The Modern Library, 1929.

*Individualism, Old and New.* 1929, 1930. Reprint. New York: Capricorn Books, 1962.

*The Influence of Darwin on Philosophy.* New York: Henry Holt and Company, 1910.

*Intelligence in the Modern World.* Edited by Joseph Ratner. New York: The Modern Library, 1939.

*Liberalism and Social Action.* 1935. Reprint. New York: Capricorn Books, 1963.

*Logic: The Theory of Inquiry.* New York: Henry Holt and Company, 1938.

*Philosophy and Civilization.* New York: Minton, Balch and Company, 1931.

*The Problems of Men.* New York: The Philosophical Library, 1946.

*The Public and Its Problems.* New York: Henry Holt and Company, 1927.

*The Quest for Certainty: A Study of the Relation of Knowledge and Action.* New York: Minton, Balch and Company, 1929.

*Reconstruction in Philosophy.* 1920. Reprint. Boston: Beacon Press, 1948.

*The School and Society.* Rev. ed. Chicago: The University of Chicago Press, 1915.

Editor. *Studies in Logical Theory.* Chicago: University of Chicago Press, 1903.

*Writings by Charles A. Beard*

## BOOKS

*A Charter for the Social Sciences*. New York: Charles Scribner's Sons, 1932.

*The Discussion of Human Affairs*. New York: The Macmillan Company, 1936.

*An Economic Interpretation of the Constitution of the United States*. New York: The Macmillan Company, 1913.

*Economic Origins of Jeffersonian Democracy*. New York: The Macmillan Company, 1915.

*A Foreign Policy for America*. New York: Alfred A. Knopf, 1940.

*John Dewey and the Promise of America*. Columbus, Ohio: Progressive Education Association, 1939.

*The Myth of Rugged American Individualism*. New York: The John Day Company, 1932.

*The Nature of the Social Sciences*. New York: Charles Scribner's Sons, 1934.

*Politics*. New York: The Columbia University Press, 1908.

*Public Policy and the General Welfare*. New York: Farrar and Rinehart, 1941.

*The Republic: Conversations on Fundamentals*. New York: Viking Press, 1962.

With Mary Beard: *America in Mid-passage*. New York: The Macmillan Company, 1939.

*American Spirit: A Study of the Idea of Civilization in the United States*. New York: Collier Books, 1962.

*The American Spirit: A Study of the Idea of Civilization in the United States*. 1942. Reprint. New York: Collier Books, 1962.

*The Rise of American Civilization*. New York: The Macmillan Company, 1927. 2 vols.

With William Beard. *The American Leviathan*. New
York: The Macmillan Company, 1930.
With James Harvey Robinson. *The Development of
Modern Europe*. New York: Ginn and Company,
1907-1908. 2 vols.
With G. H. E. Smith. *The Open Door at Home*. New
York: The Macmillan Company, 1934.

## ARTICLES

"America's Quest for Security." *Journal of the Association
of University Women* 28 (1935): 141-144.
"Creating the Good Life for America." *Journal of the
American Association of University Women* 28 (June
1935): 195-198.
"Essentials of Democracy." *School and Society* 50 (August
19, 1939): 228-235.
"A Five Year Plan for America." *Forum and Century* 81
(July 1931): 1-11.
"The Historian and Society." *Canadian Historical Review*
14 (March 1933): 1-4. (With George M. Wrong.)
"A Historian's Quest for Light." *Proceedings of the
Association of History Teachers of the Middle States and
Maryland* 29 (1931): 12-21.
"History and Social Science." *Saturday Review of Litera-
ture* 12 (August 17, 1935): 22-23.
"Limitations to the Application of Social Science
Implied in Recent Social Trends." *Social Forces* 2
(May 1933): 505-510.
"A Memorandum on Social Philosophy." *Journal of
Social Philosophy* 5 (October 1939): 7-15.
"Neglected Aspects of Political Science." *American Politi-
cal Science Review* 42 (April 1948): 211-222.
"A Plea for Greater Stress Upon the Modern Period."
*Proceedings of the Association of History Teachers of the
Middle States and Maryland* 6 (1908): 12-15.

"That Promise of American Life." *New Republic* 81 (February 6, 1935): 350-352.

"The Rise of the Democratic Idea in the United States." *Survey Graphic* 26 (April 1937): 201-203.

"Rushlights in Darkness." *Scribner's Magazine* 90 (December 1931): 577-578.

"Ruskin and the Babble of Tongues." *New Republic* 87 (August 5, 1936): 370-372.

"Search for the Centre." *Scribner's Magazine* 91 (January 1932): 2-7.

"The Task Before Us." *Social Studies* 25 (May 1934): 215-217.

"That Noble Dream." *American Historical Review* 41 (October 1935): 74-87.

"Time, Technology, and the Creative Spirit in Political Science." *American Political Science Review* 21 (February 1927): 1-11.

"The Twilight of the Social Systems." *Living Age* 357 (January 1940): 410-417.

"The World as I Want It." *Forum and Century* 91 (June 1934): 332-334.

"Written History as an Act of Faith." *American Historical Review* 39 (January 1934): 219-229.

With Alfred Vagts. "Currents of Thought in Historiography." *American Historical Review* 42 (April 1937): 460-483.

# Index